RUSH TO GLORY

RUSH TO GLORY

FORMULA 1 Racing's Greatest Rivalry

TOM RUBYTHON

Foreword by John Watson

Photographs by Rainer Schlegelmilch

LYONS PRESS
Guilford, Connecticut
An imprint of Globe Pequot Press

Copyright © 2011 Tom Rubython/Myrtle Electronic Press Ltd
Photographs © Rainer Schlegelmilch
First published in the United Kingdom in 2011 as *In the Name of Glory*
First Lyons Press Edition, 2013

Lyons Press is an imprint of Globe Pequot Press.

Project editor: Meredith Dias
Layout: Lisa Reneson

Library of Congress Cataloging-in-Publication Data

Rubython, Tom.
 Rush to glory : Formula 1 racing's greatest rivalry / Tom Rubython ;
foreword by John Watson ; photographs by Rainer Schlegelmilch.
  pages cm
Includes index.
ISBN 978-0-7627-9197-2
1. Grand Prix racing—History. 2. Formula one automobiles—History.
I. Title.
GV1029.15.R84 2013
796.72—dc23

2013015035

Printed in the United States of America

10 9 8 7 6 5 4 3 2 1

Formula 1™ is a trademark of Formula One World Championship Limited and does not imply an
endorsement of this book.

CONTENTS

CONTENTS

Contents

ACKNOWLEDGMENTS

A book like this owes so many things to so many people. But, as always with any motor racing book featuring this era, I owe John Hogan the deepest thanks. John had unique insight into both Niki Lauda and James Hunt in 1976; he was their mentor, their guru, their paymaster, and their best friend during that remarkable season.

I believe that John knows what really went on in 1976 better than any other man alive. And I am very glad that he confided in me the long-forgotten details and dramas.

It's also true to say that without John, there would have been no James Hunt. He created him, nurtured him, developed him, and saved him from himself when he needed saving, which was pretty often from what I observed.

Equally, when Niki was in trouble, he always turned to John to help him out of the holes he continually seemed to be digging for himself at certain points during 1976.

John's account of 1976 has helped blow away the myths surrounding James and Niki, of which there were many. Both drivers were lucky to have had such a wise friend on their side.

The other man who played a significant role that season was Bernie Ecclestone. He was close to both men, though not in the same way as John Hogan. Bernie wanted James and Niki to drive for his Brabham team in 1976 and made plenty of effort to try and make it happen. But for a man who likes getting what he wants, for once Bernie failed on both counts. If he hadn't, history would have been very different. We must thank him for failing; otherwise, we might have been denied the dramas of 1976.

I also have to thank previous authors, notably Gerald Donaldson and the late, great Christopher Hilton. Chris's death in 2010 was a very sad loss to the Formula One community, and his books *Portrait of a Champion* and *Memories* were extremely useful to me. This book is all the better for Chris's contribution to motor racing's history.

I am also deeply indebted to Andrew Frankl, cofounder of *Car* magazine.

Andrew has the best memory of anyone I know about what happened at the 1976 British Grand Prix at Brands Hatch. His recollections of that remarkable day bring alive a whole chapter that otherwise would have had to rely on far less reliable, less colorful, and less graphic sources.

Equally, Philippe Gurdjian's character insights into both James and Niki were incredibly valuable to me. Few people know about the unique contribution Philippe has made behind the scenes to Formula One over the years. Luckily, I do, and so did James and Niki, as two of his many beneficiaries.

Stirling Moss was in the thick of it during 1976, working for American television. He was also particularly close to James Hunt, making his background recollections a treat to include in this book.

Equally, Andrew Marriott was close to Hunt during 1976 and, as usual, saw things that others didn't see in the background—much of which make up the fabric of this book.

John Watson, as ever, was my principal guide to James and Niki's Formula One career from an insider's perspective. He was there and doing it, and therefore his recollections are invaluable. Regardless of that, John knows what he's about where motor racing is concerned. As anyone who knows him will attest, John has very particular and forthright views, and woe betide anyone who might disagree with them. Luckily, his view of things almost always coincided with my own, which made him a very good collaborator. John's greatest contribution is the time he is prepared to give to journalists and authors and the effort he puts into answering our questions.

Max Mosley was also very close to James and Niki and has unique insights of those times in the early '70s when both drivers were struggling newcomers.

Max, James, and Niki had the most unusual of relationships and shared good and bad times together on the way up the motor racing ladder. Now that Max has retired from his onerous duties, he can tell it like it was in a manner that he was not necessarily able to do in the past.

Peter Collins is an admirer of the achievements of both James Hunt and Niki Lauda, and no one can analyze a Formula One situation like Peter. People who know me will know that I value Peter's opinion most highly.

People who may have read my other books will know this is my shortest yet. That is simply because it is the story of a year and is therefore very concentrated. It may be short, but the effort expended upon it was still great, and I cannot finish here without thanking my own people who worked on the original edition of this book.

David Peett and Mary Hynes, as always, took care of sales. Ania Grzesik designed the original edition, as she does all my books, and Kiran Toor, our chief sub-editor, took care of the words, as she always does.

Thanks also to John Blunsden, my personal guru, for his wise publishing counsel. A few words from John can be worth thousands of dollars in saved costs.

For this book, I chose to work with Rainer Schlegelmilch exclusively on the photographs. Rainer is Formula One's top photographer and has been since David Phipps retired. In truth, it's wrong to describe Rainer as a photographer, as he is a true artist. His photographs are really more akin to paintings, such is the care that goes into each one. Anyone who has examined his work will know that without being told. Thanks also to Stefano Luzzatto and Boris Schlegelmilch for handling the nuts and bolts of the photographic process.

The usual thanks to David Browne, Jo Buck, Ian Foyster, and Peter Milton at our UK printers. Printing a book properly so that it is a delight in a reader's hands is no easy task, but they manage it so effortlessly and painlessly. They also made sure the UK edition arrived in the shops on time.

Martin Bilbie meticulously examined the appendices and removed any errors that may have been apparent—a thankless task.

Finally, my gracious thanks to our final proofreaders, Stephen Meakins and Vikki Brice, who are also my neighbors in the village of Castle

Ashby. As always, they get the final manuscript only a few days before printing, and their responsibilities are onerous—i.e., making sure this book goes to the printers with as few errors as is humanly possible with hardly any time to do it in.

Thanks to you all for your unstinting efforts, but, as always, the words that follow—including any errors or omissions—are my responsibility alone.

Tom Rubython
Castle Ashby
Northamptonshire
October 20, 2011

Heroic Rivals

The summer of 1976 is best remembered for the soaring heat that started around 1 May and lasted until 31 August. In many European countries, not a drop of rain fell for four months. It was the biggest heat wave in generations. In England, the roads melted and the ice cream ran out.

But the extraordinary weather, which has not been seen again since, was nothing compared to what was happening on the racetracks of Europe that summer.

No dramatist could have created a more riveting scenario or created two more heroic rivals to feature in the 1976 Formula One season. Niki Lauda, the reigning champion, led the world championship from the first race to the last race and until almost the very last lap of the season. But "almost" became the most important word in the Austrian's dictionary. He led for 274 days (equating to 6,600 hours, or 395,999 minutes) of those ten months. It was not until the very final few minutes of that ten-month period that James Hunt moved ahead of him and won the world title by a single championship point.

To lose a championship in such a way was devastating for Lauda, especially given the circumstances of what happened to him in 1976. No man is psychologically equipped to deal with maintaining a lead for so long only to lose. To be bested in such circumstances was a scenario he could never have envisaged, and when he flew out of Tokyo at the end of October 1976, he was a broken man.

No Hollywood screenwriter could have scripted such an ending or described the human drama of such a dramatic season. Just like the extraordinary weather of that summer will likely never again be matched, there can never again be such a dramatic racing season as 1976.

Many people believe that Niki Lauda's accident was the sole reason for the outcome, and most people believe that James Hunt was only champion because of it. But the cold facts don't support that. Fortune and misfortune were doled out pretty evenly that season.

When the statistics are examined, they read as follows: Niki Lauda scored five Did Not Finish (DNF) results, and James Hunt also scored five DNFs.

So each had an equal number of times when he did not make it to the checkered flag for one reason or another.

So each had an equal number of "being there at the end" opportunities: the times he could have scored points—11 each in all—and that's what counts in motor racing.

Over the whole season, both had their problems. Hunt had three races, for reasons that had nothing to do with him, in which his car rendered him absolutely uncompetitive. Lauda had three races where his physical well-being, again entirely beyond his control, rendered him absolutely uncompetitive.

And each had two races where other circumstances meant they could not take the checkered flag. Make no mistake; when everything was balanced out, this was a fight between equals. And when the final score came to be read out, the best man at that moment emerged the winner.

The 1976 racing season will be remembered for as long as people take to the tracks to race cars.

There can and will never be another season like it. It was a unique moment in time.

My Year with James and Niki

Thanks for the Memories

A lthough it didn't seem that obvious at the time, looking back, I can see how fortuitous it was to be a participant in the 1976 Grand Prix season—arguably one of the most remarkable years ever in Formula One.

For me it was very special, as it was my breakthrough season: the year I won my first Grand Prix and became a regular at the front end of the grid. No one who hasn't been there can understand the relief of winning your first Grand Prix. It's a mighty weight lifted from your shoulders.

I had much in common with James and Niki. We were all roughly the same age and born of the same generation. We were all on the way up the motor sport ladder at the same time and entered Formula One within a year or so of one another. Most of all, I counted myself lucky to consider them both as friends.

I first ran into James in 1971 when he was driving for Chris Marshall's Formula 3 race team and Irishman Brendan McInerney was his teammate. I recollect first meeting James in a restaurant in the Kings Road in Chelsea. It was one of his favorite haunts, and he was eating there with his then-girlfriend, Taormina Rieck, along with Max Mosley and Robin Herd. I recall Max telling me I should be driving a March.

I first came across Niki the same year at a Formula 2 race at Mallory Park. In those days he drove a Porsche 911S, which at the time was my ultimate road car.

I was actually the last of the three of us to get into Grand Prix racing. My first event was at Silverstone on 14 July 1973. James was in the Hesketh-March and Niki in the works BRM. I had an older Brabham-Ford BT37 sponsored by Hexagon of Highgate, but I didn't care—I was just glad to be there.

That day at Silverstone, we were all at the start of our careers and far from household names. In those days the performance of the car was in the hands of the driver, and that was visible on television as the cars really moved across the track and skill was at a premium. James was the master of Woodcote corner, and it's fair to say he went through it quicker than any of us, which is why he was always so competitive at Silverstone, whatever car he was in. That day he was easily the best of the three of us and finished fourth in the race. I remember clearly that I retired on the 36th lap in my old Brabham.

In hindsight, James did remarkably well in his first season, scoring points with relative ease and impressing everyone. It took me another year to score my first championship point, in 1974 at Monte Carlo, and I managed to score five more that year. But the vagaries of Formula One became very apparent to me in 1975, when Niki leapfrogged both of us and romped to the world championship. James managed to win his Grand Prix, whereas I managed to go the whole season without scoring a single point.

For me 1975 was a year of poignancy with the death of Mark Donohue in his Penske-Ford, an event that gave me my chance of a competitive car for the first time.

As 1976 dawned, Niki was in a different world with a very well paid drive at Ferrari and a world championship already under his belt. James was in a totally different position, and just two months earlier, it looked as though he was out of Formula One altogether. He got lucky when Emerson Fittipaldi opted to leave a competitive McLaren and drive what he must have known would be an uncompetitive Copersucar car. It was the most emotional and irrational decision he ever made in his life, but it was the best piece of luck James Hunt ever had. Emerson's inexplicable decision propelled James into a very competitive car.

All three of us witnessed the ups and downs of making it to the top and, then, surviving at the top. The difference between them and me, I guess, is that they had the good fortune (especially James) to be in the two top teams in 1976. I was with a good team, but it was new, and the car was not initially as good as the Ferrari or the McLaren.

Being toward the front of the grid that season gave me a bird's-eye view of the battle for supremacy that developed between Niki and James. There is no doubt in my mind that Niki would have been world champion but for his accident. Niki's Ferrari was incredibly reliable, and when he retired, it was a shock, as such events happened so rarely.

And then Niki's accident changed everything. I came upon the scene 20 seconds after the cars of Arturo Merzario, Brett Lunger, and Guy Edwards.

Niki's car had been on fire in the middle of the track, but the fire was out by the time I got there. Arturo had lifted Niki out of his car, and I found him lying down at the side of the track in a pool of fuel and oil. We helped him up and looked for somewhere clean and dry to lay him down. I found a clear area. He had been badly burned, but he was fully conscious, although he really didn't know what was going on. He must have been in great pain.

Somehow his helmet had been wrenched off without killing him, and it was a miracle he survived. I was just glad Niki was conscious and we could talk. I rested his head on my thighs and cradled him as best I could.

He was talking away in English to me, and I remember he asked how his face looked. In truth, it didn't look good, but I told him it was okay and not to worry.

After what seemed like a lifetime, an ambulance arrived, and Niki was on a stretcher and inside the vehicle within seconds. With that, I put my helmet on and drove back to the pits assuming that the race would be restarted.

At that stage, I had no doubt Niki would survive, as the internal injuries he had suffered were not obvious at that time. But it seemed clear he would be away from racing for a long time.

Following the accident, I indirectly helped Niki by competing as hard as I could against James in the following two races. I managed to win one of them and could have won both with better luck. Niki was delirious with joy when I beat James in Austria. The following Monday, my team manager and I called Niki in the hospital, and he thanked me for preventing James from winning another Grand Prix. I said I would do my best to repeat the performance in Holland at the next race, and I very nearly did.

But if you came up against James in the right mood—when he was ready to fight the world—he could work miracles, and I could not pull it off a second time. After a titanic battle with James for the lead, my gearbox broke and James romped to victory on his birthday—much as I tried to spoil his party.

I was, like everyone else, astonished when Niki reappeared at Monza for the Italian Grand Prix. His quick return to the cockpit from the horrible accident in Germany was the most heroic act ever witnessed in our sport.

Niki had an iron will, and no other man could have pulled it off. To finish fourth at the Italian Grand Prix barely six weeks after having received the last rites from a priest was an out-of-the-ordinary event no one could have predicted.

The final drama in Japan could not have been made up by the most imaginative fantasist, and the emotions that Niki must have experienced were simply beyond what any human being could handle.

In the end, it was the aftereffects of the accident that ruined his world championship chances. He simply had no control over the tear ducts in his right eye, and it impaired his vision in the wet. The rain was so bad that a lake formed on the circuit at the end of the main straight. It was the worst possible condition for Niki and yet another variable that made such a difference to that season's ending. If the weather had been good, Niki certainly would have wrapped up the championship in Japan. The gods smiled on James that day.

John Watson
Oxford
England
June 20, 2011

CHAPTER I

Niki and James before 1976

Years of Struggle to Succeed

1947–1975

I t was a source of permanent rankle to James Hunt that, although he was 18 months older than Niki Lauda, the Austrian beat him into Formula One by a whole 12 months. Hunt always considered Lauda his benchmark, his main contemporary and, ultimately, his chief rival. Everything he did was measured against Niki Lauda. In fact, one of the reasons that Hunt thought he could succeed in motor racing was Lauda. Hunt always thought that if Lauda could do it, then he definitely could.

The difference between the two men's characters was the sole reason that Lauda got there first and was initially more successful and ultimately enjoyed a much longer career. The difference was purely determination.

Lauda possessed an iron-willed determination to succeed, which Hunt didn't. Hunt may have been determined, but he always realized there were things in life other than motor racing, and this continually held him back.

But Hunt was, arguably, a more naturally talented driver than Lauda, and it was inevitable that he would eventually succeed.

And there was also the time lapse. Lauda wanted to be a racing driver from the age of nine and got started on his ambition then. Hunt only got the bug after his 18th birthday and began his quest from a long way back.

For Lauda, at that time, there was nothing else. In fact, Lauda's strong will became the driving force in his life. He would certainly not have become a racing driver without it.

Born on 22 February 1949, he was the son of a wealthy Viennese paper mill owner. He enjoyed a privileged upbringing at a time when much of the rest of Austria was still impoverished after the war. The family wealth had been accumulated by his grandfather, Hans Lauda, who was a very rich man with a town house in Vienna, a country estate in the Austrian countryside, and a house in St Moritz.

The young Lauda, lacking any intellectual or sporting talents, developed an affinity for cars almost from the moment he was born. On his 14th birthday, his grandparents gave him some money, which he spent on a 1949 convertible Volkswagen Beetle that was virtually a wreck. He stripped it down and dismantled the engine. Then he rebuilt it meticulously over the next two years. By the end of the process, had a really good knowledge of how cars worked. He used to drive the Volkswagen around the private roads of his grandfather's country estate long before he obtained a license.

But the young Lauda proved a severe disappointment to his family. He left school with no academic qualifications and no particular prospects. He got a job as a mechanic at a local garage. But even that did not go well; on his first job he stripped the threads on the sump of a customer's Volvo during a routine oil change, necessitating the engine to be removed to fit a new sump. The job did not last long, and he drifted, seemingly interested only in motor racing. It became his all-consuming obsession.

When he was old enough to get a provisional license, he started driving illegally on public roads before he passed his test. But after he passed, his parents refused to buy him a car unless he returned to his studies. It forced him to return to college to try to complete his education and graduate. His father told him that there would be no more money until he did. There was little chance of that, as he was not made to pass exams. So he forged a diploma that showed he had graduated when he hadn't. It fooled his parents, and they patted him on the back and released him some money.

He explained his problem with academia: "Studying or having a normal profession was totally alien to my way of thinking."

His graduation was important because it triggered a series of payments from his family and he bought his first road car, a newer Volkswagen Beetle that he could drive on the road. He then also began looking for a race car to buy.

Like James Hunt, his choice fell on a Mini as the ideal first racing car. But he promptly crashed it while driving on the road too fast in icy conditions.

After it was rebuilt, he competed in his first motor race, a hill climb on April 15, 1968. He was just 19 years old.

Lauda described his attitude in the early days: "The only thing is to go to the track, get into the car, and drive your tail off." He added: "There was not one single thing in the world that interested me even a fraction as much."

He finished second in his first race, but there was no celebrating by his parents, who were totally against his racing. They cut off all further funds to stop him. His father told him that his funding would only be resumed when he solemnly promised to stop racing. He did promise, but it was a promise he couldn't keep.

He carried on secretly and actually won his next hill climb event in the Mini. But there were journalists present, and his win was recorded in the local newspapers, which were avidly read by his father.

Lauda knew the game was up; when his father read about the race, he flew into a rage. He realized his son was dishonest. As honesty and integrity were a Lauda family tradition, his father threw him out of the family home.

As Lauda remembered: "That was it. He'd finally had enough of me."

The lack of support from his parents for his racing ambitions troubled the young man, and there was a degree of estrangement from then on that was never really reconciled. But Lauda's time at home was over, and he knew that his forced exit from the family bosom was inevitable.

Luckily, he had just started dating a girl called Mariella von Reininghaus.

Meeting Mariella was a piece of very good luck: Not only was she very beautiful, she was also financially stable. Lauda met her while she was skiing at Gastein with a group of friends from Graz, which also coincidentally included another Austrian racing driver named Helmut Marko.

Lauda took a bad fall in the snow, and when he looked up, there was Mariella staring into his eyes asking him if he was all right. Lauda didn't bother with any pleasantries and responded by asking her if she would accompany him the following week to the upcoming Vienna hunt ball.

A surprised Mariella agreed. A week later she drove down from Graz and they went to the ball together. Bored with the stuffy ball after 10 minutes, they left to go to a local bar and, from that moment, were inseparable companions. Together they rented a small apartment in the middle of Salzburg, moving from their respective homes in Vienna and Graz.

By then Lauda was absolutely determined to become a race driver, and Mariella, whose own parents were very wealthy, was able to support him day to day. He remembered: "Mariella was very pretty, intelligent, level headed, and composed. Her reasoned approach to life and her self-control rubbed off on me during these early hectic days in racing." He added: "Being around her had a pronounced influence on my character. I have much to thank her for."

Mariella gave him a new confidence, and he went to a Salzburg bank and obtained a loan for his racing. His grandfather's reputation stretched to Salzburg and meant there was no problem with the bank advancing money to a member of the Lauda family.

Just like James Hunt, he only did a few races in his Mini before realizing its limitations. He quickly traded up for a Porsche 911, which was financed by more bank loans and what can only be described as begging visits to both his grandmothers. He mainly raced the Porsche in hill climbs, popular in Austria at the time.

He may have appeared feckless, but Lauda always thought things through before he went to banks for money. Although he very rarely told them the complete truth, he never let his obsession with racing cloud his thinking. As he said: "Once in the sport, my approach has always been very level headed and pragmatic. I have always thought my career through one step at a time, dealing with each subsequent problem as and when it came up."

In 1968 he suffered a setback when his boyhood hero, Jim Clark, was killed. Clark's death reverberated throughout Europe, not least with the Lauda family. It made financing a career in racing even more difficult. No one wanted to give him the money to potentially kill himself.

In 1969 Lauda moved up to Formula Vee, the European equivalent of Formula Ford and, in 1970, to Formula 3. By this time he was deeply indebted to more than a few banks. He leveraged his family's name and reputation as far as he could to get the cash.

But Formula 3 was his entree to the big time of motor racing, and he was competing for the first time with the best young talent around. But in his first ever Formula 3 race he had his first big accident, at Nogaro circuit in the south of France. His car went over the rear wheels of another car in front and flew through the air, destroying itself on landing. He was very lucky to escape with his life, entirely uninjured. It didn't put him off at all, and he quickly paid to have the car rebuilt.

It was the first of three serious accidents that year, all of which he managed to walk away from. He wrote off another car at Brands Hatch but somehow managed to keep going. As the season wore on, he found himself competing ever more frequently against James Hunt, who was also trying to make his way in Formula 3 on the circuits of Europe that summer.

In truth, neither man distinguished himself. They were both far from successful, and neither shined. It was only Lauda's continued access to borrowed money and handouts from his grandmothers that kept him competing. Hunt only kept going thanks to his rich new patron, Lord Alexander Hesketh. And, like Lauda, Hunt kept crashing cars.

When he wrote off his third car, Lauda was forced to rethink his career. Just as James Hunt had also discovered, he too decided he was going nowhere in Formula 3 and realized he had to move up to Formula 2.

Somehow, deep within him, he believed he had what it took to succeed as a racing driver, despite the lack of any results to prove it. He decided to go for broke in 1971 and secured a new loan of $25,000 from the Erste Öesterreichische bank.

The money enabled him to buy a Formula 2 drive in the works STP-sponsored March-Ford team for the 1971 season. The bank also agreed to waive interest on the loan in exchange for a sponsorship deal. Lauda explained his deal with March: "They had young superstar Ronnie Peterson as their number one and, as a result, did not feel the need for anyone any good in the number-two slot. They were prepared to take on board someone like myself, provided, that is, I paid my way." Lauda admitted he was lucky to get the drive, but only because he was the best of a bad bunch who wanted it. As he said: "I didn't have too bad a pedigree. I was competent, and I could probably argue my candidacy better than most other 21-year-olds anxious to get out of Formula 3."

March was a new manufacturer, and 1971 was its second year of competition in Formula 2. By luck, the latest March 712 car, designed by Robin Herd, proved to be very competitive. The car gave Lauda a chance to make his name.

Lauda also formed a strong bond with Robin Herd, who found him to be an excellent test driver. It was his ability as a test driver that sustained him in the early years, when he showed little promise on track. But he did just enough in 1971 to inspire sufficient confidence in others to enable him to make the move up into Formula One the following year. In reality it was a year too early and he would have benefited from another year in Formula 2. But it was then that he first discovered that he had a real survivor's instinct to succeed. That realization drove him on when others would definitely have given up.

Somehow he managed to secure a big loan and attract personal sponsorship, which enabled him to buy a Formula One drive with March in 1972. Max Mosley offered him a driving package that included a full season of Formula One and Formula 2 for an all-in price of $100,000. Lauda responded to Mosley's offer by saying it was "no problem." In reality it was a big problem, but a problem that he knew he could solve.

He arranged a new deal with the Erste Öesterreichische bank that combined a $100,000 loan and sponsorship space to cover the interest payments. He also took out an insurance policy that guaranteed the bank repayment if anything happened to him.

But Lauda made the crucial mistake of announcing the deal with the bank and March before it was signed. Jochen Rindt's death a year earlier inspired his grandfather to take decisive action to stop his grandson's racing activities, and Hans Lauda stepped in to halt the deal.

The bank could not afford to ignore him. So after Lauda had signed the deal with Mosley, the Erste Öesterreichische bank's directors voted against granting the loan under pressure from the Lauda family.

This left Lauda in deep trouble, and he telephoned his grandfather to beg him to change his mind. But Hans told him simply, "A Lauda should be written up in the financial pages, not the sports pages." Hearing that, Lauda slammed down the telephone and never spoke to his grandfather again.

Lauda rushed round to all the other Austrian banks he knew and ended up at one called Raiffeisenkasse. Amazingly, the manager there, Karl-Heinz Oertelit, took him seriously when he asked for $100,000 for motor racing. Lauda explained, "I made the acquaintance of a man who had a very acute feel for what is feasible and what is not."

Raiffeisenkasse agreed to virtually the same deal as Erste Öesterreichische, and this time Lauda kept it secret until he had signed the loan agreements so his grandfather couldn't interfere again.

He drove to England and gave Mosley a check for the exact amount, which left him with nothing for his living expenses and around $50,000 of old debts to pay back. It was a last throw of the dice.

To pay for his living expenses, he raced saloon cars and sports cars for private owners. Private owners paid handsomely for Formula One drivers to compete in their cars, and Lauda earned $20,000 that year from this activity and also gained valuable experience. He remembered, "I had never before and have never since driven in so many races in one season as I did in 1972."

However, all the circumstances that had prevailed for him in 1971 worked against him in 1972. Robin Herd had designed a radical new Formula One car with a transverse gearbox called the March 721X.

When Lauda first tested the car, he was considerably slower than Ronnie Peterson, his teammate, who had praised it after his first drive.

Lauda thought the car was an absolute dog from the first time he drove it and couldn't understand why Peterson didn't feel the same way. For the first time in his life, Lauda experienced self-doubt and wondered whether he was as good a driver as he believed himself to be.

This was the first time he had felt that emotion, and it hit him hard. He took Mariella for a short holiday to Marbella as he thought about whether he should continue racing or not: "For the first time, I felt unsure of myself. Maybe I wasn't the fantastic driver I believed myself to be."

But it gradually began to dawn on Robin Herd that Peterson was a poor test driver and had little mechanical feel for how a car was behaving. By contrast, he realized that Lauda had a very good feel, and they soon wished they had listened to him earlier instead of Peterson.

Peterson wisely avoided racing the March 721X and raced a modified 1971 car throughout 1972. But Lauda was stuck with the 721X. Saddled with a slow car in a slow team, it seemed his career might be over. Lauda called the car "a colossal mechanical fiasco."

Lauda said, "It was obvious the car was wrong from top to bottom, and no amount of redesigning would help. The experience was certainly salutary for me. I learned that I should have more faith in my technical judgment."

The 721X nearly brought down the whole March organization and stopped Lauda's progress in its tracks. Peterson left the team at the end of the year, and Lauda blamed him for much of what had happened: "There are well-known drivers who would rather try to tame a vicious car than attempt to explain to the designer where the car's faults lie and how one can perhaps correct them."

Lauda found himself out of a drive and with debts of $80,000. By way of compensation, March offered him a Formula 2 seat for 1973 but nothing in Formula One. He argued he was due a refund for being supplied with such a terrible car, and there was a heated row with Max Mosley. Mosley told Lauda there were no guarantees and would not budge on a refund. Lauda drove away from March's Bicester factory for the final time in high dudgeon. It was the lowest point of his life, and he decided to end it all, as he remembered: "I knew there was a T-junction a few miles ahead, and all I had to do was keep my foot to the floor and there was a solid wall on the other side." As he candidly recounted later, he floored the accelerator and resolved to end his life—so desperate was his financial plight after Mosley refused to hand him a lifeline.

But in the few minutes it took him to drive the 2 miles, he somehow got himself together. As he said, "I clicked my brain back into gear in time."

He realized that he had to persist, as there was nothing else to do. He knew it would take 20 years to pay back his debts and decided he had to make his racing career work. Once again, he justified his failures in his head and decided they weren't his fault.

One thing he did know for certain was that there could be no more borrowing. He was in debt up to his neck.

Then Louis Stanley, the boss of the Marlboro-sponsored BRM team, appeared out of the blue as his savior and invited him to test the new BRM Formula One car at Paul Ricard circuit in France.

Stanley, who so often appeared to be a buffoon, was in fact sometimes very astute—he was just good at hiding it. He had heard that Lauda was an excellent test driver, and he knew that was just what BRM needed. So Stanley figured that instead of paying Lauda to test the car, he would invite him to a trial for the team. Lauda went along with it.

Lauda was kept out of the car for the first few days by niggling problems that always plagued BRM, and the driving was left to team drivers Clay Regazzoni and an Australian named Vern Schuppan. He ended up driving 20 laps on the third day of the test.

Lauda knew that he only had to be faster than one of them to be in consideration for the third car BRM was going to run that season. But more progress was made on that third day than in any previous day's testing that winter. Lauda was also considerably faster than Schuppan.

Louis Stanley was very impressed with the "Lauda package," as he called it. So he summoned Lauda to his suite at the Dorchester Hotel in London for a discussion about his future. After keeping him waiting for an hour amidst some grand theatrics, Stanley told Lauda he would drop Schuppan and that the third BRM was his, subject to certain conditions. But then came the bombshell. There would be no salary, and he would have to pay his own expenses; plus he would have to attract some sponsors. It was a deal that Lauda could just about afford to accept.

To seal the deal, he promised to go out and raise some sponsorship. Lauda knew he would have three races at least before he needed to deliver on the promise.

But before he would sign, Stanley wanted to meet the prospective sponsors. So he flew into Vienna airport, and Lauda brought along Karl-Heinz Oertel to impress him. Luckily Stanley could not understand a word of German, and somehow Lauda managed to persuade Oertel to advance him another $80,000 to up his overdraft to $160,000 in all. Stanley thought the loan was actually sponsorship and agreed to contracts being drawn up by lawyers in Vienna for signature before he went home.

While he waited, Stanley went to visit St Stephen's Cathedral to listen to the carol singers and enjoy a helping of Austria's favorite dessert—boiled chestnuts and cream. Back at the airport, he signed the contract before he flew off.

Lauda was back from the brink, and his career was on again.

But Lauda described the financial consequences of the deal as "madness," and it was only with Mariella's support that he got through it. He recalled much later how he put it all to the back of his mind: "I gave as little thought to my precarious financial position as I was to give, a couple of years later, to the fantastic amounts of money I was earning."

Lauda quickly found dealing with Louis Stanley on a day-to-day basis hilarious. Everything Stanley did was accompanied by grand theatrical gestures designed to impress. But amid it all, Lauda quickly realized that the BRM team was in terminal decline. He managed to make his first sponsorship installment but could not pay the balance, as he was using this year's debt to pay back last year's. He was sick with worry that Stanley might want the contract he had signed translated and that he would lose the drive. He was also worried he might be accused of fraud if BRM's lawyers discovered that a contract they thought was a sponsorship agreement was actually a loan agreement from a bank.

On the track, the 1973 season with BRM proved almost as big a disaster as 1972 with March. The best result the three drivers managed among them was a fourth place. Lauda's best placing was fifth at the Belgian Grand Prix, where he picked up his first ever world championship points.

His career was saved by the one outstanding performance he put in at the Monaco Grand Prix. Lauda drove perfectly that day and held a superb third place before retiring. His performance that day caught the attention of a lot of people at the race. Louis Stanley, for all his faults, suddenly recognized that Lauda was going to be a big star of the future, and he was the first person to do so. Consequently, Stanley offered Lauda a three-year contract with a salary and canceled the sponsorship agreement he had signed. Lauda was so relieved that he signed immediately.

But 1973 was the BRM team's last year in the big time, and its future prospects were poor.

Luckily for Lauda, Enzo Ferrari had watched the Monaco Grand Prix on television and, like Stanley, had been mightily impressed. Acting completely out of character, Enzo turned up at the Dutch Grand Prix at Zandvoort for the qualifying sessions specifically to meet Lauda.

Enzo became obsessed with signing Lauda to drive for Ferrari in 1974. But now Lauda had the problem of getting out of his long-term contract with BRM. Luckily, Lauda had negotiated a breach of contract penalty, and in the end he used some of his Ferrari salary to buy himself out of his BRM contract. Ferrari agreed to pay Lauda $50,000 a year to drive, and so he began to repay his debts. He had come back from the brink.

Although initially Lauda found Enzo Ferrari difficult to work with, it was clear that the Ferrari team was coming back from a very difficult period, and the only way was up. Mauro Forghieri, a 40-year-old engineering genius, had returned to be technical director, and Lauda threw himself into the task of helping Forghieri make the old car competitive and design a new car for 1975.

The other good thing that Lauda found at Ferrari was its new team manager, Luca di Montezemolo. Montezemolo was very well connected with the Agnelli family, which owned Fiat and controlled Ferrari. The downside was that he was only 26 years old and unproven. But Montezemolo seized control of the team, sidelined Enzo Ferrari, and restored sanity to the team's management.

Montezemolo was to prove the catalyst to a Ferrari revival. Montezemolo, Forghieri, and Lauda were suddenly in the right place at the right time.

Lauda also got on well with his teammate Clay Regazzoni, and they soon became very close.

Forghieri soon reengineered the car and put it on a par with the McLaren M23. It all worked so well that either Regazzoni or Lauda could have won the world championship that year—and Regazzoni, then at his peak, very nearly did. As it was, Ferrari narrowly lost the world championship to Emerson Fittipaldi's McLaren-Ford.

Lauda's life was totally transformed after he won two grand prix in Spain and Belgium and was suddenly a genuine bona fide Formula One star. And Ferrari found itself a contender again after many years in the wilderness.

The following year, in 1975, everything came right for Lauda as Forghieri introduced the new Ferrari 312T. Lauda called it "a permanent monument to Forghieri's skill, a gem of a car." Lauda completely eclipsed Regazzoni that season and won races in Monaco, Belgium, Sweden, France and America. It seemed he effortlessly annexed the world championship with little opposition. It was his year, and he was suddenly famous and successful after all those years of struggle. By the end of the year, he had paid back all his debts and had over $250,000 left in the bank. The turnaround in his life was complete. So it was with some confidence that he looked forward to 1976.

But as the 1976 season beckoned, James Hunt found himself in an entirely different position to Lauda. By contrast, his Formula One career was in ruins, and he could only look and dream of the success Lauda was having. But Hunt knew that he was every bit as good a driver as Lauda, and that gave him the renewed determination to carry on.

Hunt was born on August 29, 1947 in the southern English county of Surrey. He was the son of a successful stockbroker. His parents were solidly middle class and earned enough to educate their many children at public schools. Hunt, 18 months older than Lauda, was a gifted boy intellectually and exceptionally talented at sport. His parents had ambitions for him to become a doctor.

But just before his 18th birthday, a friend took him to see a motor race at Silverstone, and Hunt was instantly hooked on the sport. From then on, he knew he wanted to be a racing driver.

He started off in a Mini before graduating to Formula Ford and Formula 3. He quickly got himself noticed as a fast driver with an aggressive driving style. But he also gained a reputation for crashing cars and earned himself the nickname "Shunt." He seemed prone to spectacular accidents. In October 1970 he was involved in a spectacular finish-line accident with another driver, Dave Morgan. The race was televised, and Hunt flattened Morgan in front of millions of television viewers.

He spent nearly five years in Formula 3 trying to make it and failing. Just as he was about to give up, he met a young English aristocrat named Alexander Hesketh. Lord Hesketh was a young man who had inherited a great deal of money on his 21st birthday and founded his own racing team. The team was managed by Anthony "Bubbles" Horsley.

Hunt was adopted by Hesketh, who was a petrolhead. He and Hesketh were of similar age and bonded together like brothers. Together they dabbled in Formula 3 until Hunt wrote off the team's cars in spectacular crashes. Far from being discouraged, Hesketh then graduated to Formula 2 and bought a new car for Hunt to drive. After that he decided to go into Formula One. It was the break that Hunt had been looking for, and he seized it with both hands.

Lord Hesketh had enough money to build a Formula One team around Hunt. And he did just that, starting in 1973, when he bought a new March-Ford 731 car from Max Mosley for Hunt to drive.

The following season Hesketh invested a small fortune and built his very own car, the Hesketh-Ford. The first Hesketh, designed by Harvey Postlethwaite, was loosely based on the March, but faster.

For the next two years, Lord Hesketh backed Hunt all the way, and his little private team enjoyed spectacular success, with Hunt winning his first Grand Prix in Holland in 1975, beating Niki Lauda for the victory. But just as it scored its greatest success, the Hesketh team ran out of money, and Hunt found himself without a drive as 1976 dawned. By then it was too late to find another drive.

It was his own fault of course, as the writing had been on the wall at Hesketh Racing since the end of 1974, when Lord Hesketh had effectively stopped putting new money into the team. It had survived the 1975 season by using up funds left in the bank account, selling off assets, spending Hunt's prize money, and renting out its spare car at races to drivers willing to pay.

Because of the success of the team, particularly after its first Grand Prix win, Hunt believed that a sponsor would be signed with relative ease for 1976. He said, "It didn't worry us too much because we felt that we were in a very good position with the success we were getting. Bubbles particularly wanted to do that because, of course, it was his future. He knew there was going to be no long-term future with Alexander. He wouldn't just pay forever."

Hunt admitted as much to Nigel Roebuck years later: "From mid to late 1974, there was no more money really forthcoming from Alexander. He'd spent what he'd got for racing."

Although what happened in the following two months seemed like a disaster, it eventually proved to be the making of him.

Suddenly, events transpired in James Hunt's favor.

CHAPTER 2

Contrasting Fortunes

Lauda on Top of the World, Hunt Down and Out

December 1975

As Niki Lauda wrapped up his first world championship season on October 5, 1975, he was looking forward to an even more successful 1976 season. By contrast, James Hunt was down and out of Formula One.

Hunt was out of a drive as Lord Hesketh finally closed down his team after running out of money. Hunt was desperately grateful to Lord Hesketh and had hung on until it was finally confirmed that the team would close. It was an expensive gesture; by then it was too late for Hunt to get another competitive Formula One drive.

But Niki Lauda couldn't have been better positioned. He was established at Ferrari, and its designer had a brand-new car, the Ferrari 312T2, on the drawing board. Lauda could sense that the new car would be a winner. He had also negotiated a contract that would see him earn over $300,000 if he won the championship again. Not only that, he had negotiated a personal sponsorship contract with Marlboro worth another $75,000. A year earlier he had been struggling to survive; now he was a very wealthy young man with the world at his feet. He was also in love.

But suddenly Lauda received a shock that threatened to knock him off his confident perch. Luca di Montezemolo, the young Italian manager who had been responsible for the Ferrari team's renaissance, announced he was leaving the team to take a top job at the parent company, Fiat. Lauda was stunned and recalled, "The first hint of trouble came with the departure of my friend and ally Luca Montezemolo, who had to make a career for himself and couldn't afford to stay on the lower rungs of the ladder as team chief indefinitely. Luca was promoted closer to the seat of power in the Fiat dynasty." Suddenly Lauda knew that all bets were off and everything was to play for.

Montezemolo's departure was the big break James Hunt needed, although he did not yet know it.

On November 14, 1975, it was finally confirmed that Hesketh was definitely closing. Hunt, not really believing that the day had finally come, wondered what he would do.

Although it seemed the end of the world at the time, it was eventually to prove to be Hunt's salvation. If Hesketh had survived and continued, Hunt would have stayed with the team for the rest of his career and probably never won a world championship. The closedown was the catalyst for Hunt to move on to bigger and better things, although it certainly didn't feel that way at the time.

Lord Hesketh was full of remorse and said, "I am deeply grateful to James for having stayed when the going got tough. The fact that he has not secured his future drive for next year is because he believed in a dream that we all believed in."

But Hesketh's deepest thanks could not secure Hunt a drive for 1976.

As it was, there were only two less-than-desirable drives available. The first was at the Lotus team, and that was far from definite. Lotus had suffered in the economic recession and had no money to pay its drivers. As a consequence, it expected number one, Ronnie Peterson, to leave. At the end of 1975, team manager Peter Warr, desperate for cash, had hawked Peterson's Formula One contract around the Formula One paddock to the highest bidder. There were no takers for Peterson's contract, and once he learned what Warr was doing, Peterson became disillusioned with the team. Sensing, but more likely hoping, that Peterson might leave, Warr opened negotiations with Hunt on the basis that he

would agree to drive for nothing and be paid for each world championship point he scored.

But with no cash to develop the car, the Lotus would probably be
uncompetitive. And added to that the fact that Hunt did not like Peter
Warr and refused to work for nothing, it meant that there was no drive at
all. In any case, it soon became apparent that Warr was determined not to
have Hunt driving for Lotus and had only been going through the motions
of offering him a drive to make himself look good. When Hunt realized
what was happening and that he was being used, he called Warr a "pygmy."

Hunt's other offer was from the new, reconstituted Wolf-Williams
team, owned by Walter Wolf and Frank Williams. Williams had bought
the Hesketh 308C car that Hunt had driven in the last three races of
1975. Both Wolf and Williams were now keen to see Hunt drive their
cars. But Hunt believed that the 308C was a terrible car, and he would
only take the drive with Wolf-Williams as a last resort.

Hunt's only other hope was Bernie Ecclestone, the Brabham team
owner. For 1976 the Brabham team was contracted to run Alfa Romeo
engines with the Italian carmaker paying the team's bills with sponsorship
from the Martini & Rossi beverages company. The cars would be driven
by South Americans Carlos Pace and Carlos Reutemann.

Ecclestone sensed Hunt might be out of a drive and wanted to keep
him in the sport. At the time, Ecclestone was just beginning to sell Formula One's television broadcast rights, and he sensed that Hunt would be
a vital part of that, especially in Britain. In the end, Ecclestone's instincts
proved right, and Hunt emerged as the key to unlocking Formula One's
true television potential.

Ecclestone put his formidable mind toward getting Hunt a drive. He
proposed setting up a Brabham B-team, whereby Hunt would drive a
last year's Brabham car fitted with a Ford-Cosworth engine. But when
Ecclestone asked the Italians for permission to run Hunt in a separate
team, they refused point blank. They weren't about to have their Brabham
dream team upstaged by a British playboy driving last year's car and, in
all likelihood, beating them. In the end, even Ecclestone's persuasiveness
couldn't make that deal happen.

Afterwards Hunt was deeply grateful and realized that Ecclestone had placed himself in a very difficult position on his behalf: "I think Bernie was only doing it as a matter of generosity to me."

So Hunt stared unemployment in the face. And that might have been the end for Hunt in Formula One had it not been for John Hogan, who headed up motor sport for the Marlboro cigarette company, the biggest sponsors in Formula One.

By 1975 Hogan had become head of sponsorship with the task of using motor sport sponsorship to establish the Marlboro brand outside of North America. With a budget of $1 million a year to spend on Formula One, Marlboro was the title sponsor of the McLaren Formula One team, and Hogan had the two top drivers of the day, Emerson Fittipaldi and Niki Lauda, signed up to the brand.

Like Ecclestone, Hogan would have liked to give Hunt a drive. To that end, he decided to confide in Hunt some information that no one else knew. Hogan told Hunt that he had one glimmer of hope for 1976. He told him that although Emerson Fittipaldi had signed a contract for the 1976 season worth $250,000 a year to drive for the Marlboro-sponsored McLaren team, it was by no means certain he would honor it. Hogan said that there was a glitch in the paperwork that could allow Fittipaldi to walk away from McLaren.

Fittipaldi had a good reason for walking away. He had been offered $1 million a year, quadruple his existing salary, to drive for a Brazilian team sponsored by Copersucar, the Brazilian state-run sugar refiner. The team was run by his brother, Wilson Fittipaldi, which was another attraction. Fittipaldi pondered his choices. He could not be certain that the Copersucar car would be competitive, although he knew the McLaren would be.

But an extra $750,000 a year was an awful lot of money in the mid-'70s, and he was severely tempted.

Aware of the offer, Hogan and McLaren team principal, Teddy Mayer, were certain that Fittipaldi would turn it down. They were totally relaxed that Fittipaldi would drive for McLaren and put winning races before money.

But they were to be proved very wrong. Hogan, who had a reputation for infallibility where Formula One contracts were concerned, openly admitted he did not see Fittipaldi's defection coming at all. As he said, "Teddy was convinced, we were convinced he was going to drive."

It all came to a head on the evening of Saturday, November 22, when Mayer got a phone call from Fittipaldi, in São Paulo, telling him he had just signed a contract with Copersucar for 1976, and that meant he would not be driving a McLaren. He explained to Mayer that it had been his dream to drive for a Brazilian team.

Mayer could scarcely believe what he was hearing. When Fittipaldi had finished, Mayer told him bluntly that he had a contract to drive the Marlboro McLaren and that he would sue him if he didn't. Fittipaldi politely pointed out that he had not signed his McLaren contract and was sure Marlboro would release him from its contract once they knew that. Fittipaldi had it all worked out. Mayer reflected later, "I can only say he has sold out for a bag of gold."

Mayer was a brusque American, totally devoid of emotion and not one to dwell on the past. But he realized that Fittipaldi's defection was a huge loss. In his two seasons with McLaren, Fittipaldi had finished first and second in the Formula One world championship. In fact, the realization that Fittipaldi would not be driving for McLaren in 1976 hit him like a thunderbolt. He knew it was too late to sign a replacement top-line driver. Mayer picked up the phone to Hogan and asked him what to do. Mayer knew Marlboro would be very disappointed with the news.

It was a cold night, and Hogan was at home with his wife, Anne, in Reading, Berkshire. Mayer didn't waste time talking about Fittipaldi, as Hogan recalls: "Teddy rang me up and just said, 'We need to find a driver.'"

Mayer's idea was to promote Jochen Mass, a German who was McLaren's number two, to be number one driver, and the search would be for a good number two to replace Mass. But unlike Mayer, Hogan did not believe that Mass was good enough to be number one.

Hogan knew he must find a star, a proper number one. In an ideal world, his first choice would have been to lure three-time world champion, the then 37-year-old Jackie Stewart out of retirement, but Hogan knew that wasn't going to happen. As Hogan admits, as much as he may have liked it, "I couldn't see Jackie sitting in the cockpit."

Instead, as Hogan recalls, "I knew who to get instantly—James."

Hogan decided to go after him, but he was immediately met with opposition from both Mayer and Alastair Caldwell, McLaren's team manager; and he knew there would also be objections from his bosses at Marlboro headquarters in Lausanne, Switzerland.

Hogan said, "I knew I had to make it look good, because Marlboro and McLaren would have been just as happy with Jackie Ickx." In fact, Belgian veteran Jackie Ickx was immediately the bookies' favorite to get the drive. But Hogan knew what everyone else didn't: that by then, Ickx was a has-been. He was determined that Ickx did not get the drive.

Hogan had always been very focused, and now all his focus was on Hunt. He instinctively knew there wasn't a moment to lose. In his mind he could already envisage Ickx on a plane to Lausanne to sign a deal with his immediate boss, Marlboro's European vice president of marketing, Pat Duffler. That terrible thought drove him on.

But first Hogan had to find Hunt. On that cold Saturday night in November, he had no idea where Hunt might be found. First he called his home in Marbella, and the person who answered was drunk. The drunkard told Hogan, "We think he's in London." Exasperated, Hogan put down the phone and continued searching. Eventually he tracked Hunt down at Lord Hesketh's town house in London.

It turned out that Hunt already knew Fittipaldi would be leaving McLaren; the Brazilian driver had tipped him off a few days earlier. Hunt was very grateful and said, "This fine gesture by Emerson, from a business point of view, gave me warning—time to get myself ready." He added, "I knew that if Emerson didn't sign, I was going to McLaren. And I had known that since the beginning of September."

Hogan told a disbelieving Hunt, "I'm going to come see you now." Hunt thought Hogan was joking, but Hogan jumped into his Ford Escort and drove from Reading to London at high speed.

But Hunt's confidence was misplaced. Except for Hogan, no one else wanted him to have the drive. Without Hogan lobbying for him, he had little chance of getting it. Ickx was always the favored candidate. In fact, the attitude internally at McLaren at the time was "Anybody *but* Hunt." Fortunately for Hunt, Hogan's attitude was the reverse. It was "Anybody but Ickx," and Hogan ultimately had final say.

When Hogan arrived at Hesketh's house an hour and a half later, Hunt was much the worse for wear and had been smoking cannabis in the company of a girl Hogan hadn't met before, Jane Birbeck. Hunt seemed out of it and unaware of the urgency of Hogan's mission, and even less cognizant of the fact that his entire future was on the line.

Hunt behaved petulantly and refused to talk to Hogan alone, insisting he had no secrets from Jane Birbeck, even though the two hardly knew each other at that stage. On any other day, Hogan might have left and driven home. But he humored Hunt and, against his better judgment, laid out the deal in front of Birbeck. Hogan knew that if the details of a deal got out, Hunt's chances of the McLaren drive would be stone dead. But still, Hunt insisted that she remain present, as he clearly trusted her.

Then Hunt surprised Hogan again. He tried to tell Hogan he had other offers and wasn't particularly interested in the drive. He said that he was about to sign a contract with Lotus. But Hogan knew better. As he recalls: "He tried to convince me that he had a Lotus offer on the table, but I knew that wasn't going to happen."

It turned out that Hunt was overawed by the offer of a McLaren drive. One of Hunt's biggest anxieties was whether he would be able to beat his new teammate Jochen Mass. Mass had a formidable reputation in Formula 3, and Hunt's fears were not as irrational as they may now seem.

Ignoring Hunt's anxieties about Mass, Hogan spelled out what was on offer: three contracts with Marlboro, McLaren, and Texaco and a retainer of $50,000 a year. Hunt knew vaguely what Fittipaldi was earning and told Hogan that his offer was laughable. But Hogan was deadly serious.

Hogan simply reiterated that Hunt was in no position to bargain and that the retainer was $50,000 plus success bonuses, prize money, and extra fees for personal appearances. And that, he said, was that; take it or leave it—knowing all the while that Hunt could not afford to leave it.

Hogan said later, "It was very low on the money; I pushed him down to as low as I thought he would go. We realized he didn't have an option. We played it cool. I was desperate to sign him, but I didn't tell him that."

Hunt looked at his old friend and decided not to call his bluff. He nodded ascent, and with that, Hogan drove back to Reading.

The following morning, Hunt sobered up and telephoned his brother Peter with the news. Peter Hunt was delighted, as well as secretly relieved.

McLaren was the most successful Formula One team of the past five years. It had been founded by Bruce McLaren, a New Zealander who entered Formula One in 1966 and who had been killed testing a sports car at Goodwood in 1970. The team survived its founder's death and carried on, being run by Mayer from a factory at Colnbrook, near London's Heathrow Airport. By the end of 1975 the team had won 15 Formula One grand prix races, the Indianapolis 500, and the Can-Am sports car series in America several times.

On Monday, November 24, Peter Hunt rang Hogan and accepted the offer on behalf of his brother. Hogan immediately set to preparing the contracts and convincing his bosses at Marlboro in Lausanne. Hogan said, "I managed to slip and slide it through, partially on the grounds that it would give us a good story—the Brit [Hunt] against the German [Lauda]."

But Hogan still had to convince McLaren. Team manager Alastair Caldwell did not want Hunt under any circumstances. Caldwell could nix the deal if he had a mind to, as could Mayer.

Neither Mayer nor Caldwell rated Hunt, although they recognized his achievements with the small Hesketh team. So Hogan invited Caldwell to a local hotel and ordered a bottle of Absolut vodka. They drank it between them, and Caldwell was persuaded.

Afterwards Caldwell said, "We had no racing driver, and James had no seat. No option for him and no option for us."

But Caldwell said he still didn't like Hunt and insisted, "James was an ordinary driver to me. We were fairly hard-bitten, we were a professional racing team, and the golden boy–hype business at Hesketh really meant nothing to us. They were just a bunch of wankers."

But Hogan ignored Caldwell and said, "I was convinced he was the right man."

Contract details took only a few days to finalize, and Hogan got the deal done in record time. From hearing about Fittipaldi to signing a contract, it took 13 days to get Hunt's signature. Hogan fought to get Hunt signed to a driving contract before someone said he couldn't.

The contract was finally ready to sign on Friday, December 5, and Hogan took it round to Lord Hesketh's house to get Hunt's signature. When the deal was finally signed, Hunt, Hogan, and his wife donned their finery and walked to the annual British Racing Drivers' Club ball being held at the Dorchester Hotel in London's Park Lane. At the ball, David Benson read the body language and sensed what had happened.

Benson broke the story in the *Sunday Express* some three days before the official announcement. The following Wednesday, McLaren and Marlboro held a joint press conference to announce Hunt as their new driver. At the conference Mayer took all the credit for signing Hunt: "When Emerson Fittipaldi rang me to say he would not be driving for us this season, I was deeply upset, more dismayed than I cared to reveal. It was a great personal relationship, and it had suddenly been jarred. The mood lasted 27 seconds. I thought of James Hunt. I thought of Hunt's great talent, his courage, and his technique. But most of all I thought of his hunger. Like great boxers, a racing driver has to have that thing inside him which drives him on beyond his rivals."

It was utter nonsense, but only John Hogan knew that it was Mayer who had coined the phrase "Anyone but Hunt" within McLaren. Nevertheless, John Hogan stood nearby and just smiled at Mayer's audacity and didn't care to correct him.

But Hogan had one more hurdle to get over. He had to take his new driver to Lausanne to meet his bosses at Marlboro.

Rather typically, Hunt arrived at the offices of Marlboro with no shoes on. Hogan took Hunt into the office of a top Marlboro executive. After they had shaken hands, Hunt walked out of the office and, as soon as he was out of earshot, said in front of more than half a dozen other more-junior Marlboro execs, "He's a cunt." Hogan recalled: "Everybody burst into laughter, and another top Marlboro man said, 'You're absolutely right.'" Years later, the same scene was reenacted in the Jim Carrey film *Liar, Liar.* It is hardly surprising, given the story has been retold so many times, that it has become such a classic.

It was the start of a wonderful relationship and one of the best deals John Hogan ever did for Marlboro. Hunt walked the walk and smoked his Marlboros, and sales of the brand soared across Europe.

Well, actually he didn't really smoke Marlboros. Hunt preferred to smoke Rothmans. But every night, in deference to his new sponsor, Hunt would transfer his Rothmans cigarettes to a Marlboro red-and-white carton.

When all the hurdles had been cleared, both Hunt and his brother Peter were far from elated. Elation had turned into panic very quickly. They were worried that they could not live up to the deals they had signed. As Peter Hunt recalled, "Nobody really knew how good James was. Maybe the Hesketh was a super car and his driving was only average." Hunt himself, for all his self-confidence, was remarkably candid and realistic about his own abilities at the time: "If you want to be ridiculous about it, I wasn't to know if the Hesketh was a car that was three seconds a lap better than anything else and I was just driving it slowly, or vice versa—that it was three seconds a lap worse than anything else and I was driving it mighty quick. You can form opinions, but you don't know for sure."

Niki Lauda observed all these shenanigans from the island of Ibiza, where he spent most of the close season closeted secretly with his new girlfriend, Marlene. He was delighted when Emerson Fittipaldi announced that he had left McLaren, and he believed his closest rival had been sidelined. He shared Alastair Caldwell's opinion of Hunt and didn't really rate him. He had no notion that James Hunt would prove to be his closest competitor in 1976.

The most unlikely of circumstances had set up the Formula One season of 1976 to be the most remarkable ever. And so it proved.

CHAPTER 3

Hunt Astonishes McLaren and Lauda

Pole Comes from Nowhere

Brazil: January 23–25, 1976

The 1976 Brazilian Grand Prix was held at the Interlagos track, just outside São Paulo, over the third weekend of January. In those days, the season started early, and James Hunt flew from his Christmas holidays in Gstaad to South America in plenty of time to acclimatize to the heat and humidity of São Paulo. He wanted as much time as possible to get to know his new team, many of whom he hardly knew. But he also had other motives for arriving early: He wanted to party, which for him involved drinking as much as possible, cocaine, and sleeping with as many women as possible. But as debauched as he was in those two weeks, his antics were a mere shadow of what had gone on in the Hesketh days in São Paulo in 1973 and 1974.

In contrast, Niki Lauda flew to São Paulo the day before the qualifying began and locked himself in his hotel room, spending most of the time watching television, reading, and preparing for the race. When he was racing he avoided drink, drugs, or women. Instead, as a diversion, Lauda had become obsessed with flying, which he found just as fulfilling as driving a race car. He was content to spend his time immersing himself in reading aircraft manuals.

Hunt was totally the opposite; he spent hardly any time in his hotel room, and partying took precedence over racing. He loved the São Paulo social scene and had made many friends there in 1973 and 1974, when he and Alexander Hesketh had had plenty of money to spend.

With Alexander gone, Hunt spent much time in the company of Max Mosley. The 36-year-old Mosley ran the March Formula One team and was also part-time secretary of the Formula One Constructors' Association (FOCA), run by Bernie Ecclestone. He and Hunt got on very well; it was a relationship that dated from five years earlier, when Hunt had raced March cars. Hunt liked Mosley, and the two men both liked women; they also shared a similar outlook on life, although Mosley didn't indulge in drugs.

Mosley recalled a reception hosted by Marlboro cigarettes, Hunt's main sponsor. To get to the party, Mosley and Hunt decided to share a car and set off together across São Paulo. As Mosley recalled, "James said to me, 'Do you mind if I stop at one of my friends' on the way?' And I said, 'No, not at all.' So we stopped at this very posh block of flats and went up to the top floor. There was this amazing flat with an amazing view, and a very nice man. We all sat down, and the nice man got out a piece of highly polished stone and laid out on it three lines of white powder. James turned to me and said, 'You don't want yours, Max, do you?' And he did both of them. We then went happily on to the party." It was a typical incident and by no means uncommon.

Mosley also observed at close hand Hunt's remarkable capacity for women. He believed Hunt was a man totally incapable of being monogamous or faithful to one woman. In modern parlance, he believed Hunt was a sex addict, and there is no question he had a big appetite for it. Hunt's preference was for wholesome, nice girls. At races he was very successful with women, but the type of girl he liked did not always fall easily into bed with him. For those who resisted his charms, he had a fallback line that typically won them over. He would tell the women: "But I might be killed in the race."

Hunt had a girl in every port, and his main Brazilian girlfriend at the time was 19-year-old Charlene Shorto, a well-connected socialite, and they were an item for much of the time he was in South America. Shorto was the sister of Baroness Denise Thyssen, who was married to Baron Henri Thyssen, the iron and steel heir who also owned the world's most valuable art collection. But Shorto was by no means the only girl on Hunt's radar in Brazil. Jochen Mass, his teammate, recounted an anecdote that reflected Hunt's cavalier attitude toward women at the time: "There was a girl called Mercedes, and she worked for Spanish television. She said, 'Can I do an interview?' He said, 'Not a problem,' and they stood him beside the camera. And as she was asking him a question, he asked her [on camera]: 'Do you fuck?'"

Mass recalled that Hunt was never afraid of discussing sex and his requirements, even with journalists. He said sex for him was a therapeutic form of relaxation. He called it a "form of communication."

Mosley witnessed all of this in São Paulo in the week before the race and remarked, "I mean, he was just full-on into women." Hunt was very candid about his attitude toward sex during a race weekend: "I don't usually have sex before a race because I am very definitely concentrating. I find that it is the communication between two people that makes it worthwhile, and before a race I am pretty uncommunicative. However, if, say, I have an hour or so to spare before dinner on the night before a race, then I can enjoy the physical release. But I will only do it with someone who is fully understanding."

After two weeks of virtually nonstop partying, the race weekend finally arrived, which meant there was less time for hedonism.

Both Hunt and Lauda had political problems within their teams. Neither felt they had done enough testing over the winter season, and both believed that their teams were resting on their laurels.

Lauda, in particular, was reeling from the resignation of Luca di Montezemolo as Ferrari team manager.

Montezemolo had been parachuted into Ferrari by Fiat boss Gianni Agnelli at the age of 26 to effectively sideline the founder, Enzo Ferrari, and take control of the team. Before Montezemolo's arrival, the team had not won a world championship for 11 years. Agnelli, who had great respect for Enzo Ferrari, wanted the denouement done subtly with no embarrassment to the old man who, despite his many failings, Agnelli revered.

Montezemolo had owed his rise at such a young age to his special connections with the Agnelli family. His own family background had always been shrouded in some mystery. Officially he was born in Bologna and was the youngest son of Massimo Cordero dei Marchesi di Montezemolo, a minor Piedmontese aristocrat whose family was connected to Italian royalty. His mother was Clotilde Neri, who was related to the famous Italian surgeon Vincenzo Neri. The rumors were that his real father was Gianni Agnelli, who had had an affair with his mother. Those rumors are unspoken in Italy, and the real story has never been revealed.

Whatever the truth, Montezemolo more than lived up to the responsibilities he was given by Agnelli. Although ridiculously young for the role as head of Ferrari's Formula One team, Montezemolo rose to the task. His reign had been fantastically successful.

Part of the problem had been the irascibility of founder Enzo Ferrari, then in his late 70s. Enzo Ferrari was a schizophrenic. One moment he could be incredibly overbearing and pompous, a complete bully, but after he got his own way in a discussion—or at least thought he had—he turned immediately into a charming, warm human being whom no one could fail to like.

Montezemolo had succeeded brilliantly in sidelining Enzo, placing the Ferrari founder in a metaphorical box where he could do no damage but still take all the credit for the team's revival.

Montezemolo did all that was asked of him and proved a brilliant manager and, more important, a brilliant politician. Montezemolo spearheaded the revival that had culminated in Lauda's 1975 championship win and was entirely responsible for the team's renaissance after years in the Formula One wilderness.

But Montezemolo was a talented young man in a very big hurry. Running the Ferrari Formula One team, as glamorous as it was, was a small job, and he was eager to move on to bigger things. Lauda had total respect for Montezemolo and pleaded with him not to leave. But the ambitious Italian saw Formula One as a backwater and had higher ambitions within the top management at Fiat Group, which owned Ferrari. As soon as he could, he quietly left after appointing a new team manager, Daniele Audetto. But Audetto was a very strange choice and seemed to have been decided upon more by Montezemolo's personal friendship with him than by his ability to do the job.

Audetto, who had a rally background, had previously managed some of Fiat's motor sporting activities. Montezemolo was a close friend, and they had driven rally cars together in their youth. Their driving careers ended when Audetto was seriously injured in an accident that also prompted Montezemolo to retire from the sport. After Audetto recovered from the accident, he graduated from Bocconi University, and Montezemolo helped him get a job at Fiat.

Lauda had approved the appointment of Audetto on Montezemolo's advice, but it soon became apparent that although the 33-year-old Audetto was four years older than Montezemolo, he was too young and inexperienced and seemed immediately out of his depth. Audetto grated on Lauda straightaway, and Lauda described him to a friend as a "fraught personality."

The problems did not really start, however, until they got to Brazil. Lauda said later that Audetto's personality changed before his eyes. As he perfectly described: "Slowly he realized, mostly through the Italian press, who treated him with great respect, what an unbelievably important job it is to be racing team leader for Ferrari; he was quite overcome by his own importance."

In São Paulo the invitations flooded in from Brazil's great and good. Audetto loved socializing and wanted to go out every night and take Lauda, whom he saw as his employee, with him. Audetto treated Lauda as a trophy, and the driver thought this was ridiculous. Lauda resisted the invitations and flattery, and soon a split appeared.

After that, the relationship deteriorated rapidly as Audetto discovered what a difficult job he had taken on. There were additional complications. Montezemolo's departure had left a power vacuum in the team, into which stepped a newly energized Enzo Ferrari. It was not something Audetto had anticipated, nor was it something he was equipped to handle. Audetto likened the job to being a referee trying to keep order among Ferrari's feuding factions, all of whom came out to play once Montezemolo was gone.

The result was typical Italian chaos where order had previously reigned. As Lauda observed ruefully, "The loss of Luca is a great blow to me."

It also seemed clear that Audetto preferred Ferrari's number two, the Swiss driver Clay Regazzoni, to Lauda. Whereas Lauda was dismissive of Audetto and what he believed were his pompous airs and graces, Regazzoni played up to him. The 37-year-old Regazzoni secretly harbored grudges against the younger Lauda that dated back to 1973, when they had driven together in the BRM team. When they both moved to Ferrari in 1974, Regazzoni had been number one driver, but he had been completely outdriven by Lauda in 1975 and was relegated to number two status. It rankled, and when Audetto arrived, the older man saw it as his chance to push Lauda aside.

Regazzoni assiduously went about the task of undermining Lauda. Lauda believed that he pandered to Audetto's vanity. As Lauda recalled, "Audetto was naturally closer to Regazzoni than he was to me, partly because they spoke the same language but also because of Clay's more enthusiastic social life."

During the weekend, Lauda coped with the shifting political sands by completely outdriving Regazzoni on the track. It solved the immediate problem; the real difficulties would surface a few months later.

James Hunt found that he had remarkably similar problems at McLaren.

The management of the team was dominated by two men, Teddy Mayer and Alastair Caldwell. Both were talented in their own way, but both were men of extremes with, as Hunt once confided to a friend, "a capacity for competence and incompetence in equal measure."

Caldwell and Mayer had a difficult relationship themselves. They disliked each other and most of the time held each other in contempt. It was a recipe for management disaster, but somehow the team seemed to work under their complementary skills.

Mayer had graduated from Cornell Law School in New York with a law degree. But he never practiced and after graduation went to work managing the affairs of his racing driver brother, Timmy, in Australia and New Zealand.

Mayer met McLaren team founder Bruce McLaren in the early 1960s. Bruce was impressed by Mayer's sharp analytical skills, and they quickly became friends. When Timmy died after a racing accident in Tasmania, Bruce McLaren invited Mayer to come and work for him in England. Mayer bought shares in Bruce McLaren Motor Racing Ltd. and became a director. When Bruce McLaren was killed in June 1970, Mayer bought more shares and shared ownership of the team with Bruce McLaren's widow, Patty. In the five years that followed, Mayer turned McLaren into Formula One's most successful team. Whether this success was due to serendipity, the foundations laid down by Bruce, or to Mayer's own ability, no one really knew. But whatever it was, Mayer took the credit.

In all this time, Alastair Caldwell was Mayer's number two. Caldwell was a rough-hewn New Zealander steeped in motor racing. Like Mayer, he had arrived at McLaren after a tragedy; his brother Bill had been killed in a motor racing crash in 1967.

Caldwell proved to be a talented engineer, but his rise was blighted by the fact that he didn't get on with Mayer. Put simply, Mayer didn't rate him. But when Bruce McLaren was killed, Mayer increasingly appreciated Caldwell's talents and softened his attitude. Four years later, he made Caldwell manager of the Formula One team.

The record says that Caldwell's appointment was a huge success and he welded together a talented team of mechanics, including the legendary Dave Ryan, Steve Bunn, Lance Gibbs, Ray Grant, Howard Moore, and Mark Scott. But Caldwell's critics say he was made to look good by the skills of these mechanics.

And that is the situation in which James Hunt found himself when he arrived at the team in 1976.

What Hunt didn't know then was that Alastair Caldwell had told the team that Jochen Mass was the number one driver and that the mechanics should treat him accordingly. Mass had the support of the management and, in both Mayer and Caldwell's judgment, he would prove to be faster than Hunt. So although Hunt had taken the number one car, they considered Mass to be the number one driver. Instead of fighting Niki Lauda for the championship, Hunt found his first battle was with his teammate—to be number one in his own team. Both Mayer and Caldwell fully expected Mass to blow off Hunt.

It was a massive misjudgment, as 30-year-old Jochen Mass was only an average driver. Born in Munich, Mass was a year older than Hunt, although a less-experienced driver. He had started driving competitively at the age of 21 after a spell in the German merchant navy.

The matter was further complicated by the fact that Hunt had history with Mass from their Formula 3 days in 1972. Mass had taken over Hunt's March works drive, and Hunt now sensed that history was repeating itself. Indeed, Mass harbored the same secret grudge against newcomer Hunt that Regazzoni held against Lauda.

It was a difficult situation, particularly as Hunt and Mass became good friends straightaway. Mass was something of a playboy himself, and when he wasn't racing, he spent most of his time sailing in the south of France. Later Mass denied there were ever any such problems between them: "As teammates, basically we got along fine. It was a very happy team."

But not in Brazil it wasn't.

The political problems that both Hunt and Lauda were facing at McLaren and Ferrari were being fanned by the winds of economic recession blowing down the Formula One pit lane. The global recession had started with the Arab oil crisis in 1973–74 but, in true fashion, had only hit Formula One once longstanding sponsorship contracts had expired and proved difficult to renew at previous rates.

By 1976 the recession was in full swing, and every Formula One team was hit hard at the start of the season. Money was very tight, as Teddy Mayer was always reminding people. The lavish spending of the Fittipaldi era was well and truly over. But Hunt felt that Mayer had gone too far with his economizing and that it was affecting the team's performance.

McLaren had a reputation for engineering excellence, but Hunt found a complete lack of preparedness at the first race. There had been no preseason testing, as Mayer wouldn't sign off on the money needed for a proper winter testing program. Mayer believed that Emerson Fittipaldi had developed the car as far as it could go, and they didn't think a formal testing program was necessary. To some extent that was true; by 1976 the McLaren-Ford M23 was a beautifully sorted car. Fittipaldi was a brilliant test driver, and he had left behind a car with a highly sophisticated suspension system.

The lack of winter testing bothered Hunt, but he was even more troubled by the fact that McLaren had not built him a new chassis to suit his physical characteristics. Instead they gave him an old Fittipaldi chassis, no. M23/8/2, which had been built in 1975 and had seen plenty of use. Hunt was a tall man, while Fittipaldi was diminutive. But Mayer refused to authorize the building of a new chassis for Hunt on the grounds of cost.

When he first got in it for a shakedown at Silverstone, Hunt found the McLaren car not to his liking. His feet were uncomfortable on the pedals, his knees were too high in the cockpit, and his elbows didn't clear the sides of the cockpit. He also complained that the steering was heavy. He said, "The cockpit was all wrong. I literally couldn't drive the car. I was in great physical discomfort."

It was clear that the car was too small for Hunt, and the seat fitting at the factory had been less than perfect. The trouble with seat fittings was that they were done in a static car. At racing speeds, it was very different.

It was obvious that a new chassis was needed for the taller driver, and Hunt was shocked that it wasn't built. Meticulous attention to detail had always been a McLaren hallmark, and Hunt told anyone who would listen that the McLaren team under Mayer was a "rudderless ship," adding, "It didn't have any direction."

Added to that was the uncertainty of McLaren's new car, the M26, which was waiting in the wings.

Hunt was genuinely surprised to find that, in so many ways, McLaren was inferior to the Hesketh team and that the Hesketh team manager, Anthony (Bubbles) Horsley, was a superior manager to Caldwell. Hunt explained: "With Hesketh, we used to spend a lot of time examining ourselves. Bubbles used to exercise tremendous discipline."

In fact, Hunt was scathing about McLaren's approach to team discipline, as he had expected a much harsher regime. He explained: "McLaren don't give me any discipline at all. They let me do exactly what I want to do, and they don't take any notice of me."

Hunt was particularly upset about McLaren's casual attitude to debriefs. As he said, "The debriefing sessions we have at McLaren aren't the same sort of thing at all. We discuss something if we feel like it. But [here] if nobody wants to talk, we don't . . . I would actually get into trouble with Bubbles if I talked to anybody else after a practice, and before I had sat down, he would have wrung the truth from me and we would all have had a big postmortem."

Mayer and Caldwell were forced to defend themselves against Hunt's accusations, and they blamed his attitude for the problems.

Mayer said, "Possibly, James's initial shortcomings were that he didn't like taking decisions. He had been in a team where all the decisions were taken for him; where Bubbles Horsley told him exactly what to do all the time. I think that it's better for a driver to learn to take his own decisions because he has more information available to him, and this is where a more mature driver will ultimately do better." Caldwell added, "As team manager, I want to be able to contribute to the choice of tire or choice of settings on the car, but ultimately the driver has got the say, and I think initially James wanted us to do that."

Hunt complained to John Hogan of Marlboro about what was going on. He was so angry that he informed Hogan he wanted to leave McLaren and cancel his contract. Hogan sympathized and was also angry with Mayer. Marlboro's budget was generous by the standards of the day—the biggest in the paddock—and Marlboro expected the money to be spent making the car as competitive as possible. Hogan wasn't at all enamored with the penny-pinching he was witnessing.

But after a meeting with Mayer, Hogan was told that all the team's cash had been spent on developing the new car, the M26. Mayer told Hogan that he had never expected Hunt to have to race the M23. Mayer finally admitted that the new M26 had proved to be substantially slower than the M23 in testing and needed a redesign.

When Hunt learned of this, he was apoplectic and shouted at Mayer for not telling him the truth of the situation. Hunt famously told Mayer, "I'll tell you Teddy, and I've told you before, you don't know anything about motor racing whatsoever. Go and buy a new briefcase."

As soon as Caldwell had realized that the new M26 was a dog, he had embarked on a crash course to improve the M23. It was too late to build a new chassis, so Caldwell modified the existing cars. Caldwell made three principal changes to start the season. He managed to knock a staggering 40 kilos off the weight of the car, principally by redesigning the bodywork using the latest materials. He tweaked the rear suspension by reverting to the previously used lower wishbone design instead of parallel links. But his masterstroke was the introduction for the first time in Formula One of a six-speed version of the Hewland FGA box, which he had intended to debut in the new M26. The car certainly looked faster, as John Hogan had repainted the cars in Day-Glo red to make them stand out on television.

But there had been no time to test any of the modifications. So when qualifying started on Friday, January 23, Hunt immediately found that the steering was very heavy and the new bodywork cramped. On his first time out, he found himself wrestling with the steering and his hand continually hitting the cockpit sides. As a result, he badly blistered his thumb in only a few laps. He drove back into the pits, waving his blistered thumb furiously at Mayer.

Hunt went public straightaway on McLaren's unpreparedness and readily spoke his mind to journalists. John Hogan of Marlboro was on hand and advised him to quiet down. Hogan warned Hunt that he risked being fired if he carried on and that he had no other place to go if McLaren rejected him. But it was too late; the damage had been done.

Predictably, when Mayer learned what Hunt had been saying about his team, there was a furious row. For Hunt it was a pivotal moment—he could either walk away from the team at the first race, or Mayer could begin listening to him. That Friday evening, Caldwell intervened between the two men and set to work lightening the steering and modifying the cockpit to suit Hunt's requirements. Despite the problems, Hunt managed to set the seventh quickest time in the first day, although his teammate Jochen Mass was fourth fastest.

Niki Lauda had had an entirely different first day of qualifying. Ferrari had a new car under development that was still six months away from being completed. In the meantime, it would rely on last year's championship winning car, the 312T. Even though it had had minimal testing or development over the winter, it was fast straightaway. The only modification was slightly narrower track rear suspension that was supposed to lift the top speed. As a result, Lauda simply carried on where he had left off in 1975. He was fastest of all at the end of the first day, and Ferrari underlined its supremacy with Regazzoni coming in second fastest. Hunt was also outqualified by Emerson Fittipaldi in his new Copersucar-Ford car.

Caldwell and the McLaren mechanics worked all night to modify Hunt's car and presented it to him on Saturday morning with heavily modified steering and bodywork—as much as could be achieved thousands of miles away from the factory.

But Hunt's luck was out and, as the final qualifying approached, his Ford-Cosworth engine blew up. In those days, engines could be changed in less than two hours provided everything went smoothly. But the engine change didn't go as planned, and the final qualifying hour began with Hunt's car still in bits.

Predictably, the tension rose in the McLaren pit, and Mayer and Hunt started arguing again. While he was waiting, Hunt ordered his mechanics to make some suspension setup changes. But Mayer immediately countermanded the instructions and told the mechanics to leave the suspension settings alone. A furious Hunt barged into Mayer, elbowing him in the ribs. Screaming at Mayer, he told him to get out of his way. Mayer stood his ground and told Hunt he would have to go out with the car in the same spec in which the last session had ended. Hunt recalled the situation that afternoon: "I was going out with 20 minutes left on a 5-mile track. I was guessing the settings, and Mayer told me, 'You can't do that.' I told him I was driving the bloody thing. I wasn't going to be pushed around when I knew what I wanted."

The fierce arguing and physical altercation took place in front of the McLaren mechanics, who were astonished to hear their boss being shouted at. They had never seen anything like it before.

Hunt then threw Mayer's briefcase to the back of the garage and threatened him further if he didn't leave. At that point, Mayer retreated and the mechanics made the changes to the suspension that Hunt had requested.

But as soon as Mayer left, Hunt knew he was in trouble and likely to be fired if he qualified behind Mass. As he left the pit lane with 20 minutes to go, he couldn't have been more motivated to succeed.

Indeed, Hunt had read the situation correctly. A shocked Mayer went to the back of the pits and sat down on an old oil drum. He opened his briefcase and started studying the minutia of the driving contract between the team and Hunt. He fully intended to dismiss Hunt from the team as soon as qualifying was over. He studied the fine print of the contract to see what the financial consequences would be.

As Hunt left the pit lane for his warm-up lap, he was not under any illusions about what awaited him on his return. He realized that he could not treat Mayer as he had and still expect to remain on the team. He knew that keeping his job depended on him grabbing pole position for the race.

Hunt gave it all he had, and he went fastest of all on his first flying lap. Lauda was pushed into second place on the grid with only 10 minutes of the session remaining.

Hunt's time was 200th of a second better than Lauda's best. Hunt rolled back into the pits gesticulating wildly at Mayer, who was sitting open-mouthed behind the fencing, not knowing whether to believe his own eyes.

Lauda was sitting on the Ferrari pit counter. He had not intended to return to the track that day and had been saving his engine and his tires for the race, believing he had done enough to get pole. Now he realized he would have to go out again and do another flying lap. It was an inconvenient development, but he was not worried, as he knew he had not pushed the Ferrari to its limit that weekend.

As he drove out of the pits, everyone expected Lauda to grab pole back from Hunt, and that's the way it looked as he sped out—that was until halfway though his fast lap.

Just at the wrong moment, Lauda's luck changed. As he approached the Curva do Sol bend, he found the BRM of Ian Ashley in front of him. As he moved to overtake the slower car, the BRM's 12-cylinder engine blew up in the most spectacular fashion and splashed oil all over the road and smeared Lauda's visor. Any chance of a faster lap was over, and the world champion found himself second on the grid after being fastest for virtually all the qualifying sessions. Lauda got out of his car in a furious mood and threw down his helmet. He stepped out of his overalls and set off for the BRM pit, whose pit crew he blamed for his misfortune. Halfway there he stopped and turned around, realizing it was just a racing incident and that it could have happened to anyone.

Hunt's pole position was made even sweeter by the fact that he had blown off his highly vaunted teammate. He had also put his predecessor, Emerson Fittipaldi, to the sword. Driving in Fittipaldi's home country, in Fittipaldi's old car, Hunt had beaten him. All his nemeses—Mayer, Niki Lauda, Fittipaldi, and Mass—had been vanquished in one stroke.

Although Fittipaldi and Lauda were upset, Jochen Mass was devastated by Hunt's performance. He had believed he would easily outqualify Hunt and be crowned the team's number one driver.

Meanwhile, Teddy Mayer had returned to the McLaren pit after his earlier expulsion and still couldn't believe what he had just seen. Never before had he witnessed such amazing bravado and experienced such a conflict of emotions within a 20-minute time frame. Having been prepared to fire Hunt the minute he stepped out of the cockpit, Mayer completely forgot about that and was now ecstatic. He embraced Hunt with as much vigor and passion as he had ever shown toward another man.

Mayer was most excited because Fittipaldi's nose had been rubbed in it. The resentment at Fittipaldi's abrupt departure had been gnawing away at Mayer for weeks. As Hunt recalled: "In front of the Brazilian crowd, it was almost more than Mayer could take. It was not what McLaren had been used to with Emerson. But it was important psychologically, because we immediately had each other's respect."

He said, "It was my first-ever pole, which I was rather pleased about. And it impressed the boys. After that, I was very much number one."

Caldwell and the mechanics were suddenly in awe of their new driver. In that five-minute window, Hunt had established undoubted number one status, ensuring that Mass would not challenge him again.

The last-minute battle for pole revived local interest in the race and set the turnstiles rattling on race morning. Race day dawned hot and sunny as the 22 cars assembled on the grid. For Niki Lauda, who was used to sitting on the front row of the grid, it was just another race with the only difference being an unfamiliar helmet alongside him. Being beaten by Hunt in qualifying was a minor annoyance, and the two men sat on the front row of the grid glaring at each other.

But for James Hunt, his first-ever pole position in a Grand Prix was a very big deal indeed. He found he was extremely nervous. He started shaking, and three times had to go round to the back of the garages to vomit. The vomiting was normal before a race, but this time it was exacerbated by the amount of cocaine, alcohol, and nicotine circulating in his body. Aside from illness, Hunt was particularly frightened of burning his clutch on the start line and feared he would make a poor start and let Lauda lead away.

Hunt's fears became a self-fulfilling prophecy, and that is exactly what happened as Lauda went off ahead of him. Hunt said, "I erred on the side of safety; one thing I didn't want was to not get to the first corner at all."

But it was Clay Regazzoni who outran both of them. He led the opening laps, with Lauda close behind and Hunt third after a very brief challenge from Fittipaldi, which faded as quickly as it had begun.

It was immediately clear that Lauda was much quicker than Regazzoni, and so he bided his time, knowing it would come. But after seven laps, Lauda suddenly got annoyed and started harrying Regazzoni. They were looking like anything but teammates as they squabbled on the track. On lap nine, Lauda swept past and within one lap opened up a three-and-a-half-second gap, demonstrating to Audetto, who was standing in the pits with his stopwatch, how superior a driver he was.

Watching how easily Lauda had disposed of Regazzoni, Hunt saw his chance and on the next lap also went past. Regazzoni had overcooked his tires trying to stay in front and quickly lost his right front tire, which had worn to the canvas. He had to pit when the tire finally gave way.

The race seemed set for a battle royal between Hunt and Lauda, but the contest ended as quickly as it had started when Hunt's new Cosworth engine let him down. One of the eight fuel injector trumpets fell off, and the cylinder stopped firing altogether. The engine would still have taken him through to the finish if it hadn't been for the trumpet moving around and eventually dropping into the throttle slides.

Lauda was then briefly challenged by Jean-Pierre Jarier's Shadow-Ford car, which was flying and looked set to overtake him. With nine laps to go, Jarier drove the fastest lap of the race. But at that moment, Hunt inadvertently delivered to Lauda a huge favor. Hunt's throttle jammed wide open and threw him into the catch fencing at high speed. Catch fencing, widely used in that era of Formula One, had many faults; but that day it probably saved Hunt's life. That, coupled with his skill in spinning the car around, prevented what would have been a major accident. As it was, Hunt was able to get his car out of the fencing with the engine still running, and he drove it back onto the track. But the oil cooler had been ripped off, and it had deposited an oil slick on the track just as Lauda and Jarier were coming around. Lauda's greater experience and cunning enabled him to navigate his way through without mishap. But Jarier couldn't; he locked his tires and skidded off into the barrier, crumpling the car and leaving Lauda to cruise to victory.

Lauda's win had been heavily aided by the problems of Regazzoni, Hunt, and Jarier, all of whom would most likely have beaten him on the day. But Lauda didn't see it that way at all and was ecstatic that he had vanquished all his rivals, including Emerson Fittipaldi, who brought his dire Copersucar car in 13th in front of some very disappointed fans. Jochen Mass finished sixth.

Lauda didn't care how the victory had been achieved and believed he had taken on all comers and demolished them. But Hunt was brutally honest about his own performance: "I wasn't quite quick enough; I was about five seconds behind Niki when I had trouble. A trumpet fell off and the engine started misfiring, and then, not content with that, it jumped down the throttle slides, which stuck it open in the middle of a great long corner. I wasn't man enough to handle that, even though it was only on seven cylinders."

After all the drama of qualifying, Hunt was magnanimous in defeat. And any thoughts that Mayer had had of firing him were completely gone. Both men were relieved when the race was over, and discord turned to complete harmony. In post-race chats to journalists, it was all sweetness and light. In fact, Hunt seemed to have completely forgotten all the acrimony that had gone on over the previous three days: "Fortunately we got it all together, and I think everyone—particularly Teddy, John (Hogan), and me—breathed a huge sigh of relief."

Alastair Caldwell had also completely changed his tune and now declared how glad he was to have Hunt in the team. He had never imagined that Hunt would be faster than Jochen Mass, and when it happened, he was genuinely stunned. Caldwell famously said, "This unknown bloke came in and blew Mass away. It doesn't matter if the guy has got number one written on his forehead or tattooed over his whole body, if he's second fastest, he's number two—period."

The same situation, albeit in an entirely different manner, was manifesting itself in the Ferrari garage. Niki Lauda had carried on where he had left off, and Daniele Audetto had won his first race as Ferrari team manager. It seemed both of them could walk on water, and they temporarily forgot their differences.

But there was one crucial difference between the McLaren and Ferrari teams as they both packed up to leave for home: While Caldwell, Mayer, and Hunt had genuinely put their differences aside and harbored no rancor, Lauda and Audetto's rapprochement was only temporary. Audetto was seething that Regazzoni had not won, and Lauda told friends he believed Audetto was a pompous clown.

In the end, it was the politics that would decide the outcome of the 1976 Formula One world championship—not the drivers, nor the cars, nor the teams.

CHAPTER 4

Niki's Women Problems

Marlene Replaces Mariella

Summer 1975

S ometime in the middle of 1975, Niki Lauda fell out of love with his girlfriend of eight years, Mariella von Reininghaus. The sudden realization that, after all, he would not eventually marry Mariella was the equivalent to a volcanic eruption in his emotions.

As romantic as the next man but devoid of many of the emotions of normal human beings, Lauda had always struggled with his love life. He was a man whose metaphysical makeup evolved at different, inconsistent speeds over long and undefined periods of his life—sometimes suddenly changing without warning.

Emotionally he lacked consistency of purpose, which often led him into sudden decisions and diversions that defied logical analysis. It was a trait that followed him throughout his life and at times gave him that special edge that was often the difference between success and failure. When the traits were deployed well, they worked phenomenally well. But when not deployed well, they had the inevitable consequences, which often took years to play out due to the complexity of the thoughts behind them.

To understand Niki Lauda, it was necessary to know him and to have observed him over a lifetime, so unusual was his emotional makeup. In time, the giants of motor racing, including people such as Enzo Ferrari,

Bernie Ecclestone, and Ron Dennis were to run up against that curious concoction of emotions and emerge second best.

In contrast, James Hunt was a simple man: easy to understand, easy to fathom, and therefore easy to predict. But that could never be said of Niki Lauda.

The most obvious discrepancy in Lauda's character was inconsistency. Lauda very often displayed the most inconsistent urges that could possibly be present in a human being. He would strongly criticize and condemn others, sometimes publicly but often in private, and then immediately display the same foibles and failures himself.

Suffice to say that Lauda's emotional and intellectual constitution was not the standard off-the-shelf variety. And that all manifested itself in the summer of 1975, when he switched off his fiancée of eight years and flicked to another woman, whom he had met at a party.

The Lauda/von Reininghaus relationship was almost an institution within Formula One's tight-knit community. Outside the sport they were one of Europe's best-known and loved celebrity couples. In the top social salons of continental Europe, they were the top go-to couple.

Almost everyone regarded their relationship as near perfect. Mariella was an extraordinary woman in every way, striking to look at and owning a personality that was very easy to like. If Europe had then had an eligible woman league table, Mariella would have been at the top.

The fact that she was also one of the best-connected young women in Austria seemed almost inconsequential. Added to that the fact that she was the daughter of an Austrian brewery millionaire and the product of an enormously wealthy family, she was indeed the perfect woman that Lauda had always sought and seemingly found so early in his life.

If Mariella had a fault, it was with her sexuality. Outwardly she had sex appeal, but inwardly she was reserved.

They met when they were both teenagers, and she was his first girl-friend and he her first boyfriend. He was attracted to her smooth beauty and she to his dashing lifestyle. Although he was perpetually broke, he drove a Porsche 911S. She liked his seemingly endless ambition to get on at such a young age and found life around him to be exciting.

He found her totally undemanding and willing to fit in with the life of an aspiring racing driver. She was content to let him take the limelight and to settle down as his shadow. Socially, however, Lauda was in her shadow; he was not in her class.

Success in his career was the objective that both of them worked toward. Mariella devoted years to supporting her young boyfriend as he struggled to make it as a racing driver.

Lauda admitted that Mariella had all the qualities that he really looked for and respected in a woman. As he said many times: "Mariella was very disciplined, quiet, thoughtful, and with endless patience." So it was no surprise when he proposed to her soon after they met, although no wedding date was ever set.

Lauda was just as keen as Mariella toward that end, and he called his relationship with her a near-marriage. He said about her, "I was almost certain we would get married." Her personality suited his career perfectly, as Lauda always readily admitted. As he described it: "During test driving and practice, she could sit for hours on a heap of tires without moving or speaking; she was good at yoga! If I came by once an hour and gave her a kiss, she was perfectly satisfied. Her self-control was sometimes almost uncanny."

But the downside of Mariella, and an aspect Lauda railed against, was the total control she sought over his life. As he explained: "She had great influence over me and tried to have even more. Up to that point, I was glad to let this happen."

There was, however, a sting in the tail. As soon as he was successful, Mariella expected her boyfriend to retire from racing and to settle into a safer, more predictable career. While he was unsuccessful, Lauda went along with that. And he couldn't imagine being with anyone except her.

All went along swimmingly until Lauda signed for Ferrari in 1974. For the first time they had money. With some of the cash, they bought land outside Salzburg for their dream home, for when they got married and started a family. It was something that was absolutely taken for granted in the relationship.

Mariella firmly believed that once her boyfriend had achieved his goals and become world champion, he would be true to his promise made many years earlier and would give up his complete obsession with motor racing and devote himself to her and a family—she really believed that. She thought they were an unbreakable team, and so did he.

But she hadn't counted on success changing Lauda into something he wasn't when he was 18 and struggling. It has to be said: It wasn't a change for the better.

As soon as Lauda tasted success, he wanted more and more. When he had been a failure as a race driver, it was easy to think of stopping, as Lauda got no pleasure from losing. But success changed all that, and Mariella failed to notice.

Typically, racing drivers are pleasant people on the way up and after they retire. During the successful years, however, they often change into egomaniacal monsters, and Lauda, although not the worst example in history, was not immune from those pressures. It was reflected in the way Lauda often treated autograph hunters. The coldness with which he dismissed them, even young children, often shocked people.

Mariella did not notice the personality changes that were gradually starting to happen. The difference between them was that she put the relationship first, and he put motor racing first. Lauda explained: "She began to make plans for me to give up driving; become world champion, then finish it. Family, a decent job, that was her line, and she pushed it hard."

But once he had tasted that success, after years of being forced to swallow failure, Lauda was never going to give up racing. After one world championship, he simply desired a second. He was a consummate risk taker, and she failed to recognize that. Mariella simply wanted a family and a loving husband. His success and retirement to normal life was an essential part of Mariella's ambitions and her life plan, and she would make any sacrifice to get it. Lauda, however, admitted, "I had no desire to retire at the age of 26. Even though age had little to do with it, I simply didn't want to do it."

When that became clear, strife came into their relationship for the first time. Lauda even began to dislike elements of Mariella's personality—an emotion he had never felt in all the years they had been together. But she simply didn't notice.

Lauda could see that if he did not retire at the end of 1975, as Mariella expected, there would be trouble. As he said, "I dreaded the endless arguments that would ensue if, in fact, I stayed in racing after becoming world champion. We quarreled more and more often."

But having money brought matters to a head. It meant they could afford to build a dream home. The building of a new house, their eventual marital home, gave Mariella a real purpose in life for the first time, and she threw herself into it. As Lauda was winning his first world championship in 1975, Mariella was overseeing the architect building the house.

During 1975 they naturally began to see less of each other, and the split happened gradually, without either really being aware of it. As Lauda admits, the house took over Mariella's life as much as motor racing had taken over his: "Everything to do with my house, the building of which she almost took over." In 1975 they both had too much else to think about, and when they finally did look to each other, it was too late—it was already over.

There is no question that Lauda was frightened of the consequences of splitting up with Mariella. For all of his success and fame, he was no match for her as a human being. And deep down he knew it. Mariella von Reininghaus was deeply loved by everyone Lauda knew. He knew that everyone, certainly everyone who mattered, held Mariella in the very highest regard.

He too held her in the highest esteem; the only problem was that after eight years, he had fallen out of love with her, and it took the arrival of a new woman in his life for him to do anything about it.

Lauda met Marlene Knaus in the summer of 1975. She was half Latin and half Austrian and worked as a part-time actress and model. Her family was not wealthy like Mariella's, but it was very distinguished. Her grandfather was a renowned gynecologist and her father a famous Austrian painter.

The relationship started at the Salzburg home of Hollywood actor Curt Jurgens. Jurgens was one of Austria's best-known celebrities and a Hollywood superstar in his prime. Now aging and past his peak years, he was still in huge demand as a supporting actor in a variety of roles from

James Bond films to serious dramas. He had earned at least $4 million over 40 years as an actor. He was also a consummate ladies' man and a playboy and held legendary parties at his various homes.

At the time Marlene was Jurgens's regular girlfriend, but then Jurgens had a girl in every port, and it was far from a serious committed deep relationship. Jurgens was also twice Marlene's age, and she was just having fun.

It so happened that Lauda and Mariella were invited to a party at Jurgens's home, but fate dictated that Lauda went on his own.

Marlene was hosting the party, but as soon as they saw each other, she and Lauda got together straightaway. They were soon closeted in earnest conversation, and the rest of the guests were forgotten. Jurgens observed what was happening, but he didn't seem to mind at all.

Almost immediately they knew they would see each other again, even though Lauda knew about Jurgens, and Marlene was fully aware of Mariella. Lauda described that first meeting simply: "She spoke to me and a spark flew between us."

After the party they enjoyed two intimate dinners together. And then Marlene contracted pneumonia and fell very ill. Lauda visited her constantly in the hospital, sometimes running into Curt Jurgens coming down the hospital corridor the other way.

Gradually, after a few weeks, Marlene got better and discharged herself. Although still in a very weak state, she flew to the island of Ibiza to recuperate. Her parents owned a holiday home on the island, and Ibiza was her favorite place. Between races, Lauda flew there as often as he could in his airplane see her. He told Mariella a pack of lies to cover up his absences.

In fact, Lauda hardly saw Mariella during that period. Mariella, who was so busy with the construction of the house, didn't seem to notice his absence or question where he was spending his time.

This went on all summer and until early autumn, when Lauda had to leave for North America for the US and Canadian Grand Prix. He was away for three weeks and found he spent the entire time thinking about Marlene, and with that he finally realized the relationship with Mariella was over.

Marlene became the catalyst for change, and Lauda decided to end it with Mariella. As he said, "I went away more in the summer of 1975—I had to have a change."

But the relationship between Mariella and Lauda was not the work of a moment; it was a lifetime's work for both of them. Ending it was far from easy. But he was a very practical person. He had fallen out of love with Mariella and fallen in love with Marlene. For him it was black and white.

Despite the granite exterior, Lauda cared what people thought, and exiting the relationship with honor became very important to him. In pursuing that goal, however, he ended up riding roughshod over Mariella's feelings.

Lauda concocted a plan to make the split appear mutual and to reduce the impression that there was anyone else involved. He wanted it to be known that the relationship had run its course and that both parties sought an exit. He certainly did not want anyone to know he had left Mariella for another woman. So loved was Mariella that he feared the whole of Europe would turn against him if that became known.

After he arrived back in Salzburg from New York, he decided he had to end it at the first appropriate moment. According to him, the opportunity came when he returned to the apartment they shared. He went through the front door and was overwhelmed by a feeling of not wanting to be there. As he later revealed, "I draped my jacket over the back of a chair and looked at Mariella and suddenly it hit me: This won't work." He turned tail and walked out with next to no explanation. He drove away that night into Marlene's arms, never again to return, leaving behind a very confused Mariella.

Lauda proposed to Marlene that night. He told her he would not see Mariella again, and they went away to Ibiza on Lauda's airplane the following morning.

Mariella was left completely bemused as she confided to her closest friends that she had no idea what had happened. When he finally returned from Ibiza to Salzburg, Lauda saw Mariella and told her another pack of lies. He told her he was stressed and, because of that, demanded they end their eight-year relationship. He told her that he "no longer had time for emotional nonsense."

It was completely untrue. Mariella had become a burden, and after almost eight years together, he coldly dumped her in a few minutes' conversation.

As soon as he proposed, Lauda tried to marry Marlene straightaway. But he wanted it kept a secret, as he was desperately concerned that Mariella and her friends did not discover that he already had a new girlfriend.

So in November of 1975, he flew to England and met secretly with John Hogan.

Although Hogan was principally the boss of James Hunt's title sponsor, Marlboro, he was also very close to Lauda. Marlboro was also a personal sponsor of Lauda's, and the Austrian was every bit as important to Marlboro as was Hunt. Hogan was probably Lauda's best friend and closest confidant in Formula One, as well as being the man whom he completely trusted, despite his obvious closeness to his chief rival. Hogan was the man with whom Lauda thought he could discuss any problem without holding back—be it business or pleasure.

So almost from the very moment Lauda split from Mariella and took up with Marlene, Hogan was in on it. Lauda could trust Hogan because he was not judgmental. Hogan was his guru and had enormous understanding of human emotions. Hogan was also very discreet. Lauda knew instinctively he could be trusted with his biggest secret, which is what had brought him to England in the first place.

Lauda suddenly arrived at Hogan's home in Reading. Hogan remembers it well 36 years later and takes up the story: "Niki said, 'You know what I'm missing? A wife. Where can I get married in England?' It was almost comical."

But Hogan went along with it, and because Lauda had said nothing to the contrary, he presumed he was referring to getting married to Mariella. And then he brought Marlene in, who had been waiting in the car.

Hogan, momentarily stunned, knew Lauda well enough to know to not ask any questions. As he remembered: "I was living out in Reading in those days, so I said, 'Let's try Reading registry office to see what happens.'"

Lauda said there was no time to waste, so Hogan got into his car and they drove off to the center of Reading. As Hogan recalls, "So we drove up to the Reading registry office: Niki, myself, and Marlene. And this very nice gentleman said, 'I'm terribly sorry. I'd love to, but I can't.'"

The registrar told them that any marriage he performed in England would not be legal and that he would not do it. It had been a wasted mission."

So Lauda's plans were thwarted. With that, he gave up the idea of an immediate marriage and instead flew to Ibiza with Marlene, where they lived together in total secrecy over the winter. That is, until three months later, when they turned up in Kyalami.

CHAPTER 5

James's Women Problems

A Hasty Marriage Unravels

January 1976

As 1976 dawned, James Hunt's marriage to Suzy Miller was well and truly over. Barely two years after he had rethought his life and decided he needed a wife, he had rethought it again and decided he didn't. As he flew to South America for the first Grand Prix of the season in January 1976, he was just waiting for Suzy to find a new beau. And finally, much to his relief, it seemed that she had. It would end a 24-month saga in James Hunt's personal life, a period that defied any sensible logic at all.

Before he married, Hunt had given his views on matrimony and described it as a "stupid myth" that drivers had to have a stable home life in order to cope with the stresses and strains of racing. With those sorts of views, there seemed little chance he would succumb to marriage in the foreseeable future.

Hunt was certainly not ideal husband material. He had a giant appetite for sex and looked to feed it wherever he could, as frequently as he could. On a physical level, he was unequaled. Emotionally, however, he was an amateur. According to his friends, he would often suggest that he was not sure what love was. Gerald Donaldson, his biographer, confirmed: "The emotional component of a relationship for James was still virgin territory."

But when he moved from England to Spain at the beginning of 1974, Hunt dramatically and suddenly changed his mind. Seemingly out of the blue, he decided he wanted a wife to "help my career and ease my life in exile." Hunt had moved to Marbella for tax reasons, and it had nothing to do with marriage.

In fact, the last thing Hunt needed was a wife. He had never found a woman who could keep up with him. But for a brief moment, he cast aside those thoughts.

He found Suzy Miller playing tennis at the Lew Hoad club in Fuengirola, Spain. Like Hunt, Suzy had just moved to Spain for a lifestyle change and was lonely. She was a striking woman who made money modeling, and a few extraordinary months later, she became Mrs. James Hunt.

Barely 24, a year younger than Hunt, she had spent much of her childhood in Southern Rhodesia with her expatriate parents as well as her twin sister, Vivienne, and a brother, John. As a child she took piano lessons and became a concert standard pianist. She also was an excellent cook. Her father, Frederick Miller, had been a high-ranking officer in the British army and then a lawyer and barrister employed in the British colonies. Her childhood had been spent in a number of different countries. But it was under the African sun, with her father working as a judge in Kenya, that Suzy developed into a truly attractive young woman—a real "head turner," as Hunt would later describe her to his friends back in London.

Like many women approaching their mid-20s, Suzy was desperate to find a husband. As soon as she met him, she saw Hunt as perfect husband material. The fact that he was a famous racing driver held no appeal for her at all.

Content to devote her life to one man, Suzy imagined a partner who would provide her with security and whom, in return, she could look after. Somehow she envisaged that in Hunt. In Marbella, Hunt and Suzy began seeing a lot of each other, and their mutual isolation initially drew them together.

Hunt was still living out of a suitcase in a hotel, and she had an apartment on the coast overlooking the sea. He quickly moved out of his hotel and into her apartment.

Miller was very different from Hunt's previous girlfriends. Undemanding, she was quiet and had a thoughtful manner. At first Hunt attempted to treat her like all his previous flings—in a casual manner—but she bridled against it. And the more she bridled, the more Hunt wanted her. She was not prepared to be his casual girlfriend.

Initially, however, Hunt just didn't get it. And when Suzy quickly threw him out and he moved back to the hotel, it was a serious shock to his system. For the first time, he found himself feeling hurt and lovesick. Realizing that he actually might be in love with her, he said, "I talked myself back into her affections."

But Hunt had learned little and soon ended up thrown out once again and back for the third time in the hotel. The relationship continued with its ups and downs, and the more she rejected him, the more he desired her. It was an old trap, and Hunt fell right into it.

Finally in midsummer of 1974, after a three-week separation that included the weekend of the British Grand Prix at Brands Hatch, he found himself intensely missing her. All he could think of that weekend was about being next to her in bed—and this time his thoughts were not of lust but of love. Over the three days, he found he became more and more obsessive in his thoughts.

On the evening of the July 20, 1974, he arrived back in Marbella. He had flown in from London after retiring halfway through the race. He drove straight from the airport to her apartment and proposed marriage. As he remembered: "Knowing that the prospect of marriage would swing Suzy around, I went back to her and proposed." It was a desperate measure and reflected the extent of his infatuation. He had truly lost his senses. Suzy was delighted and accepted without hesitation. She immediately telephoned her parents and her sister, Vivienne, with the good news. She then watched as a sheepish Hunt also telephoned his astonished parents.

The engagement was properly announced a week later and a wedding date set for the end of the Formula One season, in October. The roller coaster had started, and there would be no getting off. An engagement party was held at his brother Peter's apartment in central London.

Lord Hesketh was delighted and offered to pay for the wedding. He appointed himself organizer of the event and transformed the wedding into one big party for himself and his friends. Although Hunt had known Hesketh for a little over 18 months, he was named as best man.

The prospect of a wedding had been haunting Hunt since the engagement party. It had also been dominating his thoughts during the closing races of the 1974 season. Hunt was well into having second and third thoughts about the marriage by the time the season ended. According to Gerald Donaldson, he wanted desperately to cut and run and get out of the whole situation but was too scared to do it. Seeing no way out of the wedding, Hunt turned to binge drinking.

Suzy was Catholic, which dictated a Catholic church, and Hunt converted to Catholicism for the ceremony. The wedding was held at the Church of the Immaculate Heart of Mary, better known as the Brompton Oratory, in Kensington. The grand setting was entirely appropriate for the society wedding of the year. The invitations stressed that nothing short of full morning suits were required. More or less every racing driver of distinction was invited, including Graham Hill, Stirling Moss, Jackie Stewart, John Watson, and Ronnie Peterson. Hesketh arranged an orchestra to play the music.

Lord Hesketh indulged Hunt through it all. He reassured him at every stage and lectured him on his obligation not to let people down. Hunt was too drunk to argue.

So James Hunt walked up the aisle to his own wedding hopelessly intoxicated. He himself would later say, "I just couldn't handle the whole scene, so I went out and got blind, roaring drunk. For four days I went on the most stupendous bender of my life."

Afterwards, Lord Hesketh admitted, "I think the truth of the matter is that James had rather changed his mind by the time he got to the church, and he wouldn't have been the first or last person to have done that and survived." But the marriage duly went ahead, and somehow Hunt managed to remain upright. How he did it no one knows.

As for Hunt, he would say afterwards that he remembered little of the event. At the wedding reception, Hesketh supported him when he had to stand up. According to other guests, he was virtually incoherent as he addressed the invitees, and it was all rather embarrassing. Suzy just smiled her way through it all, convinced it would be different now that he was a married man. Given how much he had had to drink that day, the portents were not auspicious.

The following day, they left for their honeymoon in Antigua, in the Caribbean.

The new Mrs. Hunt did attend some motor races during 1975 and did her best to be a racing driver's wife. Suzy admitted she was "bored stiff," saying to friends, "I literally felt like a spare part. I was just there for the show."

Within a few months, Suzy realized that the marriage was not going to work, although she was prepared to give it time. Mostly she led her own life and her husband led his. He became consistently unfaithful and was not particularly good at hiding his infidelities. Hunt recalled later, "It was a matter of clashing lifestyles and personalities. I am very much into racing and doing my own thing, and I move very fast. She wanted a slow pace, a good solid base and a solid relationship. Ironically, these were the very things I married her for in the first place."

The couple began to spend more and more time apart. Gerald Donaldson, a Hunt biographer, called the marriage one of "essential incompatibility."

But Hunt desperately wanted to please Suzy and was clearly in love with her. But it wasn't enough; as he said, "If she stayed at home while I rushed around the world, it was boring for her. If she came with me, it was no fun for her. I was always looking over my shoulder to see if she was there, and she was always struggling to keep up with me. It was a heavy deal for both of us."

Hunt knew he had to get out of the marriage, and he prayed for a miracle. The miracle he hoped for, quite simply, was that she would meet someone else. Hunt did not want to desert her and was also wary of the money situation. In the case of a divorce, Suzy would have been entitled to a large share of his wealth, which he had moved to Spain to protect. A divorce would have relieved him of at least half of his UK£100,000 (about $240,000 at the time) net worth just as he had started earning good money. He literally couldn't afford a divorce.

Meanwhile, Suzy began to feel the same. Facing the possibility that James was not for her and that she had likely married for the wrong reasons, she wanted out as well. Nevertheless, Suzy remained supportive and sympathetic to Hunt's feelings. But her understanding only heightened his sense of responsibility for her, as he said, "I was very, very anxious not to hurt her. There are nice ways and nasty ways to do things, and I hope I can never be a hurtful person."

The marriage may as well have ended there and then, but it dragged on for another eight months as Suzy looked for a new partner. Finally, despairing of the likelihood of a miracle, Hunt offered to buy Suzy a smart apartment in London and to give her an allowance, with a divorce to follow when it suited them. He was prepared to pay heavily to get out of the marriage, but she didn't need the money and was reluctant to make it official. Suzy was certainly not going to get divorced and be single again—that was not on the menu at all. So they continued to live together in Marbella, although by July 1975 they had for all intents and purposes gone their separate ways. However, publicly, outside the Formula One paddock, no one knew or suspected anything was amiss.

Hunt tried to explain what had gone wrong: "I thought that marriage was what I wanted and needed to give me a nice stable and quiet home life, but in fact it wasn't. And the mistake was mine. I really wanted to go racing on my own, and it wasn't much fun for Suzy to sit at home and wait for me all that time. It was also a terrible hassle for her to come racing because race meetings were probably the most relaxing time in my schedule. The rest of the time, you tend to be leaping on airplanes once a day, and that made it even worse. It's bad enough organizing one person to get on an airplane; organizing two gets to be twice as much hassle. It got to the point where it was a problem for Suzy to come traveling and a hell of a deal for her to stay at home. It was making life miserable in the extreme for her, and since I felt responsible for her, it was making me miserable too."

Meanwhile, Hunt had found a new occasional girlfriend, a young woman named Jane Birbeck, whom he saw when he was in London. But he also continued to meet with a succession of other girls when he was elsewhere. But he was careful to be discreet, as he didn't want anything in the newspapers that might upset Suzy or the Miller family—or his own family for that matter.

And that led to Christmas 1975 and the holiday season. Fatefully, both Hunt and Suzy went to Gstaad for Christmas to stay with friends. Gstaad was the place to be at yuletide. At that time of year, it was an absolutely magical place.

Equally, fate dictated that it was also the venue that Richard Burton and Elizabeth Taylor chose to spend their Christmas holidays.

James Hunt's marital problems were about to be solved.

CHAPTER 6

Lauda Sets the Order

But Hunt Is Now Number One

South Africa: March 4–6, 1976

There was a five-week gap between the Brazilian and South African Grand Prix; and in between the races, most drivers returned to Europe, including Lauda to Vienna and Hunt to Marbella. Hunt arrived in Johannesburg very early, in the middle of February, and booked into the Sleepy Hollow Hotel. Hunt was in South Africa early for the same reasons he went to São Paulo early—to have a good time. As in Brazil, he had made many friends in 1973 and 1974 when Alexander Hesketh was splashing money around like it was going out of fashion.

But as swarms of journalists descended on the hotel wanting to question him about his marriage, he moved out of the Sleepy Hollow and went to stay at the house of his friend, South African tennis player Abe Siegel.

At least 50 journalists and photographers traveled to Johannesburg specially to cover the story of Hunt's estrangement from his wife, Suzy Miller. In itself it was a nonstory, but it was Suzy's dalliance with the actor Richard Burton that caused all the fuss. The fact that Burton appeared to have dumped Elizabeth Taylor for Suzy made it into a huge story.

As news of the split finally leaked out, the journalists hounded Hunt wherever he went. The journalists were relentless, wanting to know why Hunt's wife was in New York with Richard Burton and not in Kyalami with him.

That week there was no bigger story for the world's press. As Alastair Caldwell remembered: "With that business of his wife running off with Burton, the whole bloody press world suddenly descended on us in South Africa." Once again, Teddy Mayer was entirely bemused by Hunt's antics and his enormous capacity for the opposite sex. Mayer was a reserved character who lived quietly and soberly with his wife, Sally, and enjoyed married life. He couldn't understand Hunt at all.

Once news of Hunt's marriage split was confirmed, South African girls were throwing themselves at him. First he took up with Paddy Norval, a well-known South African film actress. They toured the nightclubs of Johannesburg every night.

After a week with Siegel, Hunt moved to the Kyalami Ranch, the hotel next door to the Kyalami, where all the Formula One drivers stayed. The facilities were basic by the standards of today, but the setting and the climate were unrivaled. At that time it was a hedonist's dream: set in rolling grass with a giant swimming pool and surrounded by low-rise motel-type buildings. The drivers liked the fact that different girls were drawn in every day, and casual affairs and one-night stands were the norm. It was a place they could totally relax and enjoy the sunshine. Moreover, it was right by the circuit and they could walk to work. It was where the Formula One circus hung out when there was no racing.

As soon as he arrived at the Kyalami Ranch, Hunt quickly dumped Norval and was soon cavorting with Carmen Jardin, a beautiful Portuguese girl he had met at the hotel a few days earlier. Jardin accompanied Hunt to the circuit every day, wrapping herself around him at every opportunity for the benefit of photographers.

Niki Lauda flew in at the beginning of the week with his new fiancée, Marlene Knaus, in tow, and he booked straight into the Kyalami Ranch. It was the first time Lauda was seen in public with Knaus. They kept a very low profile, and hardly anyone noticed them sitting in a dark corner of the hotel's bar every night. When Lauda was at the track, Marlene stayed at the hotel, and hardly anyone knew who she was. At other times Lauda just sat around the hotel smooching with Marlene, while Hunt was living large with Jardin, an exotic creature whose presence got everyone excited.

The different approaches of Lauda and Hunt could not have been more contrasting. Lauda was discreet in every way, but Hunt was the complete opposite.

Meanwhile, at the track there was much drama as Ronnie Peterson resigned his position at the Lotus team, where he had been number one driver, and moved back to drive for his old team, March. Peterson was the highest paid driver in Formula One at $250,000 a year; five times Hunt's salary. He left after his salary had not been paid when it was due, on January 1, and he had taken umbrage. The financial situation at the Lotus team was really bad. There was no money, and the team was surviving on a wing and a prayer. The global recession had severely affected the entire Lotus group and led to a severe cash shortage across the whole company.

Peterson's contract stipulated that he be paid in full on January 1, but instead Chapman had unilaterally imposed a new payment system on Peterson. On the basis that there were 18 scheduled races that year, including non-championship events, Chapman had begun paying Peterson in installments, one-eighteenth of his salary—exactly $13,800.

But Peterson, who was fed up with team manager Peter Warr anyway, didn't care about Lotus's problems and was insulted. He decided to leave rather than to accept the new terms, and he did a deal with Max Mosley to drive for March.

Peterson figured he didn't have a lot to lose, as the new Lotus 77 car was uncompetitive and there was no money to develop it. Peterson's teammate, Mario Andretti, was only contracted on a race-by-race basis, and he declined to drive in South Africa, meaning Lotus had two no-hoper drivers in its cars.

The other major change in the paddock was the reemergence of the Hesketh team, now owned by its former team manager, Anthony Horsley. Horsley had managed to resurrect the Hesketh team by running the 1975 308 cars, which had been given to him by Alexander Hesketh after the team closed down. Horsley set up a new a business, running them as rent-a-cars for would-be Formula One drivers who could pay a fee. It was purely a moneymaking operation, and Horsley's Hesketh revival was destined for the back of the grid, as he readily admitted: "We had gone from the front of the grid, from being the glamor boys, to the back of the grid and being forgotten. But, on the other hand, the bank balance went from zero and filled up again." Horsley was aided by a recent prize money fund increase and the fact that some of the money was allocated retrospectively from the previous season's performance. The prize money bonus was worth about $70,000 to the team in all, and Horsley exploited it. Hunt was delighted to see Horsley and got a real boost from having his mentor and best friend around again.

The week of testing prior to the Grand Prix was totally dominated by Lauda and Hunt, with the Ferrari proving the faster all week. The week's testing proved to be a trial of strength between the two men, and at the end of it, Lauda emerged as the clear victor.

But as soon as the testing ended and qualifying started, the situation was completely reversed; Hunt was consistently the fastest in all four qualifying sessions. Either there had been a dramatic improvement in the McLaren's performance between testing and qualifying, which was unlikely, or Alastair Caldwell had been sandbagging Ferrari during testing, a technique with which he was not entirely unfamiliar. Or there was a third possibility: that Lauda began sandbagging Hunt when qualifying started.

The most likely explanation was that the McLaren team had simply got its act together and had benefited most from the testing. It had turned to focus entirely on Hunt and left Jochen Mass to fend for himself. As the undisputed number one, Hunt began to receive the star treatment. As the team's focus had automatically shifted to Hunt, the earlier problems had just melted away. Once the car had been modified to suit him physically, all the frustrations he felt went with it. Hunt's car had been entirely rebuilt to suit him, and there would be no repeat of the Interlagos fiasco. Teddy Mayer was even moved to publicly apologize to Hunt for letting him down in Brazil.

So Hunt found himself in a perfectly developed and highly competitive car, just as Fittipaldi had left it, and enhanced by the new six-speed gearbox. It was clear that the M23 was a competitive car that had been undermined by the one-off problems in Brazil. With these problems finally put right, the car was ultracompetitive and, on its day, every bit as fast as Lauda's Ferrari.

On a personal basis, things were also much improved. The McLaren mechanics got to know Hunt and began to enjoy working for him—not least of all because of the amount of available women he introduced them to. Hunt drew women to the team like a magnet. As Caldwell noted, "We were all as happy as pigs in shit."

The team was in an entirely new frame of mind, and the new superiority of McLaren in qualifying undoubtedly benefited from two significant modifications. First, there was a brand-new starter system that Caldwell had invented and was fitted to Hunt's car just for qualifying. It was a remote system that started the engine with pneumatic power rather than an onboard battery. The weight saving was considerable and undoubtedly aided Hunt in qualifying. The second was the fitting of some plastic skirts to the McLaren's underside, thereby improving the aerodynamics. Neither modification was carried over into the race due to uncertainties over their legality.

The Ferrari was unchanged. Lauda's Ferrari started the weekend in identical specification to Brazil. But in testing, the team tried a De Dion design for the rear suspension, but it proved to be slower and so they reverted back. The De Dion system had been designed for the new 1976 car, the 312T, but the 312T1 was easy to update, and the team sought a short-term advantage.

Even with all the modifications made to the M23, no one was in any doubt that the Ferrari was, on a long run, the superior car. The M23 was by now a four-year-old design, and the 312T was only a year old. In overcoming that, it was clear for the first time just how accomplished a driver James Hunt was.

So it was no surprise when Hunt, now totally comfortable with his car, effortlessly took pole position once again alongside Niki Lauda. Jochen Mass put in a superb performance to be third on the grid behind Lauda, and Regazzoni was ninth. The surprise of qualifying was Vittorio Brambilla in the works March. He had been galvanized by the arrival of Ronnie Peterson in his team, and his speed seemed to increase accordingly.

But even though Hunt was fastest, Lauda had been the star of qualifying by dint of sheer consistency of purpose. The Ferrari was the most stable car on the circuit, and while every other driver had to work hard to get their times, Lauda took it easy and seemed to be controlling the steering wheel with his little finger. But Hunt and Lauda were the only two drivers in it, and no one else had a chance. Equally, no one had any doubt who would win the race.

Surprisingly, Lauda was unhappy. He called his Ferrari 312T "shit" and declared, "It's sliding too much." But he appeared to be trying to outpsyche his opponents, and some even wondered whether he had let Hunt have pole.

Hunt was very apprehensive about the start; he was a very poor starter, and Lauda was a very good one. As Hunt said, "Niki's never been known to make a bad start yet."

On race morning, during the warm-up session Lauda had problems with an engine misfire that could not be cured. The mechanics replaced everything they could think of and hoped for the best.

True to form—with Lauda never known to make a poor start and Hunt rarely known to make a good one—both performed as predicted. Lauda dropped Hunt at the start and roared off. Hunt made a terrible start and was only good enough for fourth place on the first lap behind Lauda, Mass, and Brambilla.

A few laps later, Jochen Mass, in third, waved his team leader through. There remained only Vittorio Brambilla's March-Ford between Hunt and Lauda. On lap six, Hunt got past Brambilla and into second place, albeit seven seconds behind Lauda. He gradually closed the gap on Lauda, although he never seriously challenged him. It varied during the race from 10 seconds to 3 seconds.

But on lap 20 Lauda started to have problems. On the 20th lap his Ferrari started pulling to the left. The cause was a slow puncture in the left rear tire. Lauda also had problems with brake balance. He said, "Every couple of laps or so, I had to get used to a completely different car—every couple of laps, I had to work out a new line."

Hunt sensed that Lauda was in trouble as he closed up on him. As Lauda said, "It was just about the best moral tonic he could have hoped for, and he hounded me pitilessly." With two laps to go, Lauda realized that Hunt could take him. Then fortune played its part as they both came up to lap John Watson's Penske car. Lauda made a do-or-die thrust to get past Watson, surprising Hunt. So for the last lap, Hunt was held up by Watson's slower car, thereby enabling Lauda to hang on.

Over the line, Lauda led Hunt by 1.3 seconds at the finish. Mass was third, albeit 46 seconds behind. For Lauda it was another rout of his rivals, and he was now firm favorite to be world champion again. But despite Lauda's apparent superiority, the first two races had lit the fuse for the 1976 world championship, and it was obvious Hunt would not let Lauda have it all his own way. When he took his helmet off at the end of the race, Hunt was grinning from ear to ear with his second place.

Hunt was suddenly a genuine world championship contender, and he was strangely surprised by it. Hunt had dominated qualifying, but Lauda had dominated the racing.

CHAPTER 7

Women Problems Resolved

Marlene and Jane

April 1976

The 1976 South African Grand Prix marked a watershed in the personal lives of Niki Lauda and James Hunt. Lauda debuted his new fiancée—soon to be wife—Marlene Knaus, and it finally became apparent that James Hunt's marriage to Suzy Miller was over when she appeared in public on the arm of actor Richard Burton in New York.

The resolution of their personal circumstances was a huge relief to both men, especially to Niki Lauda, who had agonized over the dumping of his fiancée of eight years, Mariella von Reininghaus, in favor of his new love, Marlene Knaus. Equally, Hunt had been desperate to see Suzy settled into a new life.

Lauda's relief seemed more palpable in South Africa. Marlene Knaus was a very sensual woman in an ethereal way; pretty rather than beautiful, she exuded sex appeal. There was something about her that men liked, even though she invariably wore her hair in a severe, brushed-back bun at the top of her head, which made her appear a lot older than her 24 years.

In South Africa, Lauda and Marlene could be seen every night in a quiet corner of the bar of the Kyalami Ranch Hotel. They were clearly enjoying each other's company and couldn't stop exchanging reassuring glances as curious people dropped by to say "hello."

They were both nervous. Although a secret in England, Lauda's love life had been a source of speculation in continental newspapers for the past few months. But with no firm evidence, and none of the principals talking, journalists could only guess what was going on. But at Kyalami it was clear Lauda had most definitely taken up with Marlene Knaus.

The ripples in Europe's social circles were immediate. Lauda and Mariella had been one of the most important couples in Europe for the past eight years. Lauda was desperate to not appear to have left Mariella for Marlene, and it was his good luck that his new girlfriend attracted very little attention. Lauda had figured he could test the water in South Africa, away from the full glare of European journalists.

But he hadn't figured on the Hunt-Burton-Taylor story making his news a complete nonevent. Such was the buzz surrounding James Hunt that hardly anyone noticed Lauda had a new girlfriend.

The newspapers were only interested in Hunt's wife and the fact that Suzy had broken up the marriage of Richard Burton and Elizabeth Taylor. It was the perfect cover for Lauda's low-key introduction of Marlene.

To those who did notice, Lauda introduced Marlene by saying simply, "This is my lady." Remarkably, the sudden dumping of his companion of eight years and the woman he intended to marry did not seem to merit any further explanation than that. As he had been seeing Marlene for at least six months during the close season, and Mariella had already been long gone from his life, he had forgotten all about her and didn't care to discuss it. For him the transition was seamless.

But outside of Lauda's earshot, there was plenty of gossip and discussion. The truth was that no one was interested in Marlene; they all wanted to know what had happened to Mariella.

And as soon as word got around, Lauda encountered a muted but hostile reaction to Marlene from the other wives and girlfriends present. They put up a united front in support of Mariella in her absence. They were horrified when they realized what Lauda had done and plotted together as to how they could reunite the couple.

They simply couldn't believe that Lauda would dump the spectacularly striking Mariella for Marlene, who was undoubtedly attractive but not in Mariella's class in the beauty stakes. John Watson, a disinterested observer at the time, described Mariella's beauty as akin to a piece of "Dresden porcelain."

David Benson, the motoring editor of the *Daily Express*, was the journalist in the know, and he was also critical of Lauda's decision to dump Mariella, saying, "Lauda had simply removed the fuse on the emotional circuit in his brain." But when he filed the story back to his newspaper, he found the news editor was barely interested in it.

Lauda was also under fire from all quarters, including ones he never could have imagined. One vociferous critic was the architect who was building his house. Once he realized that Lauda had split with Mariella, he refused to do any more work. He told Lauda, "It's a dirty trick. I wanted to build the house for you and Fraulein Reininghaus." He told Lauda he would not finish the house because of how he had treated Mariella. The architect's opinion reflected what everyone else thought. They all sided with Mariella, and some were quite hostile to Marlene.

But as people got to know Marlene, they warmed to her, including David Benson, who said, "I established a friendly relationship with Marlene when the other people on the racing circuit cold-shouldered her, thinking she was merely some local pickup." But Benson could sense that Marlene was more than a casual fling—although he had no idea how much more.

Mariella may have gone quietly, but she was very popular on the Formula One scene, and others were resolutely determined to save the relationship. In fact, people went out of their way to try to mend the relationship. The wives and girlfriends worked fervently behind the scenes to dispatch Marlene and reinstall Mariella at Lauda's side. They believed Lauda would come to his senses quickly if pressure was placed on him and if news of the relationship leaked out and he saw peoples' reactions. For a few weeks there was still a great deal of fevered speculation about whether Lauda and Mariella would get back together again.

Nina Rindt, widow of Jochen Rindt, took direct action and invited people to a party where she hoped to reunite the couple. The party was at her house, overlooking Lake Geneva. Helen Stewart, Jackie Stewart's wife, offered to get in touch with both Mariella and Lauda and to try and heal the breach. Helen was nominated by the others to directly intervene. But they were all laboring under the impression that Lauda and Marlene had just met and had no idea what had occurred the previous year in Reading. And they didn't count on Lauda's reaction to the scheming.

When news of the women's summit and the party at Lake Geneva reached him the next day, Lauda decided to take action. He didn't want a media circus, and he knew the Austrian and German press would take Mariella's side against his. So Lauda went as quietly as he could to a registry office in Vienna-Neustadt and married Marlene. The registrar agreed to perform a special ceremony outside normal hours, and astonishingly it remained a secret for nearly a month, by which time journalists accepted it as a fait accompli, making further speculation effectively unnecessary.

With that, speculation about a reunion ceased and Mariella was forgotten. And James Hunt continued to hog the headlines, which suited Lauda just fine.

And those headlines kept coming, for it was a far juicier story than anything Niki Lauda was getting up to in the bedroom.

It was pure coincidence that Richard Burton and his wife, actress Elizabeth Taylor, were spending the 1975–76 winter holiday season in Gstaad at the same time as James Hunt and Suzy Miller.

Although the Hunts had agreed to be together for the holidays, their marriage to all intents and purposes had ended the previous summer. Hunt had spent much of the summer with Jane Birbeck in London, while Suzy moped around in Marbella wondering what to do next.

When they got to Gstaad, Suzy and Hunt immediately went their separate ways, hardly seeing each other. Hunt was in serious training for the 1976 Formula One season and spent all day at the gym or running. At night he didn't drink and, consequently, didn't socialize. Without alcohol, Hunt was a different man. But Suzy knew he was surreptitiously seeing local girls during the day, and she ended up very depressed for the first time in her life. She spent most of her time wandering around Gstaad on her own. Hunt was unhappy that she was unhappy and wished their situation could be resolved. On a whim, Suzy decided to stay on in Gstaad when her husband jetted off to South America for the Brazilian Grand Prix in early January. Anyway, Gstaad could be great fun in January, and Suzy needed some fun in her life.

Suzy was well aware that Burton and Taylor were in town, as was everyone. They were the most famous people in the world and had just been married for the second time the previous October. But Suzy had heard that the new Burton-Taylor reunion was not going well. She had always found Richard Burton very attractive and had vague connections to him though Brook Williams, who was a friend. Williams was Burton's closest aide, and she wondered whether she might get to meet Burton one day.

But what happened next she did not expect.

Suzy first set eyes on Burton as they were going opposite ways on a ski cable lift. Their eyes met, and Suzy smiled. Burton flashed back his trademark smile, and there was an instant attraction. He recognized the signs, and she made a huge impact on him straightaway. When she had gone past, Burton turned to Williams and asked, "Who is that vision that just passed by?"

Burton was transfixed, as he would say later: "I turned around and there was this gorgeous creature, about 9 feet tall. She could stop a stampede." Burton immediately sought an introduction and asked Brook Williams to fix it for him. He said he would.

Burton was staying with Taylor at her house in Gstaad, called Chalet Arial, and Williams soon engineered another meeting. He invited Suzy to a party at the château. Suzy quickly discovered that Burton and Taylor were already leading separate lives and that the remarriage had not worked out. Burton was sleeping in a room at one end of the château and Taylor in a room at the other end.

The affair between Burton and Suzy began almost immediately. From the day they were introduced, Burton and Suzy became virtually inseparable. He was 50 and she was 26. Burton remembered: "She started coming to the house two, three, and then four times a week."

Eventually Elizabeth Taylor noticed the Englishwoman coming to the house every day. She immediately realized what was going on and said to Suzy, "You'll only last six months with Richard." To which Suzy replied, "Perhaps, but those six months will be very worthwhile." With that, Taylor went out and found herself another boyfriend at a local disco, clearing the way for Suzy and Burton to take their relationship forward unhindered.

Burton invited Suzy to join him in New York, where he was due to star in Peter Shaffer's play *Equus* on Broadway. She accepted but said she would have to ask her husband's permission.

As the affair developed, Suzy was keeping James Hunt, in Brazil, fully informed over the telephone of her developing situation. To say that he was delighted would have been an understatement. In fact, when she first told him that Burton had invited her to go to New York, he had simply replied, "Fine, off you go." Burton opened to rave reviews in *Equus* and was the talk of the city. But, perhaps unsurprisingly, journalists in New York soon began to ask who the blond was that accompanied him everywhere. They had absolutely no idea who she was, and uncaptioned photographs started appearing in New York newspapers.

When Hunt headed home from South America, he found his house empty. By then Suzy was spending most of her time with Richard Burton in New York. After a few weeks, he left for South Africa early and was soon parading around Johannesburg with different women. All this was going on despite the fact that, as far as the rest of the world was concerned, Hunt and Suzy were still happily married.

Eventually the New York journalists worked out that the striking blond was the wife of racing driver James Hunt and that she had clearly broken up Burton's marriage to Elizabeth Taylor. There was no bigger media story than that in the last week of February 1976.

With the news suddenly out, and Suzy and Burton no longer a secret, Hunt was in for a shock in South Africa. He was suddenly being followed by journalists, who had flown in specifically to work on the story. His hotel was staked out by a throng of jostling journalists and photographers—none of them interested in the race. Alastair Caldwell remembers: "Suddenly we had huge media interest. We had the *Sydney Morning Herald* and the *Punjabi Times;* we had every daily newspaper in the world, even Mexico. All were trying to interview us and talk to James. They were being flown in by the planeload." It became so bad that Hunt had to move out of his hotel.

Once again it was David Benson who was ahead of the story and gave the *Daily Express* its biggest ever show business scoop. Benson wrote a story that appeared on the front page of the *Daily Express* on February 26, 1976. It was headlined: "Suzy To Marry Burton." The story read: "Suzy Hunt, wife of British racing driver James Hunt, is seeking a quickie divorce in America so that she can marry Richard Burton. This follows the actor's latest breakup with his second-time wife Liz Taylor. He and 27-year-old Suzy are staying at the same New York hotel. Burton, too, was said to be in a hurry to get a divorce."

The article finally legitimized the story and made it official. James Hunt was finally free of his marriage and officially a single man again. To celebrate, he went to the gym. It was one of the most satisfying workouts of his life. He was finally free, exactly 16 months after his wedding day in London.

Richard Burton telephoned Hunt in Kyalami, ostensibly to apologize for what had happened. Hunt remembered Burton being rather embarrassed and tongue-tied on the telephone, which he found strange. Hunt assured Burton that, far from being upset, he was delighted about the situation.

Burton couldn't quite believe that Hunt was being so casual about letting go of his wife. He expected Hunt to be bitter toward him and devastated. But Hunt simply said to Burton: "Relax, Richard. You've done me a wonderful turn by taking on the most alarming expense account in the country." A bemused and somewhat relieved Burton replaced the receiver in his hotel room and turned to Suzy and smiled. She said to him, "I told you James is fine about all this."

When the news was out, a relieved Hunt spoke to journalists: "Her running off with Burton is a great relief to me. It actually reduces the number of problems I have to face outside my racing. I am mainly concerned that everyone comes out of it happy and settled." In fact, there was no disguising Hunt's utter relief at what had transpired, as he confessed:

"I prefer to be on my own at races because, really, there's enough to do looking after me. It's more than I can handle to keep myself under control at a race meeting without trying to look after someone else as well and have more responsibilities and worries. I find that if I want an early night before a race, or if I want a couple of hours to cool off and relax before dinner, I can do no better than to read a book or listen to music and, therefore, it's better to be on my own." Resolving not to get tempted into marriage again, he told journalists: "Meanwhile, it is probably a good thing that I am still technically married. I have that as a safety valve. It will stop me from doing anything silly again."

Hunt flew straight back into London from Johannesburg to stay with his parents, where he was due to drive at the non-championship Race of Champions at nearby Brands Hatch. While there, he realized that he must meet Burton to firm up the arrangements for the divorce. He was very anxious for nothing to go wrong and for Suzy not to become his responsibility again. He was also anxious to sort out the financial arrangements and to find out how much the divorce would cost him.

After the race he was helicoptered away from Brands Hatch straight to London's Heathrow Airport, where he flew to New York to discuss the details with Burton face to face. In New York, a nervous Hunt was shocked to find himself again surrounded by photographers and journalists asking him questions about his wife and Burton.

At their meeting, Burton thanked Hunt for having given him Suzy. Amazingly, Richard Burton told James Hunt that he would pay for the divorce and provide Suzy's settlement for him. Burton estimated that she would have received $500,000, and he settled that amount for her on Hunt's behalf. The divorce did not cost Hunt a penny. Hunt was impressed by Burton's sensitivity. Thoroughly approving of Burton, Hunt said he hoped to meet him again soon.

Soon afterwards, returning to London, Suzy was interviewed by David Benson, to whom she said: "All I want now is to complete the separation with as much dignity and friendship as possible. James and I are still good friends, and I hope we will remain so. He tried awfully hard not to hurt me. Fortunately, everything has turned out for the best for all of us. James is happy, and I am happy. It sounds corny, but, put this down David, he [Richard] is a very special person and we are very, very happy together."

It was all finalized in June 1976 in Port-au-Prince, the capital of Haiti, in the Caribbean. Burton arranged that the divorces of both Taylor and Burton and Hunt and Miller were completed on the same day. (In Haiti, foreigners could be divorced in a day.)

On Saturday August 21, Suzy and Burton were married in Arlington, Virginia. Virginia was one of only three states in the United States that recognized a Haitian divorce. At the precise moment of their wedding, Hunt was relaxing in Scotland. He was playing golf at Gleneagles. For the record, he told a local journalist, "Richard Burton came along and solved all the problems. I learned an awful lot about myself and life, and I think Suzy did too. We all ended up happy, anyway, which is more than can be said for a lot of marriages." For Hunt it was the final release. As he said afterwards: "For the first time, I am mentally content with my private life. Suzy is largely responsible for that."

The last word was left to James Hunt's mother, Susan Hunt. She made it clear that she was entirely on Suzy's side. She knew precisely where in the marriage the fault lay, conceding, "Suzy is absolutely gorgeous; most of his girls are. But I can see that, for James, to be married is impossible. His lifestyle doesn't suit it. I'm bound to say I love him dearly, but I'd hate to have him for a husband."

The wedding of Burton and Suzy cleared the path for Hunt to reveal Jane Birbeck as his new girlfriend.

In reality, Hunt and Birbeck had been going out for more than six months, but Hunt had kept the relationship quiet out of respect to Suzy.

The two had met a year earlier, at which time Birbeck was having an affair with the 45-year-old Mark McCormack, the chairman of International Management Group (IMG), the world's biggest sports sponsorship and management agency. IMG managed some of Hunt's affairs, and he first saw Birbeck at a distance at IMG's offices in London when she was with McCormack.

The American was a legend in the sports industry and generally regarded as the most powerful man in sports. He was manager to all of the world's top golf and tennis stars and an author of the best-selling book *What They Don't Teach You At Harvard Business School.* The book sold millions based on the precept of how to negotiate a deal. But he was also married to Nancy Breckenridge and had three small children, who lived in Cleveland. Breckenridge was a stay-at-home housewife, bringing up the children and never accompanying her husband on his travels. Her husband was very discreet, and she never asked and she was never told about what he got up to.

McCormack and Birbeck had originally met at IMG's office in London. But like Curt Jurgens's affair with Marlene, the relationship was not serious, as McCormack also seemed to have a girl in every port and Birbeck was his London girl. When she became close to Hunt, McCormack didn't stand in her way, just as Jurgens didn't stand in the way of Marlene's union with Lauda. McCormack, always the perfect gentleman and a very considerate individual, despite his ruthless reputation in business, could also sense that she was uncomfortable about seeing a married man with three children and stood aside.

Hunt first got together with Birbeck at a backgammon tournament in Spain at the Marbella Club. But by all accounts, she had captivated him that day. When it was time to leave the Marbella Club, Jane told Hunt she was returning to London with McCormack the following day but invited him to look her up.

When he was in London again, he did look her up; and so began a relationship that would last for more than half a decade. But it all started off very slowly and very properly, which was unusual for Hunt. It was a full six months after they met that he and Birbeck went to bed together. Hunt had wanted to make sure that McCormack was off the scene completely. Only when that was certain did he proceed.

Recalling how long it took Hunt to make his move, Birbeck said, "I was sure he was gay because he never made a move on me for so long. It was a rather bizarre courtship. We had plenty to talk about, but that's all we ever did. He liked conversation and would talk endlessly to me on the telephone. When we got together, we'd have supper and talk into the small hours. There was no deep urge, particularly on his part, to make a permanent relationship."

Birbeck was 24 years old at the time and a stunning woman. Her beauty was always understated because she usually dressed like a tomboy. But when she got dressed up, she was a very impressive woman indeed. Hunt's friend John Richardson described her as "a very cool, a very English, ice maiden."

Hunt quickly nicknamed her "Hot loins," which got shortened to "Hottie." The nickname was picked up by the British media, and she never shook it off. Richardson remembers: "The name stuck, and the press picked it up and ran with it." Gerald Donaldson described her as "adventurous and fun-loving . . . with very obvious feminine charms."

Jane was the daughter of a military man, a brigadier, named Nigel Birbeck. The family was well off, and she was educated at a boarding school in Kent. Nigel Birbeck was renowned as a former deputy fortress commander of Gibraltar, where the family had lived for a long period. She spent her teenage years on the Costa del Sol. When the family moved back to Britain, they took up residence in Buckinghamshire and she started to spend a lot of time in London. She worked as an au pair for a while before taking a secretarial course.

From the end of 1975, Hunt and Birbeck were seeing each other regularly when Hunt was in London. She avoided Spain, as Hunt was publicly still married to Suzy Miller and was living with her at the Spanish house. The last thing she wanted was to be known as the girl who broke up his marriage.

But when Suzy got together publicly with Richard Burton in early 1976, there was no further need for secrecy, and the two of them became an item and began being photographed together. At first no one knew who Birbeck was, and Hunt wasn't in a rush to enlighten the paparazzi.

But the relationship was soon serious and passionate. She also had a very fierce independent streak, which Hunt adored as an antidote to Suzy's neediness. He always felt the failure of his marriage was primarily because he could not cater to Suzy's need for constant attention. Jane

Birbeck required none of that and was a total opposite to Suzy. Although she lacked Suzy's poise and ethereal presence, Hunt liked Jane's bohemian style and her undeniable sex appeal. He said of her: "She has a strong personality, the strongest one I've ever met and the only one who could stand up to my strength, which is why we have such a good balance. I've never wanted to use or abuse women, but if you have a stronger personality, you can't help but be the dominant one. And the moment that happens, you have no relationship. I don't want someone to live for me."

And so it was that the two drivers, both very happy for entirely different reasons, got down to the serious business of fighting for the Formula One world championship with new partners and settled love lives.

CHAPTER 8

Three in a Row for Ferrari

Angry Man Loses the Plot

Long Beach: March 26–28, 1976

James Hunt flew back to London from Johannesburg to compete in the Race of Champions non-championship race at Brands Hatch in England. From Heathrow Airport, he went straight to his parents' house in the county of Surrey, not far from the Brands Hatch circuit.

His parents' house was a safe refuge from journalists enquiring about the state of his crumbling marriage.

Lauda and Hunt squared up to each other at Brands, and both were eager to use the race for a test session for the British Grand Prix that was due to be held at the same circuit later in the year.

Surprisingly, neither Hunt nor Lauda dominated qualifying, and Jody Scheckter vanquished both of them in his Tyrrell-Ford. Lauda had to be content with second, and Hunt could only manage fifth. In the race, however, they dominated; Hunt beat Niki Lauda fair and square in a straight fight for the first time, although Lauda eventually retired after 17 laps with brake problems.

Afterwards, Hunt helicoptered straight to London's Heathrow Airport and flew to New York to meet his wife, Suzy, to discuss a divorce. It was there that he also met Richard Burton for the first time. From New York he flew to Los Angeles, and a Marlboro minibus picked him up from LAX and took him straight to the small town of Long Beach, where the first ever United States Grand Prix West was due to be staged on a converted street circuit.

Hunt had a very nasty flight across America and had taken too many painkillers for a headache likely caused by a heavy drinking session with Burton before his departure. He had severe stomach pains and as a result was in poor shape by the time he reached his hotel bedroom in Long Beach. Luckily he had a few days to recover.

The US Grand Prix West was a brand-new event, a second race in America at a circuit carved out of public streets in the little-known Los Angeles suburb of Long Beach. Long Beach was billed as an American version of the Monaco Grand Prix. In truth, the two locations shared only a proximity to water. The harbor was filthy and the surrounding buildings decrepit. Downtown Long Beach consisted of run-down motels, dirty apartment blocks, and old warehouses, some of which had been converted into cinemas showing pornographic movies. The circuit was worn-out tarmac bordered by concrete walls and vertical catch fencing. Long Beach turned out to be a seedy low-rent resort, nothing at all like Monaco. The town was best known as the retirement home of the ex-Cunard cruise liner, the *Queen Mary,* which had been converted into a hotel.

The race had been the improbable dream of an improbable character named Chris Pook. Pook was a gray-bearded expatriate Englishman. He was an opportunist who was perennially short of cash but had somehow raised the funds from the Long Beach local authority to accede to the demands of Bernie Ecclestone of FOCA to pay out $500,000 to host the event. It made his vision of a world championship Grand Prix around the streets into a reality.

The Long Beach local council was keen to promote the town's tourism, and they had watched as Pook tested the concept at a smaller race the year before.

Despite Pook's best efforts, however, right up to the few hours before the weekend began, there were doubts that the track could be made safe enough around its 2-mile length. But that applied to all street circuits.

Niki Lauda and the Ferrari team had high hopes for success in Long Beach. The 312T's shorter wheelbase chassis was ideal for a tight street circuit, and Lauda's driving skill was proven on tighter tracks. Conversely, James Hunt and the McLaren team did not expect to do well in Long Beach on its tight twisty track with the guardrails inches from the action. The McLaren-Ford M23 was ill suited to slow twisty tracks and, with its long wheelbase, had primarily been designed for the fast-sweeping tracks of Europe. Not only that, but Hunt hated street tracks, and despite three previous attempts, he had never managed to finish the Monaco Grand Prix.

So when qualifying was over, Hunt was very surprised when he found he had qualified third behind Regazzoni's Ferrari and Patrick Depailler's Tyrrell-Ford and, most surprisingly, found that he had also beaten Niki Lauda's time.

Niki Lauda had a very troubled time throughout qualifying. For the first time in many races, he was not a force and had to settle for a place alongside Hunt on the second row of the grid. In the end, only three-tenths of a second covered the first three cars. As Hunt said, "It was one of those sessions where everyone was getting quicker all the time, and we were as good as anybody. The four of us had been fast, swapping times, and there was really nothing to choose between us." Lauda simply said, "I hit a lot of snags."

Lauda was under a lot of pressure in Long Beach. The laid-back Californian fans expected more of the drivers at this event than at any other. Lauda refused to take part in organized autograph sessions, and he upset Chris Pook. He demanded a huge sum of money to participate, to which Pook refused. Lauda said, "I have to force myself to go to an autograph session. That's real hard labor, and I admit I put a high price on it." He added, "That's one of the primitive laws of business life: that you take note of your market value. After all, people wouldn't pay me so much if I wasn't worth it to them."

But there were deeper political dramas playing out at the Ferrari team other than arguments about autograph sessions. Astonishingly, Daniele Audetto took Lauda to one side in California and told him that he had "won enough" races and that it was now his teammate Clay Regazzoni's "turn" to take the checkered flag. He told him that Regazzoni "must be allowed to win."

Lauda was completely shocked and said to Audetto, "Are you mad? These points will be needed to win the world championship."

Audetto inferred that the world championship was already in the bag, but Lauda told him to put such ideas out of his head, insisting he did not understand the vagaries of Formula One.

Lauda refused to let Regazzoni win, and the two men did not part as friends. The situation remained unresolved. As it was, Audetto's wish came true by accident rather than by design, as Clay Regazzoni dominated qualifying and easily took pole position on the grid.

With the pressure off, James Hunt made an uncharacteristic good start in the race after Regazzoni led off, followed by Patrick Depailler, then Hunt, with Lauda fourth.

Almost straightaway, Hunt passed Depailler's Tyrrell-Ford and set off after Regazzoni. But there was a vapor lock in the fuel system, and his Ford-Cosworth engine started spluttering, which enabled Depailler to get past again. The engine soon cleared, but Hunt's efforts came to naught on the third lap when, as he was attempting to overtake Depailler's Tyrrell for the second time, the Frenchman suddenly moved after appearing to clip a barrier and inadvertently pushed Hunt's McLaren off the track. His car was shunted headfirst into the wall. It had been at slow speed, so there was little damage.

Everyone expected Hunt to dust himself off and drive on, but Hunt didn't move off again. What the spectators didn't know was that a red mist had descended over Hunt's helmet visor and he had decided to stay put, seething inside the cockpit. It transpired that Hunt was determined to play the victim that day and so temporarily lost the capacity for reasonable thought.

Eventually a furious Hunt undid his seat belts and leapt from his car. He ran to the middle of the track and just stood there, more or less on the racing line, and started a tirade of fist shaking and abuse directed at Depailler. Hunt continued this for three laps before he was dragged off the track by burly American marshals. It was a ludicrous display of truculence and observed by all the drivers, including Lauda, who was snickering under his visor at his rival's stupidity.

Lauda inherited second place, and it stayed that way for the rest of the race, with Regazzoni leading him home. There was a chance that Lauda could have pushed and overtaken Regazzoni, but 15 laps before the finish, the Ferrari's gearbox started making peculiar noises, which prompted Lauda to ease off. He slowed his lap times by as much as three seconds as Regazzoni pulled away.

In the event, Regazzoni and Lauda cruised to victory, scoring a 1-2 for Ferrari, with Depailler, who kept going, third. Lauda admitted he had been lucky and said, "I just about managed to finish."

But the best action was still to come for both drivers. As Lauda and Regazzoni celebrated the first Ferrari 1-2 of the year, Daniele Audetto strutted his stuff down the pit lane alongside his elegant wife, Delphine. Lauda mocked them, saying, "He was naturally enormously pleased and walked about more proudly than ever."

As for Hunt, he had not calmed down in the intervening two hours. If anything, he had grown more enraged. He shoved security men aside and stormed into the post-race press conference. In front of the world's media, he grabbed a startled Patrick Depailler and asked him what he thought he had been playing at. Enraged further by Depailler's initial response, Hunt shouted at him: "It was just flagrant stupidity. I came alongside you and you saw me, but you just moved over and squeezed me out. You made a complete cock-up of that corner, and the first thing you should do when you make a cock-up is to look where all the others are. The first thing you must do is to bloody well learn to drive."

Depailler said, "Look, James, I am desolate at what has happened. I am so sorry." Hunt said, "I am bloody well sorry too. Just watch it in future." With that, he stormed off. Outside, Hunt told journalists that Depailler was a "crazy frog driver" who had robbed him of a certain second place.

In the end, though, most people took Depailler's side, and James Hunt received very bad press in the following week. Even his close friend Jody Scheckter was quoted as describing his antics that day as "very foolish."

But the final denouncement came from Hunt's own team. When the McLaren mechanics brought Hunt's car back to the pits, the only damage they could find was a crumpled nose; they reported to Alastair Caldwell that the car was perfectly drivable. It was clear that Hunt could have continued in the race if his anger and sheer petulance had not overpowered his sense of reason.

As dusk fell and Hunt continued making his case to journalists, he eventually admitted he had made a mistake trying to pass Depailler at that corner, but he still blamed him for the accident.

But Alastair Caldwell and Teddy Mayer were furious with him for prematurely retiring his car. All the previous goodwill he had earned with the team's management evaporated.

His world championship hopes were also evaporating, as Lauda left America with 24 points and Hunt only had 6. Hunt wasn't even second or third in the world championship rankings; he was not even fourth. Outwardly it was a desperate situation, and he was by now eager to win a Grand Prix for McLaren. As he said, "I need a victory to make Niki sweat, and I need one to know I can do it."

It was a still very angry James Hunt who flew back to Britain to take part in the non-championship International Trophy Formula One race at Silverstone. Niki Lauda did not appear, and Ferrari sent a single car for its reserve driver. Free from any pressure, Hunt duly won it in style. In a display of driving perfection, he completely dominated the race in front of 75,000 almost out of control, screaming fans.

The International Trophy had been renamed the Graham Hill Trophy in memory of the late champion, and the trophy was presented to Hunt by Bette Hill. Hunt, as she later revealed, had whispered to her on the podium: "If I can achieve only a small percentage of what Graham achieved in his life, I will be happy." Journalist Ian Phillips wrote in *Autosport* magazine: "His style was impeccable, both on and off the track, which should shut up the childish newspaper critics for good and all."

Daily Express motoring editor David Benson witnessing it all, said: "That weekend James gave one of the most impressive displays of high-speed Formula One driving I have ever witnessed. From the moment he went out onto the track for the first of the two practice sessions on Saturday, he was clearly the fastest man on the track. He was beautifully controlled. It was smooth, clean driving without a hint of overexuberance."

After Silverstone, Hunt was riding the crest of a wave. From having been a little-known playboy racing driver, he was now internationally famous—not least because of his wife's affair with Richard Burton. As a genuine world championship contender, he was now recognized wherever he went and was enjoying it immensely. When it got too much, he retreated to Marbella, where he was left alone. Moreover, with his wife gone, he could smoke as much cannabis and drink as much beer as he liked; he could also sleep with as many girls as he liked—often two or three together, if it took his fancy.

Meanwhile, Niki Lauda had slinked off to get married to Marlene away from the public gaze.

CHAPTER 9

Ferrari Shoots Itself

Enzo Ferrari Wages War against Lauda

Maranello: April 1976

After Niki Lauda returned from California at the conclusion of the early season flyaway races, he was contemplating the start of the European season with some real confidence. The loss of Luca di Montezemolo as Ferrari's team manager was not proving as catastrophic as it might have. He had known for a long time that Montezemolo's eventual departure was inevitable and had tried to stave it off as long as he could. But now that it had come, the consequences were actually nowhere near as bad as Lauda had thought.

In fact, everything within Ferrari looked good as, after all, the team had won the first three races of the year in convincing style. But although Lauda knew better, and he knew what had gone on behind the scenes in those first three races had not been good, he was still relieved. As he said, "I won the first two races and Regazzoni the third, but in hindsight, everything was going just a shade too smoothly."

In reality, Lauda couldn't have liked Montezemolo's replacement, Daniele Audetto, any less, and he believed Enzo Ferrari was just an old buffoon. And worse, he believed the combination of the two of them managing the team, despite the good start to the season, could be fatal to his world championship chances.

But those thoughts were far away as, back home in Austria, Lauda contemplated his future as a happily married man. Niki and Marlene

Lauda had moved into Lauda's new house near Salzburg. Lauda had built the house on a site he had originally purchased with his former girlfriend, Mariella Reininghaus.

The new house was built in Salzburgerland on a site between Fuchslee and Thalgau in the hamlet of Hof. It was ideal, situated only 10 minutes from Salzburg Airport, where Lauda flew in and out of in his Cessna Golden Eagle airplane.

Construction of the house had been fraught with difficulty, and Lauda had fallen out with the architect after he found he couldn't get his Range Rover into the garage, as the roof was too low. He appointed Mariella's brother, who was a painter, to finish off the house.

Although they had known each other for less than a year, Lauda and Marlene were hopelessly in love and both keen to cement that love by starting a family as soon as possible. Lauda's new house was perfect and very suitable for the large family they envisaged. Among a host of improvements, he was keen to add a swimming pool. In fact, with summer approaching, it was the first priority, and Lauda decided to do some of the work himself. It proved to be a big mistake.

Lauda had been on a tractor with a hydraulic scoop attached at the front, shifting earth and helping dig the hole for the pool. Unfamiliar with the changing dynamics of a tractor with a load, he lost control and the tractor overturned. It tipped over with a load of earth piled high in the scoop. He explained: "I was trying to shift a mound of earth from the meadow in front of my house when I somehow managed to tip the tractor right over on top of myself."

As the tractor rolled forward, he somehow fell in between the seat and the transmission. For a brief moment, the scene was still and Lauda was motionless. He was covered in a pile of earth, and workmen rushed to help. As they rushed over, the workmen feared the worst, but Lauda eventually struggled clear, with earth caked over his eyes and in his mouth. But he was badly shaken and in pain, as he had suffered a compound fracture of his ribs. There was blood everywhere, as the ends of the ribs had penetrated his skin.

As he recalled: "A couple of inches either way and it would have been really serious. As it was, I was pinned to the ground and ended up with two broken ribs—all things considered, not too bad for a shunt with a 1.8 ton tractor."

He was very lucky not to have been killed, as he admitted: "If I had been sitting in it in the ordinary way, I would have been killed. But I had the luck to fall between the caterpillar wheels, so I didn't get the whole weight on me. Also, the earth was fairly soft, so my head was buried in a cushion."

In reality, Lauda was extremely fortunate to escape with two badly broken ribs. He was immediately bound up by a doctor and given some routine painkilling injections. Lauda later referred to the incident as "the ridiculous business with the tractor." But it was far from ridiculous, and although the injury itself was not serious, he was in terrible pain and confined to bed. He admitted to friends at the time: "The pain was excruciating. There was blood everywhere, and I can't get up without help."

It was a very debilitating injury, and immediately afterwards it looked as though Lauda could be out of Formula One for at least a month. Doctors told him that although his ribs would heal in two weeks, he would be immobilized for six weeks. There was little hope that he would be able to race his Ferrari in Spain at the next race in just two weeks' time.

As soon as word got out as to the seriousness of the situation, it caused a sensation in Italy and set in motion a series of events that completely served to destabilize the Ferrari team. The team, which had already been in difficulties internally, was now wracked with internal strife.

The tractor incident was the spark that set off a fire.

It quickly emerged that there was much jealousy within the team over Lauda's success and his internal detractors wanted an Italian driver to win in the Italian car. The internal detractors, led by Enzo Ferrari and let loose since Montezemolo's departure, believed Lauda's success had been due to the car and not the driver. Despite his success, they actually wanted Lauda out and saw the tractor accident as their opportunity. Lauda recalled: "The Italian press got hold of the story—you can hardly blame them; a Formula One world champion crushed by a tractor makes pretty good copy."

Audetto threw himself into the day-to-day intrigues at the factory in Maranello as Lauda lay in bed at home in Austria. He fueled the flames and, according to Lauda, briefed the rabid Italian journalists every day. Audetto loved the attention and adulation he received from the Italian media. Lauda believes that Audetto couldn't help himself and that he briefed against him continually in that period. As a direct result, Italian journalists started clamoring for Lauda to be sacked and replaced with an Italian. Believing him to be overrated, they maintained that an Italian could do better in such a good car. Lauda said, "All races I had won for Ferrari had still not silenced one particular section of the Italian press, which constantly clamored for an Italian driver."

And the Italian press, seemingly put up to it by Audetto, had a ready-made replacement in a young Italian driver named Maurizio Flammini. Flammini was a 26-year-old who had won a couple of races in Italian Formula 2 racing. The campaign to install Flammini in Lauda's car was led by the editor of *Autosprint,* the Italian motor racing magazine. The magazine urged Italians to "stick together."

Lauda remembered: "As soon as the news leaked out about my accident with the tractor, they sensed an opportunity to promote an Italian into the cockpit. There just happened to be a young lad around called Flammini, who had had a good result in Formula 2; he would be an automatic choice." But Lauda knew the notion to be ridiculous, as he said: "Such a silly idea, halfway through the season to have a completely inexperienced driver in Formula One. No Italian was bad or inexperienced enough not to be put forward as an alternative."

Lauda grew increasingly incensed by what was happening. His world championship and early season domination seemed to count for nothing. As he said, "I had a comfortable lead in the world championship: 24 points after three races, with the second place man on 10 points. But there were panic stations at Ferrari, and I felt the pressure." He added, "It was a fascinating situation—yesterday a hero; but as soon as I was lying on my back, I'd had my chips. One of the main reasons for the chaos and muddles was that the old man [Enzo Ferrari] and his people take what they see in the newspapers so terribly seriously."

It was obvious that someone had done a number on the Italian press, as the journalists were all coming out with the same story and theme time and time again: that the car was good and the driver was average, and that it was the car not the driver that had won the races. Lauda knew that was nonsense, and so did Clay Regazzoni, but he kept quiet as the controversy raged. Regazzoni and Lauda's relationship, which had been as good as it gets, in 1975 now became strained. He said, "Tempers ran high, and in the heat of the moment, I paid scant attention to what he said."

The feeling was that if Lauda wasn't fit to drive in Spain, Ferrari would replace him, probably for good. By this time, Lauda was fed up with Ferrari's politics and initially couldn't care less what was being written, and so he ignored it.

But eventually Lauda found he could not ignore what was being written every day. He was under pressure at home as some Italian newspapers sent representatives to Austria. Four journalists booked in at the local inn and began calling Lauda's house every hour for updates and begging for interviews. Photographers set up on a hill with telephoto lenses.

He finally snapped while speaking to a journalist from the leading Italian sports newspaper, *Gazzetta dello Sport*. As he said, "I came out with a few choice remarks, notably to the effect that [Enzo] Ferrari could take a long walk off a short pier, and *Gazzetta dello Sport* ran that in a banner headline." He added to the controversy when he was asked about the possibility of the young Flammini replacing him, to which he replied, "Italians are only good for driving round the church."

Lauda had put the match to the fuse, as he remembered: "All Italy was up in arms." Aroused by his entry into the war of words, Lauda was so upset by the resulting negative publicity that he threw caution to the wind and decided to challenge Enzo Ferrari publicly. Via the newspapers, he gave Enzo Ferrari an ultimatum. He said he would be available for the next Grand Prix in Spain and stated, "but only if and when Ferrari required him."

Enzo Ferrari was shocked by Lauda's announcement and suddenly realized he could lose him. Lauda's declaration that he would be fit and ready for the Spanish Grand Prix changed the dynamics of the affair. Enzo suddenly realized that if he replaced Lauda with Flammini and

Flammini was slower, then he would become the laughing stock of all Italy. And deep down, Enzo Ferrari knew this would probably be the outcome.

Lauda's statement successfully spooked Enzo Ferrari, who now changed tack completely and panicked. He told Audetto to do something, and he dispatched a Ferrari public relations executive, Sante Ghedini, to go and see Lauda to get a firsthand report of the situation in Austria. Ghedini was chosen because of his closeness to Lauda.

Ghedini left the Ferrari factory immediately and drove overnight from Maranello to Salzburg. He arrived in the early hours of the next morning at Lauda's home. His job was to liaise with Lauda and provide regular bulletins of his medical condition. When he arrived at Lauda's house the following morning, he found journalists and photographers camped out at his gates. The colorful Ghedini grabbed a yard broom and charged the journalists, scattering them. They packed up their things and left.

Lauda and Ghedini plotted together, as Lauda remembered: "There were panic stations at Ferrari, and I was determined to do everything I could to start in the next race." Ghedini spoke to Audetto every day, making reports on Lauda's condition. But he did not tell him the absolute truth.

If he had told him the truth, Lauda immediately would have been replaced for the Spanish Grand Prix, as the situation did not look very good. Lauda was bedridden and in total agony from his badly broken ribs. There appeared to be no way he could drive in Spain, although Ghedini, under instructions from Lauda, kept up the pretense that there was. Lauda recalled the reality of the situation: "I was lying in bed hardly able to move because the pain was so intense."

Driving in Spain looked nigh on impossible until a man named Willy Dungl arrived at Lauda's bedside. Dungl was a world-class masseur and had a very high reputation due to his long, successful association with the Austrian winter Olympics team. Dungl was introduced to Lauda by a journalist friend, a radio reporter. Lauda remembered: "I had never met Dungl, but I had heard a tremendous amount about him: masseur, guru, dietician, layer-on-of-hands, and miracle worker."

But their first meeting was hardly auspicious. Lauda was in his best curmudgeonly mood and did not endear himself to Dungl. He said, "Dungl was badly dressed and grumpy." In response, Dungl told Lauda: "I can't do a thing for you. If you want me to try, you'll have to get yourself to Vienna." With that, Dungl left. Lauda remembered his initial thoughts: "There must be the world's biggest pain in the ass."

But Lauda realized that there was no way he could drive in Spain, and after consulting with Ghedini and Marlene, he decided to get himself to Vienna and put himself in the hands of Dungl as a last throw of the dice. A private ambulance was hired, and Lauda made the difficult journey to Vienna. But Dungl placed many conditions on his agreeing to help. He told Lauda that up to now he had regarded him as an "arrogant type of sportsman who neglected his body." He told him he would help him only if he was "willing to do something for his physical well-being from then on." Lauda had no choice but to agree to his conditions.

Dungl sought out an Austrian surgeon with whom he had worked previously on accident cases, and the two of them got to work. Straightaway, Lauda realized he had come to the right place. He said, "He helped me to rediscover my own body . . . and convinced me to alter my eating habits and in each instance explained the reason for the change in a way that I could understand and accept."

But Lauda found Dungl a very testy individual indeed, as he explained: "Willy is one of the most bad-tempered people in the world. It is virtually impossible to hold a telephone conversation with him. He is so unfriendly you feel like hanging up after a couple of seconds."

But despite all the problems from that first meeting, Dungl hardly left Lauda's side; he kept him in tip-top physical condition for the rest of his career. Lauda said in his autobiography, *To Hell and Back:* "Willy Dungl has been one of the most important people in my career and my life. There is no one to touch him; he is simply a genius. His knowledge, his sensitivity, his touch, and his methods—I simply cannot imagine that there is another like him anywhere in the world."

Dungl, with the help of the Austrian surgeon, had Lauda back on the grid two weeks after the accident. As Lauda said so succinctly, "After two long painful weeks, many Dungl tricks and hard clenching of teeth, I went to Spain."

With that, it was over as soon as it had begun, and two humiliated Italians, Enzo Ferrari and Daniele Audetto, withdrew from the fray, telling their fellow Italians it had all been a mistake. But the whole event turned into an Italian farce and seriously destabilized the team.

As for Enzo Ferrari, it was just another conflagration in a career seemingly full of them. As he had once said of himself: "When I look in the mirror in the morning, even I don't understand myself. Some things in life are truly inexplicable." His reaction to Lauda's tractor accident had certainly been one of the most inexplicable events in his life.

CHAPTER 10

Hunt Wins, Then He Doesn't

Caldwell Messes Up in Spain

Spain: April 30–May 2, 1976

The Spanish Grand Prix, held over the first weekend of May, was the first race of the new European season and it was being held at the Jarama circuit, just outside Madrid. By the fourth round of the 1976 world championship, James Hunt had made himself familiar to everyone and was the center of attention in the Formula One paddock. As a front-runner, he attracted far more attention in the paddock than the reigning world champion, who was increasingly being regarded as a curmudgeon. And certainly Hunt was responsible for a lot of that.

Although Lauda and Hunt were firm friends, Lauda resented the challenge on the tracks. With his qualifying performances, many media people regarded Hunt as the faster driver, and that rankled Lauda more than he cared to admit.

Both Hunt and Lauda, aside from their own personal battle, found they had renewed troubles with their teammates.

Jochen Mass was ready to reassert himself in Spain. He had won the race the previous year and believed himself a Spanish expert. It was also the anniversary of his first (and only) Grand Prix win, and he was determined to reestablish himself in the team by winning the race. There was added needle, as Mass was actually leading Hunt in the world championship; Mass was fourth in the championship with seven points, while

Hunt was only fifth with six points. While Hunt had been getting up pole positions and making the front running in the opening races, Mass had actually scored more points: from a sixth place in Brazil, a third in South Africa, and a fifth in Long Beach.

With that in his head, Mass was entirely confident that he would beat Hunt at Jarama. It set the scene for some real aggravation between the teammates, especially as it had been previously established that whoever achieved a lead on points early in the season would be regarded as number one driver and would then be backed up by the other driver for the world championship. Hunt was worried that Mass might want to enforce that provision, even though he was clearly the quicker driver. Going down to Madrid, there is no doubt that Mass saw the race as his chance to regain team leadership with a win.

Mass was wrestling with his own ego and internal demons. He was all psyched up and had plenty of difficulty trying to understand how Hunt possibly could be faster than him in equal cars. He eventually came to the conclusion that his car, the McLaren-Ford M23 chassis number 6, must be the reason. So he told Alastair Caldwell that he wanted to make the team's spare car, M23 chassis number 9, his regular race car. Caldwell reluctantly agreed and modified it to suit Mass, thereby starting the fairly big job of adapting Mass's old car to Hunt's specification as the spare.

Hunt observed all this with a mischievous manner and was determined to teach the German a lesson he wouldn't forget at Jarama; he wanted to end the inter-team rivalry once and for all.

Lauda's problems with his teammates were eerily similar. Regazzoni, boosted by his Long Beach win, strutted up and down the paddock and pouted like an overstuffed peacock, seemingly aided and abetted by Daniele Audetto, who was now openly showing his preference for the Swiss driver and his disapproval of Lauda's attitude.

Lauda also believed that Audetto had briefed Italian journalists unfavorably after his tractor accident at home. Audetto apparently informed the media that he expected Regazzoni to beat Lauda again in Jarama. Lauda also believed, without any evidence, that Audetto had poisoned Enzo Ferrari's mind against him.

For his part, Lauda was openly contemptuous of Audetto and his continual preening. He didn't like the way he lauded it over the Ferrari team or the way he showed his apparent contempt for his number one driver. Lauda believed that Audetto thought he was socially beneath him, and treated him as such. Lauda also didn't care much for Audetto's well-heeled, statuesque, and beautiful wife, Delphine. He questioned why she attended races at all. He thought she distracted her husband while he was supposed to be at work.

For Ferrari the 1976 Spanish Grand Prix was a very important race, as it marked the debut of designer Mauro Forghieri's brand-new car, the 312T2. It was the second in a series of 312T cars. There would eventually be three models of the 312T series, spanning five highly successful seasons.

Lauda, with plenty of testing under his belt, had the new car working well straightaway. Interestingly, the car was introduced without the De Dion design suspension for which it had been designed. Lauda had thoroughly tested it and found it neither slower nor faster, and it was therefore abandoned after Ferrari had spent a great deal of money developing it. Lauda shrugged when asked about it, saying, "The De Dion was good, but it was not better." With time on its side, Ferrari arrived with new models for both Lauda and Regazzoni to drive. But there was no spare car.

The Spanish Grand Prix also marked the date for a series of regulatory changes, which were bizarrely due to come into force two-thirds through the race weekend, on May 1. The new regulations changed the permitted dimensions for oil coolers and tanks, rear-wing endplates, and airboxes. Rollover hoop regulations were also tightened. The existing cars were legal for qualifying but not for the race.

The new Ferrari had been built for the new regulations, and its debut was timed deliberately to coincide with the race. The two McLaren race cars, chassis 8 and 9, had to be modified to suit. But the spare car, chassis 5, was kept in old specifications, as it could be used legally for the two qualifying days.

In addition to modifying the cars to suit the new regulations, McLaren designer Gordon Coppuck had been messing around with the cars' wheelbases and had added as much as 5 centimeters (1.97 inches), despite the overall length of the car remaining the same. The purpose was apparently to improve airflow over the rear wing.

But it was the new regulations specifying the maximum length and width of the cars that would cause the most controversy. These regulation changes had taken place at the beginning of the season and, up until then, had not really been enforced. At the start of 1976, the CSI, the sport's governing body, had become concerned that cars were getting wider and longer and going faster with more downforce and were thereby becoming more dangerous. To counter that, a revised set of measurement regulations aimed at keeping cars within specified limits and simplifying the technical regulations was agreed upon.

To establish the maximum allowable width, CSI officials measured the widest car—the McLaren-Ford M23—and declared it the limit. Likewise, the longest car was measured and its length written in as the maximum for all cars. Alastair Caldwell remembers it very clearly: "Our car had been measured by the authorities at the Nürburgring in 1975 as the widest. They said, 'Okay, we'll make that the maximum width for 1976.' We said, 'Come on, mate, give us a centimeter,' and they replied, 'Okay, your car measured 2.9; we'll make the rule 2.10.' In 1976 the rule came in."

The new Ferrari was built within these limits, but McLaren didn't bother to change or even measure their car, arguing that since it was the benchmark, it couldn't be illegal under the new rules. What Alastair Caldwell hadn't realized, or hadn't focused on, was that the new Goodyear tires bulged out more than they had in the past. Technically, the extra bulge made the McLarens illegal—but no one at the team spotted it.

Officials of the sporting division of the CSI were rigorous in inspecting the cars at Jarama. The CSI sent three of its top officials to Spain in the shape of France's Jabby Crombac, Kirt Schildt of Switzerland, and Baron de Knyff from Holland.

The three men had plenty to think about, as the Spanish Grand Prix marked the introduction of the first six-wheeled car in Formula One. The new six-wheeled Tyrrell-Ford car was to be driven by Patrick Depailler. The six-wheeler had been designed specifically with the new regulations in mind.

As qualifying began, Niki Lauda found his cracked ribs extremely uncomfortable in the car and was well below his best. However, he was spurred on by the thought of Regazzoni and Audetto. So as not to give them any encouragement or satisfaction, Lauda, with his physiotherapist Willie Dungl in close attendance, pretended he was unaffected, saying, "It's a problem, sure. I don't feel any pain where it's broken, because the doctors have killed the nerve, but it does hurt a little bit above and below there. It hurts mostly when I am sliding the car and when I stop the slide. Your side pushes against the side of the seat then, of course. Also, I can feel the ends of the broken ribs grinding against each other. It must be slowing me down a little bit, sure, but I don't know how much."

The situation could not have been more different for James Hunt. His weekend began well, and he was fastest straightaway. As the weekend wore on, Lauda swapped the top-qualifying slot with Hunt. Perhaps more important for both of them, in every session and throughout the weekend, Lauda was quicker than Regazzoni and Hunt was quicker than Mass.

The new regulations had done their job and slowed down the cars. None of the drivers approached their times of the previous year, and Hunt's eventual pole time was slower than the qualifying record of two years earlier. His pole-winning lap, Hunt's third pole in four races, was three-tenths of a second faster than Lauda in the Ferrari beside him. Mass was third, and the two McLarens sandwiched Lauda's Ferrari on the starting grid.

Race day dawned with sunny and clear weather, typical in Spain in early May. The start was delayed while King Juan Carlos, a keen Formula One fan, arrived with his family in his helicopter.

Hunt, fearful of his clutch, was slow to get away from the start, while Lauda, high on painkillers, stormed into the lead for the first 31 laps as Hunt was again beaten off the line.

But Lauda could feel his broken, jagged rib-ends grinding together under the G-forces in hard cornering, and as the painkillers wore off, he found it increasingly difficult to control the car. Hunt was content to play a waiting game, knowing that Lauda's ribs simply wouldn't let him continue at that pace for the entire race. Hunt said later, "Niki was motoring hard at the start, and I was able to tuck in behind quite comfortably. I couldn't do anything about passing him; it was just a case of waiting until his ribs started to hurt and I'd be able to nip through." And so it proved, as Hunt went past on lap 32, followed by Mass a few laps later. Mass's engine failed with a few laps to go, and Hunt crossed the line to take his first Grand Prix victory for McLaren. Lauda crawled in for second place, 31 seconds behind and in absolute agony.

Hunt was ecstatic about beating Lauda and his teammate but afterwards was totally exhausted from having wrestled the McLaren round the difficult Jarama circuit for 75 laps. On the way to the podium, he punched a spectator in pure frustration.

But bigger problems than a wayward spectator lay ahead in post-race scrutineering.

Peter Jowitt, a Farnborough-based scientist, had been employed as a consultant by FOCA as a technical consultant. He worked for the teams, and his brief was to check car dimensions, investigate causes of accidents, and suggest modifications for safety. Jowitt was not a scrutineer and had no official powers at all. But when he measured Hunt's McLaren-Ford, he noticed that the McLaren was 1.8 centimeters (0.71 inch) too wide across the rear wheels. Jowitt innocently brought the problem to the attention of the Spanish scrutineers, thinking they would merely inform the McLaren team of the error and ask the team to correct it. Jowitt was said to be horrified when they disqualified the car on the basis of his discovery.

Hunt's celebrations in the Marlboro motor home in the Spanish paddock were curtailed shortly after eight o'clock, when *Daily Express* motoring editor David Benson delivered the bad news. Hunt was relaxing and wearing only a pair of jeans, talking to his teammate, some girls, and his normal retinue of hangers-on. What he heard shocked him, and he immediately grabbed a shirt, shouted over to Teddy Mayer, and ran to the steward's office in the race control tower.

Benson had somehow sensed trouble and gone to the scrutineers garage purely on a whim. By then it had just been announced in the press room that the stewards had ruled Hunt's car to be illegal and that he was therefore disqualified. The scrutineers had ruled that the rear tires of Hunt's M23 extended 1.8 centimeters wider than allowed by the new regulations. After a series of measurements and remeasurements, the McLaren-Ford M23 was deemed undeniably too wide across the rear wheels. The stewards announced Lauda as the new winner of the race. It was the first time the cars had been rigorously checked under the new rules, and the CSI had asked the scrutineers to carefully check the dimensions of each car.

Teddy Mayer argued with the stewards in vain. He told them that such a small discrepancy couldn't give Hunt's McLaren any advantage and that the ruling was "unbelievably harsh and unjustified."

Hunt was distraught, and tears welled in his eyes. He said, "It's stupid. It does not affect the performance of the car or make it any faster. Not even the Ferrari team protested, and they were the ones who had the most to win."

Niki Lauda had already left the circuit by helicopter. He was on his way to the airport to fly back to Austria for further medical treatment on his ribs. He learned that he had been declared the winner of the race from air traffic controllers at Salzburg Airport as he was landing his plane. Lauda's attitude to it was perfectly straightforward: "A rule is a rule. The McLaren was illegal and therefore it should have been disqualified. I am very sorry for James; he drove very well, but the car was not legal. If the same had happened to my Ferrari, I would accept the ruling."

Teddy Mayer, apoplectic toward the stewards, filed an official protest and muttered something to journalists about a conspiracy by Ferrari. In fact, Hunt's car had been measured twice in pre-race scrutineering and had been found legal. But there was now no doubt that McLaren was guilty. As Caldwell freely admitted: "We thought we had no worries because our car was exactly the same. Like idiots, we didn't even bother to measure it—my fault—because as far as I was concerned, the car had been measured and the rule based on it. However, over the winter, Goodyear developed the tires and made them with wider sidewalls. I didn't realize that the tires had been made this much wider. We got caught out."

Mayer, caught in a very tricky situation, put out a press release: "The entire McLaren team extends its sympathy to James Hunt." Stating he would appeal against the severity of the sentence rather than the correctness of the decision, he went on to say it was like being hanged for a parking offense. Mayer maintained that since the minute oversight could have given Hunt no possible advantage, he should at least be able to keep his driver's points.

After his initial disappointment, Hunt became surprisingly sanguine about the entire affair, although he did call his team's failure to ensure the car was the correct width "a fantastically sloppy performance." Hunt said years later, "The point was they'd taken the current widest car in the business and the current longest because they didn't want them to go much wider, like someone suddenly worked out if you had it twice as wide it would have twice as good road holding; likewise if you made it two yards longer. The point was the McLaren was the widest car in the business at the time. But McLaren didn't bother to check the width of its car because it had established the standard the previous year when it was all checked. The only problem was we were using slightly different tires, which had a bigger bulge. And that's the widest point on the car. It was in fact 1.8 centimeters too wide, and that was purely the bulge."

On May 13, a Spanish tribunal confirmed the disqualification, but Teddy Mayer said that the proceedings were a travesty of justice, as he had not been allowed to take McLaren's Spanish-speaking lawyer to the hearing. Mayer later described the tone of the tribunal hearings as follows: "The judges said, 'Do you know the rule about the width of the car?' I said, 'Yes.' They said, 'And do you realize that your car was wider?' I said, 'Yes' again. And they said, 'Right, thank you, Mr. Mayer.'" Mayer was the only person called on to give evidence. Mayer launched another appeal to the FIA in Paris about the tribunal's decision.

Alastair Caldwell simply accepted the blame and admitted there was no doubt the car had been too wide. He had failed to allow for the new design of Goodyear tires.

CHAPTER 11

Ferrari Ascendant, McLaren in Chaos

Ferrari's Fifth Straight Win

Belgium: May 14–16, 1976

Ferrari was in ecstasy and McLaren was in despair after the Spanish Grand Prix. Team manager Alastair Caldwell had been completely surprised and devastated, and he admitted that he had never known a more difficult time in his life. Not only was the position of his team looking precarious, but his own personal credibility was on the line as well.

The normally highly efficient Caldwell was mortified by the turn of events and by James Hunt's disqualification from the Spanish Grand Prix. His troubled emotional state affected his decision making, and instead of taking time to consider a response and course of action, he reacted by erring on the side of caution and instigating a crash program to ensure the car fully complied with the rules—with no shortcuts.

Caldwell's extreme was to have dire consequences for the team and for Hunt's world championship chances. Forgetting that all Formula One cars go fast by being barely legal and by pushing the envelope as far as it will go, his decisions were to cost McLaren and Hunt even more dearly than the forfeited Spanish points.

Back at the McLaren factory in Colnbrook, the repentant Caldwell went on a binge to make his car legal beyond doubt. Caldwell already had a marginally excessive character defect, but he now became utterly and totally obsessed with having a legal car. There was no rationality of thought at all, and he became determined to make the car legally watertight. First he declared that an oil cooler modification he had made earlier in the season was also potentially illegal. The oil coolers had been moved toward the back of the car, but Caldwell ordered them to be moved forward to their original position.

He also ordered the lowering of the rear wing and moved it forward as well for good measure. He then reduced the track of the car by two centimeters. He explained his rationale: "We had a little conference and said, 'Okay, next race we must be absolutely 100 percent safe, not get caught again. We'll narrow the car, bring the wing down just on the limit, and put the oil coolers back where they were before, on the back of the car.'" Caldwell achieved 100 percent legality, but at a huge cost to the team and to his number one driver. The changes rendered the car immediately uncompetitive. Assessing the changes, Hunt called his revised car "utterly hopeless"—just how hopeless would become apparent at the upcoming Belgian Grand Prix.

The Belgian Grand Prix that year was held at Zolder on May 16. It was a 2.6-mile tight, featureless, and artificial track with few passing opportunities. It was the sort of track James Hunt despised, entirely different in character from the sweeping Spa-Francorchamps circuit where the Belgian Grand Prix had traditionally been held but which was now excluded from hosting the race for understandable safety reasons.

While McLaren had their technical problems, Ferrari's troubles were confined to Niki Lauda's physical condition. He was still in a lot of pain from his broken ribs, and recovery had been hindered greatly by his driving in the Spanish Grand Prix. The two weeks in between had brought no respite at all. For the Belgian Grand Prix, Lauda received a painkilling injection that was supposed to last for four days. It didn't, so he called in a doctor who gave him electroshock treatment, which deadened the pain. Lauda admitted that the pain was so bad he would not have been able to drive the car that weekend without the treatment.

Ferrari was still using the old-model 312T car as the spare and was relying on serendipity to get them through. As it was, Lauda was forced to use it for part of qualifying after he lost an engine in his regular car. In a bizarre incident, the wire grid covering one of the fuel injector trumpets somehow got inside the engine when it was running and mangled the innards.

Amazingly, with his car in such poor shape, Hunt managed to top the qualifying charts on the first day of practice, ahead of Clay Regazzoni's Ferrari and Jody Scheckter's Tyrrell-Ford. But there was good reason for that: Caldwell had not had time to complete all the modifications at the factory and planned to move the oil coolers on the Friday afternoon during the first day of qualifying. There simply had not been time at the McLaren factory for the oil coolers to be moved; hence the arrangements were made to modify them at the track.

So between the morning and afternoon sessions, the mechanics shifted the oil coolers back to their old position below the rear wing. Hunt said, "We put them back virtually where they had been, under the wing, but because the wing had been moved forward, the coolers were now about an inch away from their old position."

That alteration, along with the combined effect of Caldwell's other modifications, completely changed the car's aerodynamic setup. Hunt recalled: "In order to make it narrower, they unnecessarily moved radiators around and things like that. But they hadn't checked it out and completely ruined the performance of the rear wing. As a result, the aerodynamics of the car overall were hopeless." The final changes had turned his McLaren-Ford M23 into an ill-handling brute. A journalist standing out on the track described Hunt's revised car as a "bucking bronco."

So much so that in the second session, Hunt was ninth fastest, and in the final session, he was eleventh. But he managed to line up on the second row of the grid by virtue of his time in the first session—before the oil coolers had been moved.

Afterwards, Caldwell sought to defend his radical changes: "We had several things on the car which were reasonably dodgy. You couldn't have oil fittings above a certain width from the center of the car, let's say 80 centimeters, which meant the oil coolers in front of the rear wheels could be—*could be*—construed as illegal."

Hunt was deeply depressed about his chances in the race. His only solace was that his chief rival was not having a particularly good time of it either, although the definition of Niki Lauda not having a good time of it was a resounding pole position, with his teammate Clay Regazzoni alongside him on the front row of the grid.

For once, Hunt made a good start off the grid and the flag. He somehow managed to clamber past Regazzoni into second place behind Lauda's Ferrari. But Lauda quickly built up a huge lead and pulled away from Hunt at the rate of one and a half seconds a lap. Hunt was holding up the rest of the cars, which were queued up behind him. Gradually, Regazzoni, Jacques Laffite in the Ligier, Patrick Depailler, and Scheckter all passed him. He was sixth when his car's gearbox seized up, and he retired from the race at exactly half-distance.

For Niki Lauda, it became an almost accidental afternoon. For reasons he knew not, he found himself in an early lead dominating the field. He had no idea how he was managing to maintain such a comfortable lead. But 20 laps from the end, he had a reality check when his new Ferrari 312T2 began wildly oversteering, again for no apparent reason. He remembered: "I was lying well out in front when my car suddenly began oversteering 20 laps from the finish."

With Hunt out of the race, Lauda knew he had time to pit and probably get out again in front after Hunt's McLaren had held up all the challengers. But just before veering off, he decided to try one more lap, and the car did not get any worse. As he said, "I assumed that the tires or suspension had bought it and was about to head for the pits, but instead I drove carefully for a few laps." Lauda found the car stayed consistent, and so he decided to carry on. He had a scare in the final few laps when an unknown car laid oil all over three corners.

Lauda easily went on to win from Regazzoni for another Ferrari 1-2. Jacques Laffite came home in third place and Scheckter fourth.

On the podium, Lauda was utterly bemused that he had won. He simply could not understand it; as he said, "I managed to come first after all."

After the race, Hunt was forced to reassess his own driving tactics after an onslaught from the drivers he had held up during the race due to his car's slowness. He had upset many of the drivers by employing some dubious driving maneuvers to prevent them from overtaking him. Several times, Jody Scheckter's Tyrrell-Ford was nearly shoved off the road, and Jacques Laffite's Ligier was hit by Hunt's front wheel when he attempted to pass. It was also Patrick Depailler's turn to be angry with Hunt: "Hunt was driving very wildly, holding everybody back. If Hunt says all these things about crazy French drivers, he should not drive in the same way himself." The other drivers had a good case against Hunt and, once again, it was not his finest hour in Formula One.

But that was far from James Hunt's biggest concern. Lauda now had 42 points in the world championship, with the next best-placed driver, his teammate Regazzoni, on 15 points. Hunt was seventh in the standings with six points, with Jochen Mass ahead of him in fourth, with eight points. In truth, Lauda looked as though he was home and dry for the world championship, and no one in the Formula One paddock would have taken bets on James Hunt even being in the top three.

There was also much chatter about the dominance of the 12-cylinder engine in Formula One. It had won every single race so far in 1976. In Belgium, 12-cylinder engines had dominated, and only Jody Scheckter's fourth-placed Tyrrell-Ford was not lapped in the race by the 12-cylinder cars. People believed the era of the Ford-Cosworth V8 was over. They truly did.

CHAPTER 12

Lauda's Magic around Monte Carlo

The Austrian Dominates Again

Monaco: May 27–30, 1976

The Monaco Grand Prix dawned on the weekend of the May 26–30. Monaco is everyone's favorite race, and it is eagerly anticipated each year by everyone in Formula One, from the mechanics to the drivers. It is the one race where the socializing is more important than the racing, and a very good time is had by all.

Around 200 of the grandest yachts in the world descend on the principality and are tied up adjacent to the waterside. As night falls, the in-crowd and Europe's glitterati hop from boat to boat in one long party that starts at six o'clock and ends around 4 a.m., when everyone finally goes to bed.

Niki Lauda dreaded it; he hated the false glamor of Monaco. In contrast, James Hunt couldn't wait to get started.

And socializing on the Marlboro yacht was all McLaren had to offer in 1976. Even before a wheel was turned, the team knew that the car would be uncompetitive. And worse, no one knew why. Alastair Caldwell simply had no clues as to what had caused the car suddenly to become uncompetitive in Belgium. The team had completely lost its way, and back in England at the McLaren factory in Colnbrook, Caldwell and his men were running around like headless chickens.

Having concentrated so hard on making the car legal rather than making it fast, Caldwell had briefly forgotten what Formula One was about.

Meanwhile, Hunt was having his own personal problems. He had become disenchanted with Mark McCormack's management of his commercial affairs and wanted to get out of the contract. He wanted his brother Peter, to take over as his manager. Although it was a relatively minor issue, it gnawed away at Hunt all weekend and added to the team's other problems.

Caldwell was in a foul temper as Hunt set out to have a good time in Monaco's harbor and virtually ignored his team commitments. Hunt, after three years of partying with Alexander Hesketh, was an expert on Monaco's social scene. He met up with former Formula One racer Johnny Servoz-Gavin. Servoz-Gavin, who had retired from Formula One in 1970, now lived on a yacht in Monte Carlo harbor. He and Hunt had been friends for years. They were joined by Philippe Gurdjian, a French mover and shaker. Gurdjian remembers: "They were very close, and I was very close to James."

The three young men painted Monte Carlo red on Wednesday evening. The following night, they jointly hosted a huge party on the boat, which ended up with many of the guests naked.

Gurdjian remembers it as if it was yesterday: "We finished the party the night before the Grand Prix at four in the morning, and they were all racing the day after without any problems. Now it's completely different, and you cannot imagine that."

That night, Hunt promised Gurdjian he would give him his race helmet when the Grand prix was over. The Frenchman still has it today, a prized possession from Hunt's championship year. Gurdjian still remembers his friend fondly: "He was very friendly, he had a real face, and it's a pity we don't have more guys like that."

For the serious business of racing, Hunt's car was in exactly the same specification and setup as it had been in Zolder. For reasons best known to himself, Caldwell had done nothing to the car, even though he knew it had severe self-inflicted problems. He was in a state of total denial and wasn't ready to listen to anyone's opinion about what might be wrong, especially his number one driver. The McLaren-Ford M23, which had been so fast earlier in the season, was now a pig to drive, and for no good reason that anyone could identify.

Monaco was the worst possible place to have an uncompetitive car. It was the one race where it was important to qualify well. Without retirements, the cars would normally finish the Monaco Grand Prix where they had been placed on the grid, since overtaking was virtually impossible.

Ferrari was in great shape for Monaco and finally had a spare 312T2 chassis on hand. The new car had a heavily modified monocoque that had been built without internal bracing, deemed unnecessary and at a considerable saving in weight. Clay Regazzoni quickly grabbed the new car (chassis number 27) as his race car, and his old car became the spare. Niki Lauda was unhappy about this but resigned himself to it, as he knew he could beat Regazzoni even in the older model Ferrari. Sometimes Lauda couldn't even be bothered to speak to Daniele Audetto about it. By now, he had little time for the Italian.

Even without Hunt in the reckoning, Lauda still faced a stiff qualifying challenge from the six-wheeled Tyrrell cars. The six-wheelers proved very adept around Monaco for both Jody Scheckter and Patrick Depailler. But Lauda was still quickest on Thursday and was quickest again on Saturday by a fairly wide margin. Halfway through the final Saturday afternoon qualifying session, he pulled up in the pits, got out of the car, and changed out of his overalls, totally confident that no one else was going to come close to his times. It was all so easy.

During qualifying, Lauda received some bad news from Vienna. His wife, Marlene, who was a few months pregnant, had been rushed to hospital with complications and subsequently suffered a miscarriage. Lauda wanted to abandon the race and return home. But he knew he couldn't. He considered going and returning overnight but quickly ruled it out when he realized he would get no sleep at all. Instead he vowed to get out of Monaco just as quickly as he could on Sunday and booked a helicopter to rush him to Nice airport when the checkered flag dropped.

Hunt had no such problems, and his only decision was which girl he would spend that night with. But on the track, it was hopeless. He had been used to battling for pole all season and was now not even in contention for the first half of the grid. He nursed private doubts about whether he could even qualify. The team tried a special Monaco mod by moving the rear wing to increase downforce, but it made no difference. In addition to all his other woes, the gearbox selector mechanism kept jamming up, causing some disconcerting moments on the track.

In the end, he finished in 13th place on the seventh row of the grid on a circuit where grid position was paramount. He said of his car: "It's not nice," and added, "The dreadful problem was that I was so far back on the grid I wouldn't be able to pass anybody simply because there isn't anywhere to pass at Monaco without doing anything risky or stupid. It's a pretty stupid way to have a race."

On race morning, a desperate Alastair Caldwell ordered the removal of the airbox from the engine and found it immediately improved airflow and the performance of the rear wing. He had been scratching around overnight trying to find solutions to problems, and removing the airbox was a last desperate measure.

But his solution to the problem made McLaren look like amateurs, and up and down the makeshift pit lane, technical directors couldn't believe it. Interestingly, Colin Chapman of Lotus thought he knew exactly what McLaren's problem was. But he wasn't about to tell Caldwell.

To be fair to Caldwell, McLaren was not the only top team experiencing excruciating technical difficulties. There were also problems at Brabham. Team owner Bernie Ecclestone had made a huge mistake in choosing to use Alfa Romeo engines for the 1976 season. The cars were having to start races with 10 gallons more fuel than the Ferrari, Matra, and Ford-engine cars: a weight penalty of about 65 kilograms (143 pounds). Even with that extra fuel, they were still regularly running out of fuel if they lasted to the end the race. The team's number one driver, Carlos Reutemann, was looking to leave as a result.

Like Reutemann, who was dead last on the starting grid, Hunt was dejected and knew he was finished even before the race began. The only plus point was that his car handled better with a full tank of fuel, giving him hope for the early part of the race.

When the race started, Lauda streaked off the grid, already on his way to victory. He left the rest behind to squabble among one another. Hunt was stuck in twelfth place, although with full tanks, his car was the fastest on the track. He remembered: "I was running two seconds a lap slower than I wanted to simply because there was nowhere to pass." He quickly lost concentration and spun off, but he avoided hitting the wall: "I have to say that I spun the car through my lack of interest and sheer bloody frustration." When he recovered and restarted, he was dead last and going nowhere. But at least he was clear of traffic and found he was lapping as fast as Lauda, who was effortlessly leading the race. On the 24th lap, Hunt was put out of his misery when his Ford-Cosworth engine blew up, spilling oil all over the track.

Not for the first time that season, Lauda spotted the oil first and threaded his way through. But second-placed man Ronnie Peterson fell right into it and spun, hitting the barrier and retiring instantly. The oil also eventually caused Clay Regazzoni, who was running third, to crash out.

Lauda described the technique he used for handling the oil on the track: "I thought about the oil on the first lap, and on the next lap, where the car now stood, I thought there must be more oil. I got the car more or less clean through, but I looked in the mirror: no Peterson, a nice surprise."

As soon as he got out of the car, Hunt punched the air and acted just like he had won the race. He was delighted to be out and immediately went off to the harbor to begin celebrating his dismal weekend.

The race itself proved to be a procession and one of the most boring races ever held around the streets of Monte Carlo. Needless to say, Niki Lauda won, followed across the line by the Tyrrell-Fords of Scheckter and Depailler. Interestingly, only the Tyrrells were still on the same lap as Lauda at the finish. He had lapped every other one of the 12 finishers.

Lauda didn't have much to say at the finish but claimed that his victory had been "hard work" and that it had demanded "terrific concentration." But in truth he had had great difficulty staying awake. He admitted he did have one tricky moment, 15 laps before the end, when he slipped the car into second gear instead of third. Inside the cockpit, Lauda was furious with himself and admitted he had almost fallen asleep with the boredom. But the moment brought him wide awake. As he said, "It was a shock to my whole body. Fury with myself gave me the strength to overcome my exhaustion."

It turned out to be a minor blip of no consequence. But if Peterson had still been running, he probably would have been able to get past. Afterwards, Lauda admitted: "It was one of those victories which are a bit of a bore—'once again first from beginning to end,' said the reports."

As he circulated on the post-race victory procession, Lauda was fired up with adrenalin. But inside he was exhausted and just wanted to leave Monte Carlo and return to his wife, Marlene, who by then had been discharged from the hospital. He said, "Everything overwhelmed me at once; the noise, the people, the pushing and shoving and slapping on the back.

But there was plenty of compensation for the discomfort. Lauda now had 51 points to Hunt's 6. Any notion that Hunt was a world championship contender was simply forgotten. No man had ever before won the championship from his position with six races gone.

In the paddock later that evening, there was much speculation as to the reasons for Lauda's success. Many were of the opinion that he was just a very lucky driver. But certainly not Walter Hayes, who ran the Ford Motor Company's motor sport division worldwide and who was responsible for the Ford-Cosworth engine. Hayes was in awe of Lauda; as he said, "People overlook the enormous amount of work that Lauda does for his team. Without Lauda, Ferrari would probably fall apart. Lauda makes his own luck through his own efforts. Most of the people racing today want to get rich first and win next. Lauda wants to win." These words from Hayes, one of the most respected individuals in motor sport, were printed in the *Daily Express* newspaper, much to the chagrin of Daniele Audetto.

But Lauda was by now barely speaking to his team manager. At Zolder, and again in Monaco, Audetto had ordered Lauda to let Clay Regazzoni win, arguing that the victories and the glory must be shared equally by the teammates. Lauda told Audetto that his views were "nonsense and cheating the public." Audetto ignored him, saying, "You must stay second." Audetto told Lauda he would hang out pit boards to give him instructions during the race. Lauda's exact reply to that was not

LAUDA'S MAGIC AROUND MONTE CARLO

recorded, but he later said his response to Audetto's instructions was: "I told him he could hang out any notice board he liked—yellow, green, or red, with plus and minus and double minus—I shouldn't look at it. And that's what happened." Lauda was at a loss to explain it and said, "Audetto had a sort of new-boy complex and thought he must be a great team leader with a great strategy."

By the end of the Monaco Grand Prix, Lauda had completely had it with Audetto, and he stated, "One of the two of us would have to leave at the end of the season; that much was obvious."

Finally Lauda managed to escape from Monaco after his victory lap. Not for him Hunt's celebrations. He got on a helicopter at the heliport and flew straight to Nice airport, where he got on his own plane and flew back to Vienna. He said, "Joy over the victory had simply no chance to get through. Marlene needed me and I needed her, and waking next morning was lovely."

CHAPTER 13

Lauda Has an Off Day

Alastair Caldwell in Denial

Sweden: June 11–13, 1976

There was only one opinion prevailing in the paddock as the Formula One circus assembled at Anderstorp for the Swedish Grand Prix on June 13: that Niki Lauda was already as good as world champion and that James Hunt was a busted flush. At that stage it seemed there could be no other possible outcome to the world championship. Hunt was seventh in the championship standings with 6 points, and Lauda was top with 51 points after six races.

Hunt's own teammate, Jochen Mass, thought so as well and engaged in some very defeatist talk with journalists in the paddock, saying, "You have to be lucky and catch Niki on a bad day if you are going to beat him. Only a puncture or a mechanical failure can stop him these days."

Lauda and the Ferrari team were exhibiting what was eloquently described in the *Daily Express* as "the charisma of superiority."

But history would show that Sweden was Ferrari's most disappointing performance of the year, as well as McLaren's, as the race weekend turned into a fight between the resurgent Lotus and Tyrrell teams. The bizarre change of fortune was reflected by the fact that Chris Amon, in his Ensign-Ford car, qualified quicker than both Lauda and Hunt.

But on Friday, the first day of qualifying, it was business as usual, with Lauda on provisional pole. Conversely, Hunt was having a dreadful time and spun his car a total of six times in practice and qualifying. There was a terrible lack of rear-end adhesion, and he was 14th in the first session, 11th in the second session, and 8th in the final session, for a grid position on the fourth row.

Lauda fell apart on the second day of qualifying when the track conditions were significantly faster.

He had plenty to say about the performance of his car, which he described as a "compromise." For some reason, the track at its optimum did not suit the Ferrari at its optimum. Lauda explained: "It's going to be as good as it should be. It's oversteering and understeering like all the others. But you expect that here and you set up the car in a compromise and just drive it." He added, just so no one was in any doubt, "I'm trying bloody hard." But it was only good enough for fifth on the grid as the Ferrari team's confidence suddenly vanished. It was a serious wake-up call and probably saved the rest of their season, as Daniele Audetto realized that Formula One was not a one-way street in Ferrari's favor and that things could change very quickly and often did. Jody Scheckter's six-wheeled Tyrrell-Ford qualified on pole, with Mario Andretti's Lotus-Ford alongside him.

Alastair Caldwell was still in denial about McLaren's severe technical problems. His was a "wood and trees" problem according to Hunt. But between the second and final qualifying sessions on Saturday, it finally dawned on Caldwell that the car's problems might have something to do with the changes he had ordered after Spain. So on race morning he woke up his mechanics and ordered the car to be put back to its previous specifications and setup, except for the oil coolers, which couldn't be changed at the track. Hunt recalled: "We decided in desperation to put the car back exactly to Spanish settings, but it made no difference to the car at all." McLaren was only saved from total humiliation by the problems that Ferrari was also having.

Race day dawned significantly colder, and that hindered Ferrari even more. For McLaren it didn't matter; the car was so bad they could not distinguish the change. Lauda was having severe problem with tire temperatures in warm-up; they were 20 degrees lower than they should have been. The car was a mixture of severe understeer and oversteer.

Mario Andretti was the driver of the day. He stormed off into the lead but was then penalized by a minute for a false start. After that, Jody Scheckter led, and on the 45th lap, Andretti, trying so hard to catch him, over-revved his Ford-Cosworth engine and blew it up. So Scheckter and his teammate, Patrick Depailler, scored a Tyrrell-Ford 1-2, with Lauda third and Hunt fifth.

Lauda had driven like a hero to finish third and stepped out of his cockpit in an optimistic mood, as he realized what could be achieved when everything was stacked against him. Hunt was equally optimistic and shared Lauda's thoughts, saying, "My best drive of the year; I finished miles behind in a very undrivable car." He had gained two hard-earned points as he had wrestled his car around the Anderstorp track. Those two points earned in Sweden would prove absolutely vital a few months later. Afterwards, Hunt made sure that journalists knew how bad the car really was. It was the only way he felt he could put pressure on Alastair Caldwell to fix the problems, which were by now obviously related to the positioning of the oil coolers.

As the race ended, Lauda was leading Hunt by 47 points in the world championship and Jody Scheckter appeared to be Lauda's challenger for the world crown. Hunt could have had no ambitions for the championship.

CHAPTER 14

Blood in the Garages

Caldwell and Hunt Sort It Out

Paul Ricard: June 1976

After three disastrous races in a row, Alastair Caldwell was having a personal crisis. Something had happened to the McLaren M23 to turn it from being the most competitive car on the grid to a dog. The lack of competiveness was threatening to ruin James Hunt's season as the Belgian, Monaco, and Swedish Grand Prix came and went, with only 2 points scored out of a possible 27. Even worse, Lauda scored 22 points out of a possible 27 in those three races. The damage that had been done to Hunt's championship chances couldn't have been starker.

Back at the factory in England, Caldwell and the McLaren mechanics were panicking after Sweden. It seemed the last person to know what was wrong was Caldwell, and the mechanics had lost confidence in their team manager. A furious Teddy Mayer put Caldwell under intolerable pressure to fix the problems. Caldwell told friends that he feared for his job if he couldn't work out a fix for the car's problems. Caldwell was right to be fearful for his future. Mayer was so frustrated that he was considering taking direct control of the team himself. In that scenario, he had confided to Hunt that he would promote one of the mechanics to be the new team manager. Hunt was on Mayer's side and, at that point of the season, would not have been unhappy to see the back of his team manager, whom he blamed personally for the problems.

In fact, Hunt was sure he knew what the problem was. He told Caldwell time and time again to put the car back to the original specs where it had been before the Spanish disqualification. Hunt believed that Caldwell had been overzealous in his attempts to make the car 100 percent legal.

But Caldwell simply wouldn't listen to Hunt, or to anyone. But suddenly Teddy Mayer did. As Hunt recalled: "It was one of the problems I had with McLaren: trying to persuade them to do anything. Straightaway I said to them this ⅜ inch on the rear track is screwing up the car. Something fundamental has changed, so why don't we put it back to exactly how it was for Spain, except to be within the width limit?"

Mayer's support forced Caldwell to take notice of Hunt. The mechanics had already put the car back to the Spanish Grand Prix configuration—apart from remounting the oil coolers. But Caldwell was sure that the mounting of the oil coolers wasn't the problem, as outwardly there was nothing to suggest that it could be. Hunt recalled: "They had been moved so minutely from their old position relative to the wing that we couldn't believe it could be that."

In the end, Caldwell, under unrelenting pressure from Hunt and Mayer, was forced to put the oil coolers back to where they had been. With that, Teddy Mayer authorized an expensive test session at the Paul Ricard circuit in the south of France to try out the car in the revised configuration. There were a few days left when the team could test legally before the French Grand Prix proper. Caldwell remembered: "We went down there with a car and James."

Caldwell recalled that when the team got the revised car to the Paul Ricard track, it was clear within a handful of laps that they had sorted the problem simply by reverting to the pre-Spain specification. Caldwell said, "We ran with the coolers on the back—James driving—then put them on the side, and James went a second and a half quicker."

Caldwell said that Hunt was not immediately convinced, however, believing that the changing track conditions were affecting his time. Caldwell said he told him: "No, no, no. It's not the car; it's me. The track is cleaning up; the tires are working better." Caldwell replied, "Ah, well, just to check, we'll switch them to the back again." According to Caldwell, Hunt then said, "No, no. No need to do that." Caldwell responded, "Well, we'll do it anyway." The mechanics moved them back, and Hunt went out again. When he returned, Hunt asked, "What happened there?" Caldwell replied, "You were two seconds slower again." Caldwell recalls that Hunt still did not get it, saying, "The track's worse. It's not the coolers; they have no effect at all." Caldwell said, "Okay, we'll change them back again."

Hunt was becoming increasingly angry, and he said, "I won't drive the car," to which Caldwell replied, "Oh yes, you will." The mechanics changed the coolers, and as Caldwell recounts: "James went one and a half, maybe 1.8 seconds quicker. That proved it to us."

But that is Alastair Caldwell's version of events, and many people dispute it. Some people present at the test session that day say that Caldwell rewrote history in his version of the events. In actual fact, they recollect things happening the other way around, with Caldwell not wanting to make the changes and Hunt forcing him to do so.

Caldwell made his comments to author Christopher Hilton after Hunt was dead and he was therefore unable to set the record straight. But before he died, Hunt had always been very clear about his version of what happened. As he said, "We were still struggling disastrously until, finally, I persuaded them [to make the changes]."

Hunt revealed that the McLaren mechanics finally worked out that changing the position of the oil coolers by less than 2 centimeters had been enough to upset the extremely sensitive pressure area under the rear wing and disrupt the airflow. Soon after, the McLaren-Ford M23 was a potential race winner again, and Hunt could feel it. It was a lesson in aerodynamics the team was never to forget.

And that is the version most people choose to believe, not Alastair Caldwell's.

After the problems were sorted out, there was a huge feeling of relief and a sort of rapprochement between Hunt and Caldwell, with both men thankful that the problem had gone away. But scratch beneath the surface and it was clear that Caldwell carried a grudge against Hunt from that point on. He was frequently scathing of his abilities as a test driver, saying, "James was not a good test driver—lazy, never interested in testing, and the results he gave us were dubious." He added, "He tried to be professional. But he was always lazy. We should have hired a more competent test driver and got the car quicker. Then on race day we could have dragged James in on his leash, strapped him into the car, and let him loose like a mad dog."

But Peter Collins, the former team principal of Lotus and later a close personal friend of Hunt's, disagreed strongly and said, "James was an extremely intelligent individual who thought about the science of motor racing. From my memory, James was very voluble about the problems after Spain and just wanted the car returned to its previous spec."

Harvey Postlethwaite, who had worked with Hunt at Hesketh between 1973 and 1975, also disagreed strongly with Caldwell's remarks: "James could talk about racing cars, about driving, understeer and oversteer, whatever. He was a super guy to work with; very English, very pragmatic, intelligent. One realized how technically good he was. He understood racing cars and he did not believe in the bullshit, and I found that refreshing."

Whatever the truth of it, what couldn't be hidden was the fact that inside six weeks, McLaren had almost ruined its world championship chances by its own hand. So much so that Hunt no longer considered himself in contention for the world championship title. As he said, "We lost Belgium, Monte Carlo, and Sweden as a result of that, which was extremely crucial to the championship. We were totally uncompetitive."

Worse still, the team had a public relations problem on its hands. Caldwell and Mayer had told the world and the FIA that the 2 centimeters by which the car had been too wide had actually made no difference to its performance. But since they had reduced the width of the car, the car had actually become uncompetitive. The discrepancy did not bode well for the team's chances of winning its upcoming appeal against the disqualification. Between the Swedish and French races, there were scores of newspaper articles on the subject—most of them condemning McLaren.

But at least the car was competitive again, which James Hunt would resoundingly prove at the upcoming French Grand Prix.

CHAPTER 15

Hunt's First Proper Win

Ferrari Suffer from Engine Malaise

France: July 2–4, 1976

There was a three-week break between the Swedish Grand Prix and the French Grand Prix, scheduled for July 4. The race was due to be held on the 3.6-mile Paul Ricard circuit at Le Castellet, and James Hunt spent plenty of time testing and getting his McLaren sorted. By the time the pre-race test sessions at Paul Ricard were over, the cars had been examined meticulously and restored to their pre-Spain specifications.

Ferrari made a tactical error when it elected not to test at Paul Ricard, and instead it booked test sessions at Österreichring in Austria and the Nürburgring in Germany with Goodyear.

When Lauda didn't arrive to test, Hunt realized it was a mistake and was delighted that Ferrari was absent from the test sessions. He knew that it would hand him an advantage, and he intended to make full use of it. To his credit, Daniele Audetto wanted to go to Paul Ricard and test with Hunt, but Goodyear boss, Bert Baldwin, persuaded him it was unnecessary. To soothe his fears, Baldwin bet Audetto $20 that Lauda would get pole position in France and that there was nothing to worry about.

After testing was over and in the few days before the race, Hunt went looking for some fun. He checked into the Ile Rousse Hotel, which overlooked a beach full of topless bathers. It was five days of pure hedonism, and he was in his element: inspecting his potential conquests by day, without the inconvenience of them being clothed, and bedding them by night. That carried on all weekend. But he overindulged on foie gras and made himself ill for the weekend of the race.

Niki Lauda had similar health worries and had spent the gap between races at home with Marlene, who was still recovering from her miscarriage. Lauda's rib cage had healed, and he was suffering no pain for the first time in two months. But the rib problem had been replaced by a terrible dose of the flu, and Lauda was sniffling all weekend.

Like McLaren, the Ferrari factory in Maranello, Italy, had been very busy indeed during the three-week gap. Stung by its humiliating reverses in Sweden, Ferrari introduced a major redesign of its flat-12 engine, which was significantly more powerful—this despite the fact that it was already the most powerful engine on the grid. The mechanics had also revived the De Dion suspension and fitted it to the spare car for tryout during the practice periods. There were also modifications to the front suspension that were ruled illegal by Jabby Crombac, the official representing the CSI. Crombac told Audetto that the modifications infringed the rule about movable aerodynamic devices.

James Hunt started qualifying in a confident mood. In the first qualifying session, he was second fastest to Carlos Pace's Brabham-Alfa Romeo. In the second session he was fastest ahead of Niki Lauda's Ferrari. The times from the first day were the fastest of qualifying and were carried through to a slower final session on Saturday to put Hunt on pole position. It was immediately clear that McLaren was back as a force, and the sense of relief that permeated through the whole team that afternoon in France was almost palpable.

Niki Lauda was not having such a good time. Ferrari's engine technicians were very cautious about the introduction of the new engine. The engineers imposed a rev limit on the engines and increased it gradually as the weekend progressed and as they became more confident. But the limits hampered Lauda's effort to get a good grid position, especially when the first day's times proved the faster.

Without the engine restrictions and the disqualified times, Lauda and Regazzoni would undoubtedly have been sharing the front row. They might also have had some prior notice of the engine problems they would encounter the following day.

Throughout qualifying, Lauda was far from happy with his car. The Paul Ricard circuit was windswept and had changing conditions, which once again did not suit the Ferrari, which thrived on stable track conditions. Lauda kept moaning: "One day it's hot and the car handles in a certain way. The next day it's cold and the car handles differently. Then they have more stupid races and the track becomes covered in oil. So the guy who understands his car the best . . . will win the race."

With the technical problems all solved, Alastair Caldwell was back at his best in charge of the McLaren team, and all his usual astuteness came to the fore. As qualifying progressed, his sharp eye noticed that the Goodyear tires Hunt was using were behaving strangely. He spotted that once they had been on the car for a few laps, they were a lot quicker and more consistent. He also noticed that the new cold tires were very unstable.

Caldwell called the team together and told them they would gamble on starting the race with a set of part-worn tires, which he thought would stay consistent throughout the race. Hunt thought about it and agreed with Caldwell's analysis of the situation and agreed to start the race on worn tires. As he said, "We could be pretty confident of our handling staying consistent throughout the race."

Sadly for Ferrari, Daniele Audetto was none the wiser, so Lauda started as usual with a new set of tires. Indeed, Audetto was astonished as he walked the grid and noticed that Hunt and Mass were starting on old tires. Lauda was on brand-new tires that had been lightly scrubbed in during the earlier warm-up session.

The new tires were the best choice at the start, and Lauda made the best of it and disappeared into the distance, easily outdragging Hunt off the line and expanding his lead by a second every lap. But Hunt noticed straightaway that there were problems with Lauda's engine. There was a vapor trail from the exhausts, which meant trouble. So he bided his time in second place. After seven laps, Hunt could see quite clearly that Lauda's engine was losing oil and water out of the back, and he knew it was just a matter of time before it blew up.

At the very start of lap nine, Lauda's engine seized, and he managed to dip the clutch quickly enough before he was punted off the track. He called the experience "terrifying" and said, "Bang in the middle of the Mitral straight, it happened right out of the blue: sudden silence, and my rear wheels locked. The Ferrari spun out of control and ran right across the track. I don't think I have ever stamped on a clutch so fast in my life before."

Lauda coasted to a halt with a broken crankshaft. He sat in the cockpit, quite unable to believe what had happened. He had forgotten what it was like to retire from a race and not score any points. The broken engine ended a run of 17 successive grand prix races without a retirement. The Monaco Grand Prix of 1975 had been the last time he had suffered a mechanical failure.

Teammate Clay Regazzoni was ordered by the Ferrari pit to attack Hunt, and he took over the lead using every bit of power in the revised Ferrari engine on the long Paul Ricard straights to extend his advantage over Hunt's McLaren. Eleven laps later, Regazzoni's Ferrari suffered its own crankshaft failure, and the engine seized up. But Regazzoni was not as nifty as Lauda and didn't get his clutch down in time. Regazzoni spun wildly, and it looked as though there would be a serious accident. But somehow the speed was scrubbed off, and the car got caught by the catch fencing and came to rest safely. Ferrari mechanics were devastated that both of their cars had retired. The engineers had got it totally wrong. After the disappointments in Sweden, they had introduced the new engine too quickly, been too cautious in qualifying, and paid the price in the race with two retirements. It was an own goal. Lauda simply said, "We realized that our attempts to squeeze a few more horsepower out of the engines had overdone it for the time being."

After that, Hunt led comfortably from Patrick Depailler in the six-wheeled Tyrrell-Ford until the 40th lap, when he began to feel ill and was sick inside his helmet. He was not helped by the fact that he had hardly anything to do for the last two-thirds of the race and barely made it to the checkered flag, with Depailler 12 seconds behind him in second place. John Watson came home third and Carlos Pace fourth. Despite the comfortable victory, Hunt knew it had been a lucky win, saying, "It was all rather depressing for the first laps of the race because of Ferrari's special engines. They just disappeared from me, and there was nothing I could do. It was simply just a matter of power as they whizzed off down the straight, and they really got a big lead. But you have to give credit to their quality control, because it handed me the race on a plate, and I absolutely needed it."

After the podium celebrations, there was a fright as John Watson was initially disqualified after his rear wing was found to be too high. The stewards also announced they weren't sure about the legality of Hunt's rear wing either. Hunt spent an uncomfortable two hours waiting for the verdict, which eventually put him in the clear. When the stewards made their announcement, wild celebrations broke out among the McLaren mechanics as they packed up the cars.

The story of France was the story of McLaren's comeback. Its Spanish Grand Prix victory was restored along with the nine points that shot Hunt up the world championship table to second place, only 26 points behind Lauda. The restoration had a double whammy effect. Hunt gained nine points and Lauda lost three, so Hunt effectively gained 12 overall.

CHAPTER 16

FIA Restores Hunt's Points

Turnaround in Paris

Paris: July 1976

At the end of the French Grand Prix, James Hunt went back to his hotel with the McLaren mechanics and celebrated with the girls from the beach, although not as late as he would have liked, because he and Teddy Mayer were due to fly to Paris for the appeal hearing against McLaren's Spanish Grand Prix disqualification the next morning.

Mayer had filed the appeal directly after the Spanish disqualification, and his objective was clear: to get Hunt's victory reinstated and the punishment reduced to a small fine. As Mayer said, "I'm not denying the car was technically infringing the rule book, but you could have disqualified every car on the grid in Spain for some minor rule infringement. What we want is a reduction of the punishment meted out to James." Mayer's strategy was an excellent one, because it precluded any debate or judgment about the offense and merely questioned the punishment.

At dawn the following morning, Hunt, Mayer, and Lotus boss Colin Chapman flew to Paris in Chapman's airplane. Chapman had generously agreed to testify on McLaren's behalf concerning the technical issues that had led to Hunt's disqualification. Dean Delamont, secretary of the Royal Automobile Club in London, was also a witness.

The hearing was held at the FIA's headquarters in Place de la Concorde in front of five FIA-appointed judges. Chapman and Delamont were the star witnesses and supported the argument that the penalty had been too severe.

At the end, Mayer, an accomplished lawyer, summed up very eloquently with an end message that was simple and to the point: "The punishment did not fit the crime." Mayer asked the judges to substitute the disqualification for a fine instead, and he could tell that his words resonated with the judges. Mayer walked out of the building greatly encouraged by the impartiality of the judges. As he said afterwards, "They obviously hadn't prejudged the matter."

The five judges went away to deliberate for over 24 hours.

On the Tuesday morning, Jean-Jacques Freville, Secretary General of the FIA, came out of the FIA building and told waiting journalists that Hunt's McLaren was "only minimally in excess." His statement read: "The exclusion incurred by the McLaren car driven by James Hunt, who had won the event, is annulled, with all the consequences that this measure entails." Hunt's championship points were reinstated, and the team was fined $3,000 instead. According to Caldwell, the win in France—with the car back to the original pre-Spain specification—had been the reason for their successful appeal. He said, "I'm certain the psychological advantage of us winning the day before proved decisive. If we hadn't, Ferrari would have carried the day. They would have been able to say, 'Look, these bastards are uncompetitive because they've narrowed their car, so they did have an unfair advantage when it was wider in Spain. They shouldn't get their points back.' But we proved by winning with the narrower car that it made no difference, and the hearing said 'okay.'"

James Hunt, not quite able to believe the turn of events, simply said, "It has been a pleasant surprise being reinstated in Spain."

Added to the points won in France, Hunt now had 18 extra points and Lauda had lost three. In the space of two days, Hunt had effectively moved 21 points closer to Lauda. With Lauda now at 52 points, Hunt was up to 26.

At the halfway point in the season, winning the world championship no longer seemed as impossible as it had only 48 hours earlier.

CHAPTER 17

Fiasco on Home Ground

An Extraordinary Sunday Afternoon

Brands Hatch: July 16–18, 1976

After the race in France, James Hunt was only 26 points behind Niki Lauda in the world championship. With eight races to go and a potential 72 points to play for, it was game on.

Hunt's victory in France set the scene for the upcoming British Grand Prix at Brands Hatch as a grudge match between Hunt and Lauda, and between Ferrari and McLaren.

British newspapers were full of inevitable speculation about Hunt's chances of winning the British Grand Prix. The last English, as opposed to British, driver to win it had been the late Peter Collins, driving a Ferrari in 1958, some 18 years earlier.

The Italian press was also in action, stirring up a campaign of hatred against Hunt among native Italians. Enzo Ferrari kicked off the hate-fueled weekend when he told Italian journalists that the decision to reinstate Hunt into the Spanish Grand Prix results was "a wicked verdict" and that the perfect revenge would be for his cars to trounce McLaren at its home race.

Niki Lauda was hunkered down at home in Vienna, enjoying the long hot summer of 1976 beside his newly completed swimming pool. He planned to do nothing before the race aside from a day's testing on the private Ferrari test track at Fiorano.

In contrast, James Hunt flew straight to London from Nice for 10 days of nonstop activity before the race. In the past few months, he had become a national celebrity in Britain, and his principal sponsors, Texaco, Vauxhall, and Marlboro, were taking full advantage with a huge program of events planned for him.

He was the star turn at a big televised event at London's Albert Hall called "Grand Prix Night with the Stars." The Albert Hall's private boxes were packed with celebrities in evening dress who had paid UK£500 (approximately $1,200 at the time) for a box principally to get a glimpse of the new British hero. Hunt obliged them by playing the trumpet onstage.

Hunt also drove a Vauxhall in the Texaco Tour of Britain, an informal pro-am rally for road cars driven by celebrity drivers. His codriver was BBC radio presenter Noel Edmonds, and sensationalist newspaper headlines about Hunt and Edmonds accompanied every incident-packed day of the event. In the end, his Vauxhall fell so far behind with all the duo's mishaps that it had to retire from the event early.

The British public identified with Hunt more than they had with any previous British driver. He was loved because he was different: different because he wore T-shirts and jeans, walked barefoot, chain-smoked cigarettes, and drank lots of beer. His television appearance playing the trumpet also had an enormous impact.

After the rally was over, Hunt returned to his parents' house in Surrey to rest. As he explained: "I realized I had been living my life up to the red line, and I had drained myself completely. The peace and quiet was like a cocoon to me. I needed my solitude. I needed to wind down totally before cranking myself up to the intense pitch which is vital to a good result in the race."

Niki Lauda was very anxious before the race. Although he was comfortably ensconced at the top of the world championship points table, he could sense Hunt was on a winning streak. He also knew he was hampered by his own team's politics; a disaster, he thought, was waiting to happen. He knew he could lose the championship because of his own team, regardless of any opposition from Hunt. Lauda also thought the British officials might try and favor Hunt and McLaren, thereby disadvantaging himself and Ferrari. He was certain that would be the case, with the Italian officials in his favor, when the Italian Grand Prix came around.

To counter that, Lauda got on the telephone to Luca de Montezemolo, the former Ferrari team manager, in Turin and begged him to come to Britain for the weekend to help him out. Surprisingly, Montezemolo agreed to come so long as Lauda would pick him up in his airplane and fly him in. Lauda agreed.

Brands Hatch was packed every day from Thursday to Sunday for the grand prix weekend. The maximum capacity was around 80,000, and it had been years since the race had attracted so many spectators.

The fact that the race was being held at the twisty Brands Hatch track, and not Silverstone, favored Lauda. Brands Hatch was not Hunt's favorite type of track, and it wasn't suited to the longer wheelbase McLaren car.

Ferrari prepared for the race the best it could. They built a brand new car for Lauda, called chassis number 28, and held a test session at Fiorano to bed it in. The new car was lighter, as it did not have the internal framework that stiffened the chassis of Lauda's previous car. The extra stiffening had proved unnecessary. Lauda spent the first morning of qualifying bedding his new car in.

With Montezemolo present, Lauda was transformed from the morose character he had been of late into a happy-go-lucky, fun-loving fellow. Montezemolo stoked controversy by telling journalists that he was present to "guard Ferrari's interests against local officials."

The battle for pole was always going to be between the two men. No other driver got a look in. Lauda swapped around between cars and at one point thought his engine was about to blow up. But then he changed his mind and kept to the newer car. Hunt concentrated on his regular car, getting his time up every lap.

On the first day, Hunt squeaked past Lauda for the quickest time, with Ronnie Peterson the next fastest. But on Saturday, as Lauda finally got his new chassis sorted, it was no surprise when he took pole with Hunt second fastest, six-hundredths of a second slower round the 2.6-mile track.

But Lauda's pole was not such an advantage at Brands, as he was on the wrong side of the front row. Pole meant an inside run to the first corner, a drop-away right-hander. But the track at the start line was slightly banked, and it was possible to slide sideways toward the verge on the slope of the road if the wheels spun at the start. The second spot was in fact a better grid slot. Aware of this, Lauda elected, as was his right, to start from the left-hand slot—the higher side—to get a long angled run into Paddock Bend.

So Hunt was effectively on pole even though he was only second fastest, and some observers felt Hunt had been sandbagging in qualifying because this is what he had wanted all along; he had been playing games with Lauda, who might have been second-guessing which position Hunt would choose. Regazzoni's Ferrari had been third fastest behind Hunt, with Mario Andretti's Lotus fourth. The 26-car grid was very competitive, achieving times that were all within three seconds of one another.

Brands Hatch circuit is set in a natural amphitheater and has an atmosphere like no other circuit in the world, but that day it was unparalleled by anything seen in Britain before or since. As race day dawned, the roads were jammed with a capacity crowd trying to get in to see their hero, and anticipation reached fever pitch as fans eagerly awaited the battle between Hunt and Lauda.

The atmosphere was electric as the cars stood on the grid and Hunt waved to the crowd. Unsurprisingly, Hunt made his usual poor start, but Clay Regazzoni made a storming start from the second row and ran straight into his own teammate's car. As Hunt described it: "Clay had made a super start—a real stormer. He went up on the left of me, sliced back in front of my car and dived at the inside of Niki from way too far back. It was quite ridiculous. Niki was already turning into the corner, and Clay dived in and hit him."

For a split second, Hunt was elated, as it looked as though Lauda was out already at the hands of his teammate. He remembered: "I was able to enjoy it for, I suppose, half a second because it was wonderful and extremely funny for me to see the two Ferrari drivers take each other off the road. But it quickly became obvious that I was in it too. I got on the brakes because there was no way through, and I was punted up the rear. Then all hell broke loose. I was into Regazzoni's car, which was sliding backwards, and my rear wheel climbed over his. My car was in the air, flying, and then it crashed down again on its wheels. I didn't have a chance to be frightened or to realize that I could have been on my head." The accident had been spectacular, and Hunt described Regazzoni's driving as "a serious bout of brain fade."

Although Hunt's McLaren was launched into the air, it impacted the ground squarely the right way up on its wheels. He kept his engine running, put it into gear, and let out the clutch. The car moved, but it was obvious that the steering and the front suspension were both seriously damaged.

In fact, Hunt's car was quite badly damaged. As he described: "It launched my car up in the air, and as it came down, it broke the front suspension. I had to limp in at the back of the circuit."

As he limped through the part of the circuit called Druids Loop, Hunt saw the red flag; the race had been stopped and a restart ordered. He remembered: "I gave a whoop of delight. I thought all my birthdays had come at once. One second, I was despairing of my luck, and now it was all on again. I turned into the back road to the pits, because the car wasn't steering properly. I abandoned the car and ran down the pit road to tell the lads to come and do something about it." As he was walking back, a journalist asked him a question about what had happened, and Hunt said: "Forget that. Haven't got a cigarette, have you, old boy?"

His humor hid the fact that he was in some pain; his right thumb had been hit by the spinning steering wheel while the car was airborne, but this was going to turn out to be the least of his problems.

Amazingly, most of the other drivers had maneuvered safely around the scene of the accident, which was littered with debris. The marshals were quickly in action, and within a minute and a half, the track was totally clear. It also became very clear that the stewards had been premature in stopping the race, since the crashed cars and debris had been swiftly cleared away. With the track cleared, the race need not have been stopped at all.

Daniele Audetto ran over to the control tower when he saw what had happened and went berserk. He alleged that the British stewards had deliberately ordered the race to be stopped in order to give Hunt's McLaren a chance of restarting.

Alan Henry, the well-known journalist, had a good vantage point that day, and didn't believe that Hunt was still running when the red flag was shown. As he says: "I think James knew absolutely that he was out of that race, and that he'd actually stopped. He should never have been allowed to restart it, and I think the force of Teddy Mayer, particularly, bullying the stewards got him back in."

Hunt believed differently and was genuinely unaware that it was against the regulations for him to restart. His initial thought was to switch to his spare car for the restart. But no one was quite sure whether the first race had been completely aborted.

Everyone had an opinion about what would happen next. Most of the team managers and race officials were now congregated in race control in the Brands Hatch tower, directly overlooking the start line.

The rules were unclear about what happened when a lap of a race had not been completed.

As it could have been declared an aborted start, Alastair Caldwell decided to keep his options open. As Hunt's mechanics descended on his race car to repair it, Caldwell ordered others to get the spare car ready. Hunt recalled: "They didn't know exactly which car we would be able to run at the restart." In fact, the McLaren mechanics took the spare car to the grid and put it in position while arguments went on about whether or not it was eligible.

Hunt remembered: "The stewards couldn't decide what to do because the rule book was unclear, and of course with that, there were also a lot of Formula One team managers with a lot of words to say on the subject. The stewards were confused and the rulebook was confusing, so chaos reigned."

The rulebook actually stated: "When a red flag is displayed, the race must stop immediately, and if there is a restart to the race, all people who are competing at the time are allowed to restart."

Caldwell and Mayer knew exactly what they had to do; they had to delay a restart as long as possible. So they deliberately inflamed the

131

argument in the control tower in order to gain their mechanics valuable time to repair Hunt's car. Every quarter of an hour, Caldwell was running back and forth from the pits to the tower, reporting to Mayer on the situation with the repairs.

The grounds for not allowing Hunt to restart were complex, but the essence was that he had not completed a lap at the time of the accident. He had also entered the pits from the wrong direction, but in reality, in the heat of this situation, no one was going to disqualify him for that.

Hunt's contention was that he had seen the red flag displayed and had been obeying this instruction by stopping racing immediately. The rival team managers contended that a driver who hasn't yet completed a lap is not competing. They also firmly stated that Hunt should be disqualified for entering the pits from the wrong direction as, at no time may a car be driven deliberately in the opposite direction during a race. That rule was clear.

Caldwell and Mayer argued that the obvious solution was to declare the first race null and void. For a race to be stopped after 140 meters (459 feet) was unheard of in Formula One racing. But the stewards decided that the race had gone on longer, as Lauda had managed to keep moving and had threaded his car out of trouble after the initial contact from Regazzoni, and that he had been the leader when the race was red-flagged.

Three cars—Hunt's McLaren, Regazzoni's Ferrari, and Jacques Laffite's Ligier—had been damaged in the accident, and so when the cars were called back to the grid 30 minutes later, all three drivers appeared in their spare cars. The race was ready to restart, and it was officially announced over the circuit loudspeakers that the race would proceed as though the first lap had not occurred. However, this was followed by the announcement that no car would be allowed to restart that had not completed the first lap. The restart of the race, it had been decided, would include neither Hunt, Regazzoni, nor Laffite.

The British crowd had been watching and listening in silence. Initially they appeared stoic and ready to accept the decision to exclude Hunt.

But there was a troublemaker in their midst that day: a man who was determined that James Hunt would restart the race.

He was Andrew Frankl, a Hungarian-born publisher who was acting as a photographer for the race weekend. Frankl was the founder of *Car* magazine. He had volunteered for photography duties, as the position came with a much sought after pass that enabled the holder to go anywhere during the race. Frankl was a petrolhead and wandered around that weekend enjoying himself and talking to pretty girls in the crowd. The charmer had a certain way with the opposite sex.

But more seriously, Frankl also had a history. As a young man he had been a participant in the 1956 Hungarian uprising against the Russians. His participation had caused him to have to leave Hungary and flee to Britain. He knew how to stir up a crowd as a result of his experiences back home.

At the time of the incident, Frankl was on the inside of the circuit, near the pit lane. Upon hearing that Hunt was to be excluded, he became angry and decided he would do something about it. He leaned over the fence into the public area and shouted to some fans to gather round him. Amazingly, they obeyed him. The Hungarian's natural authoritativeness meant they did exactly as they were told. Frankl told them to start chanting: "We want James." Soon 30 or so fans had taken up the chant, with Frankl conducting them with a stick he had picked up off the ground. Frankl was aided by Anthony Marsh, the circuit commentator, who helped him stoke up the crowd. Marsh himself began chanting through the 100-odd loudspeakers that lined the circuit.

Hearing the chant, the remaining 80,000 fans quickly joined in, and soon the words "We want James" reverberated around the circuit until it was deafening.

The roar of 80,000 fans shouting in perfect unison was extraordinary. The British stewards couldn't hear themselves talking in the control tower. After 10 minutes, Frankl told his group to start a slow handclap. Gradually the crowd caught on and started clapping slowly and perfectly in time. Frankl believes that it was the first time 80,000 people had slow handclapped in the open air before in Britain, and it had an extraordinary effect.

But the demonstration did not remain entirely good-natured. The fans soon turned nasty and began throwing bottles and cans onto the track. The crowd in the main grandstands opposite the pit looked likely to storm the barriers in their quest to block the track and to prevent a restart without Hunt. As missiles of every description rained down onto the track stewards, the stewards were scared by what might happen.

Hunt was by now resigned to his fate, but the fans' reaction stirred the caveman instinct in him. The support moved him and made him even more determined to start the race.

In the absence of Mayer and Caldwell, busy with their delaying tactics in the tower, Hunt took charge. He ordered his mechanics to leave the spare car on the grid and not to move it off despite the stewards' orders. He told his mechanics that nothing and nobody would prevent him from starting the race—even if he was disqualified afterwards. Ferrari and Ligier mechanics, following Hunt's example, did the same.

Hunt knew he had the support of 80,000 people.

The stewards down on the grid were frightened by what would happen if Hunt didn't race and appeared to be aware of the frantic efforts to get his car repaired; and they became almost coconspirators in the delay. Hunt said, "It was a fantastic feeling for me as I sat in my car to know I had all this support—really quite incredible."

Sensing what might be about to happen, Daniele Audetto rushed back to the control tower and was adamant that if Hunt started in his spare car, so too would Regazzoni. Alastair Caldwell disputed it to keep the argument going, even though it was obvious they would be disqualified later.

But Caldwell wasn't interested in running the spare car; it was a red herring. Caldwell knew that if Hunt started in the spare car, he would certainly be black-flagged. But a repaired race car meant all bets were off, as it would almost certainly be allowed.

Hunt explained: "We had realized that the spare car was out of the question. In the meantime, we were naturally trying to keep the argument going because they were hastily getting my car repaired in the pits."

Meanwhile, John Webb, the managing director of the owners of the circuit and the man ultimately responsible for the crowd's safety, recognized that Hunt would have to be allowed to race. Webb asked the stewards, on advice from the local police, to let Hunt start.

Webb remembers: "At the time, I don't think they regarded it as terribly serious because British crowds at motor race meetings don't get out of control. It was purely the James Hunt factor."

Hunt said, "The organizers, rather than the officials, decided the only way they were going to get the race started was to start me, whatever happened, because [the crowd] were throwing beer cans on the track."

In the control tower, the stewards consulted the FIA rulebook, watched by the team managers, all of whom seemed to have a different opinion about what should happen. The rulebook simply did not cover this situation.

The other team managers had also become aware of Caldwell's tactics of blatantly playing for time. But by now they were on Caldwell's side as the crowd turned increasingly ugly. Hunt remembered: "The crowd went completely hooligan. I'd never known anything like it. They'd got fed up with the rules and they didn't want any more rubbish. They wanted to see a motor race."

After an hour's prevarication, Hunt's race car was finally pushed back onto the grid and the spare car wheeled away. A new steering arm and front suspension had been fitted to his car.

With Hunt's race car repaired, Caldwell now returned to the control tower and tried to have Regazzoni excluded from the start. Daniele Audetto stared at him in disbelief as Caldwell started arguing against spare cars being allowed to run. Audetto screamed at the stewards, who ruled to let both Regazzoni and Laffite restart in their spare cars.

So after 90 minutes, the start of the second race was on. The cars were allowed another warm-up lap, and Hunt found his car to be in good shape. As he said, "The boys didn't have time to track it out, but we tweaked it a bit after the warm-up lap. It wasn't very good to start off with, but then the car began to settle and then started going really well."

Niki Lauda made the best of the restart and got off ahead of Hunt and Regazzoni. Carrying a full tank of fuel, Hunt's hastily rebuilt car was not nearly as fast, but as the fuel load started to drop, Hunt found that he could throw the car around more and go faster. At half-distance Lauda was leading, but Hunt closed in on him. Hunt recalled: "I'd been catching

Lauda steadily but not enough, and then I was helped by a couple of back markers trailing the field. He got the worst of that, and about five laps after that, I started stabbing at him."

As Hunt began to seek ways past the Ferrari, the fans began cheering. The noise from the crowd was so loud he could hear it above the sound of his engine. On the 45th lap Hunt finally drove inside Lauda and passed him on the climbing approach to Druids Hill. The crowd was wild with joy, and emotions were overflowing. He said, "I knew I'd got him. I knew I was getting on top and our lap times were coming down. It was quite fantastic. We were racing at around 1 minute 19 seconds for a lap of Brands, the sort of time with which Niki and I had qualified with light fuel loads in practice."

Rather fittingly, the man who had been responsible for Hunt being able to restart—Andrew Frankl—was in exactly the right place at the right time and got the only photograph of Hunt's overtaking maneuver.

After he was passed, Lauda didn't fight back and settled in to finish second. Regazzoni and Laffite dropped out with mechanical problems in their spare cars, thus saving the stewards the trouble of disqualifying them.

As he crossed the line and saw the checkered flag, Hunt raised both arms aloft to acknowledge the ecstatic fans. He said, "Brands is such an intimate circuit anyway, and you feel the crowd more than you do anywhere else. You can sense the emotion and the movement all the time, even though you are not necessarily looking at the crowd. It's there, and you respond to it."

As far as Hunt was concerned, he had properly and legally won the British Grand Prix. But not everyone thought that, and certainly not Daniele Audetto. Initially the Ferrari, Tyrrell, and Copersucar teams lodged official protests against Hunt's victory. These three teams all stood to gain points if Hunt was disqualified. Tyrrell and Copersucar eventually withdrew their protests, and the stewards rejected Ferrari's claim. Ferrari said it would take the matter under appeal to the FIA court in Paris, but no one took that threat too seriously. Since, Audetto had earlier been arguing vigorously that Regazzoni should be allowed to restart in his spare car, Caldwell asked him how he could now appeal against Hunt starting again in his race car. Audetto gasped at the hypocrisy, remembering how Caldwell had reversed his own spare car argument as soon as Hunt's race car was repaired. He just stared at Caldwell and said three words: "It's my job." With that, he stalked away.

With the victory, Hunt had earned nine points and brought his total to 35 points against Lauda's 58. He was now only 23 points behind.

CHAPTER 18

Enzo Ferrari Woos Lauda

New Contract Signed

July 1976

Only a few months earlier, Enzo Ferrari had wanted to sack Niki Lauda as team leader of Ferrari and replace him with an inexperienced young Italian named Maurizio Flammini. Now he had completely changed his mind and wanted Lauda to extend his contract. Enzo initially asked Daniele Audetto to deal with the matter of having the contract extended.

So Audetto went to Lauda and informally offered him a retainer of approximately $300,000 for 1977. But Lauda told Audetto he wasn't interested in negotiating with him and any meaningful negotiations would be a "no-no." Lauda spoke to Audetto as little as possible and wanted to keep it that way. There was simply no chance of his negotiating a contract with him.

Lauda's refusal to negotiate infuriated Enzo.

The reason the contract extension became so urgent was simple: Lauda was leading the world championship with 61 points and had just scored two quick victories in Belgium and Monaco and second places in Spain and Britain. He led the championship from James Hunt by 36 points, a seemingly insurmountable lead, and he looked certain to be champion for the second year in a row. He had also vanquished his teammate, Clay Regazzoni, whom Lauda had made to look very second rate.

Ferrari also knew Lauda was being wooed by Brabham team boss Bernie Ecclestone to drive for him in 1977. As Brabham had Italian Alfa Romeo engines, that would have been a public relations disaster.

But Enzo was in a difficult position. After the fiasco with Flammini, he knew Lauda had lost respect for him. And that troubled him, as Enzo prized his relationship with his drivers and liked to be in charge of it. With Lauda, this clearly wasn't the case.

Lauda had first met Enzo Ferrari in 1973, when he was 75 years old. He exuded great dignity, and like Lauda's previous employer, Louis Stanley of BRM, he was the master of making a public entrance. When he came into a room it seemed almost like he had rehearsed it first. Once Lauda visited Ferrari in his garden, and while he sat waiting outside, Enzo preened himself before making a tour of the perimeter on his way to enter Lauda's presence on the lawn. At their first-ever meeting, one of Ferrari's aides had primed Lauda and told him, "He is the figurehead; he is the marquee; he is life itself."

But once the glitz and pomp was stripped away, Lauda found him less than impressive. As he said, "He had a couple of off habits; he would scratch himself in the most unlikely places and hawk and spit for minutes on end with obvious relish into a giant handkerchief, which, unfolded, was the size of a flag." But Lauda still respected him, saying, "He still had all his wits about him, and his remarks were perceptive and amusing. He retained a fine sense of gentle irony."

But Lauda had great difficulty taking him completely seriously, and when he asked him what he thought would happen to Ferrari after his death, Enzo replied, "I feel no excitement at the prospect of what may come after me."

The legend of Enzo Ferrari had always been embellished by his refusal to attend races and travel outside his immediate home. Apart from the rarest of occasions, he never left the Modena region of Italy. Virtually the sole exception was to attend the Friday qualifying day of the Italian Grand Prix at Monza, and that could not be guaranteed.

And it was his dislike of travel and subsequent isolation that caused most of his problems.

He lived in his own world, entirely dependent on others for his opinions or on what he read in the newspapers. Lauda said, "His information was supplied by lackeys."

In July, as Lauda had moved from zero to hero, the same Italian journalists who had wanted him replaced began clamoring for his contract to be extended lest he move to Brabham. As usual, Enzo Ferrari reacted to the newspapers and called Lauda in.

Enzo was frantically worried about losing Lauda, who he knew was unhappy after Luca di Montezemolo's departure. He was also scared by talk of big money offers from Ecclestone's Brabham. The fact that Brabham had Italian engines made that notion completely unacceptable.

But Enzo was most concerned that there had been friction between Lauda and Daniele Audetto. For all these reasons, he was desperate to get Lauda's signature on a contract for 1977.

Renegotiating a contract midseason was a major departure from normal Ferrari practice. This was not Enzo Ferrari's usual style; he normally liked to keep his drivers on the hook until there were no other drives available, thereby limiting their bargaining ability and pushing down their retainers.

In fact, Enzo considered himself a very shrewd tactician where drivers' contracts were concerned. But this time his street smarts deserted him. With Lauda refusing to negotiate with Audetto, Ferrari asked his son, Piero, to join the meeting to help out.

So in late June, Lauda finally sat down for negotiations with Enzo and Piero in the back room of the Cavallino Restaurant, situated opposite the Ferrari factory in Maranello. Ferrari's son was mainly there to interpret Enzo's Italian into English. While Lauda's Italian was pretty good, Enzo always professed to speak no English, so the role of an interpreter appeared vital to the theater of the negotiation.

But negotiating it with the then 78-year-old Enzo and his son, Piero, was the stuff of pantomime. Enzo was not known as *Il commendatore* for nothing, and he loved to play the part during the negotiations.

Lauda told Enzo straightaway that part of his contract must ensure that the team be limited to two drivers in a two-car team. Enzo agreed but rejected Lauda's attempt to keep Clay Regazzoni as his teammate for 1977. Enzo told him straight out that Regazzoni would be fired at the end of the season. In truth, Lauda wasn't terribly upset about that after Regazzoni's games with Audetto in Long Beach, and he conceded the point.

Enzo then asked Lauda how much money he wanted, to which Lauda replied with an amount in Austrian schillings. As Lauda recalled in his autobiography, *To Hell and Back:* "[Mr. Ferrari] said nothing, but he stands up, goes over to the telephone, calls his accountant, Signor Della Casa, and asks him how much so and so many million schillings are in lire? He waits for a reply, replaces the receiver, walks back across the room, and sits down facing me."

Lauda recalled that Enzo was silent for a moment and then, after a pause, suddenly screamed in Italian at the very top of his voice: "You insolent pig! How dare you? Are you crazy? We have nothing more to say to each other! We are parting company as of this minute." Or words to that effect. His son rapidly translated the string of obscenities, and Lauda later recalled that having an interpreter somehow made the expletives more abstract. Admittedly, for Lauda the spectacle of a 78-year-old man, a legend in motor racing and a hero for all Italy, shouting at him in an unpleasant manner was very disconcerting. And that was how Enzo had planned it. But Lauda had come prepared as well. Remaining completely calm, he replied in English and said to Enzo's son, "Please tell him that, as we are parting company, I'll be flying home immediately." But Piero, realizing that Lauda was not joking, said of his own volition, "Sit where you are."

Lauda did sit, but the row continued until he invited Enzo to make him a counteroffer. Enzo, by now realizing that his intimidating tactics were not working, tried a new approach of conciliation and reasonableness. He replied that he could not make a counteroffer because he only wanted his drivers to be happy, and any counteroffer he made would only make Lauda unhappy. Lauda then said, "In that case, I really will fly home, because there's surely no point to this if you won't accept my price and you won't make a counteroffer."

After a long pause, Enzo finally offered him a contract with a retainer at 25 percent less than the figure Lauda had originally named, believed to be $300,000. It was now Lauda's turn to get angry. He told Enzo that Daniele Audetto, in the previous informal conversations, had already offered him much more and added, "Are you trying to make a fool of me?" Feeling that Enzo was being disrespectful, he said, "You want to buy my services, and that is what they cost." Enzo, believing Lauda was bluffing, yelled at him again: "What is that you say about Audetto?" With that, Enzo rose and called Audetto on the telephone. He ordered him to come to the Cavallino and explain himself. He was calling Lauda's bluff. But when the hapless team manager arrived at the restaurant, he confirmed he had already offered Lauda that sum informally. Enzo scowled at Audetto, but with a twinkle in his eye. He looked at Lauda and said, "Well, if one of my employees is mad enough to offer that kind of money, I guess I'll have to go along with it. But that's my final offer."

It still wasn't high enough for Lauda, who made a counteroffer. Calling him "incorrigible," Enzo reminded him of his blood pressure. He asked if Lauda was trying to kill him with such unreasonable demands. Lauda said to his son, "Tell him you would never have been world champion without me." But Piero refused to translate it, knowing his father would explode again. Lauda later claimed that Enzo's subsequent rant, heard by the entire restaurant, lasted at least half an hour.

After he had calmed down, there followed another half hour of relatively more reasonable negotiations. Finally Enzo said, "How much do you want?"

Lauda dropped his original price by 4 percent and said, "My final offer." Enzo replied: "Okay, Jew boy."

And, with that, the pantomime was over.

Lauda did not take offense at Enzo's last remark and shook his hand. His new deal, at the then exchange rates, was worth a shade under $345,000. As soon as the deal was agreed, Ferrari embraced Lauda warmly and openly, as if they had just enjoyed a convivial lunch together. As Lauda recalled: "The next moment he was a charming old man, the most delightful company anyone could imagine."

But Enzo Ferrari would come to regret signing that contract, which included many other Lauda demands that would later save his career after he was injured. Without it, there is little doubt he would have been fired and replaced with Carlos Reutemann, and James Hunt would have been world champion long before the final race in Japan.

That new contract, signed on the eve of the German Grand Prix at Nürburgring, was to save Lauda's career.

CHAPTER 19

Hunt Takes Full Advantage

Hunt Wins as Lauda Crashes

Nürburgring: July 30–August 1, 1976

Midmorning on Thursday July 29, 1976, Niki Lauda sat caught up in a traffic jam outside the entrance to the famous Nürburgring circuit in Germany. As he sat there, stationary in his car with the window open, a fan approached and showed him a photograph of Jochen Rindt's grave. As the fan stared at Lauda, presumably seeking a reaction, Lauda looked at the picture bewildered; he wondered what the point of it was. How was he was supposed to react? Pleased with himself, the fan walked off, but the incident stuck in Lauda's mind. Rindt was a fellow Austrian and had been world champion in 1970, but he was killed that same year at the Italian Grand Prix in Monza, only two years before Lauda had entered Formula One. Lauda hated omens and immediately wondered whether this was one.

It signaled the start of what would be the most difficult weekend of Lauda's life. He had been a firm opponent of competing on the Nürburgring circuit on safety grounds and had wanted it closed. Thinking it far too dangerous, Lauda had voiced his concerns in public and had taken a lot of criticism in the media for his views. He was wondering what to expect at the Nürburgring and what sort of welcome he would get.

A recent television documentary had shown German fans accusing him of being "chicken-hearted" and "cowardly" because of his views of

144

their beloved circuit. One particular fan interviewed said that if Lauda was so terrified of the ring, he should get out of Formula One. Lauda had watched the program in Germany sitting in a hotel room on his own. Outraged by it, he said afterwards, "I was absolutely livid, knotted with rage at my inability to defend myself."

The Nürburgring, where the 1976 German Grand Prix was scheduled to be raced on August 1, was a very different track in those days. The old Nürburgring was 14.2 miles long and unlike any other circuit in the world. Situated in the heavily forested Eiffel Mountains west of Koblenz, it was possibly the least suitable venue for a modern-day Formula One grand prix. The circuit, which had opened in 1920, was usually covered in mist and fog and was often damp, with varying weather conditions at each end. The 14.2 miles contained a staggering 177 corners.

It was without doubt the most dangerous circuit in the world. By 1976 over 140 drivers had been killed in 56 years, an average of nearly three a year. It was not until 1974, after a campaign by Jackie Stewart, that safety was addressed. Miles of catch fencing and steel guardrails were installed, finally stopping cars from flying off the circuit into the trees.

Lauda had first visited Nürburgring in 1969 as a 20-year-old driver in Formula Vee, the German equivalent of Formula Ford in Britain. His views were very different back then. As he remembers: "We didn't think it was at all bad, only exciting." In fact, for a long time Lauda was a big fan of the circuit, and one of his ambitions was to drive the ring perfectly. He believed it offered a challenge unlike any other. In 1973 he took a BMW saloon car round in 8 minutes and 17.4 seconds, then a record time for that class of car.

Later that same year, and again in 1974, Lauda was involved in several incidents at the circuit. It was a period when drivers were being killed on a regular basis. As lap times became faster, nothing was done about safety. Especially after Jackie Stewart had retired in 1973, the risk factor had become too high. Lauda recalls: "We were endangering not only our lives but the sport of motor racing itself by failing to do something about track safety."

Despite the installation of catch fencing and barriers, the problems at the Nürburgring were obvious. It was impossible to make safe such a long circuit, especially as much of it was tree lined. Even with the improvements, the circuit was under constant threat of the FIA withdrawing its racing license. Finally, in 1974 a three-year program was launched to make safety improvements.

Nineteen seventy-five saw the first-ever Nürburgring lap of under seven minutes, which Lauda referred to as the "ultimate madness." Poignantly, it was Lauda himself who drove the lap, and it has not been bettered since. He said, "It was possible only because I was in a special sort of mood that day and ready to go for broke to an extent I have never permitted myself since. As I flashed past the pits, I glanced in my rearview mirror and saw the mechanics waving their hands in the air. I knew then that I had cracked the seven-minute barrier. To be exact, my new Formula One lap record was 6 minutes 58.6 seconds. And that's how it stands to this day—no one has ever driven the ring faster."

It was a whole minute faster than when Jackie Stewart had driven his Matra155 Ford in 1968, seven years earlier. He continues: "My brain kept telling me it was sheer stupidity. I knew every driver was taking his life in his hands to the most ludicrous degree."

Jackie Stewart, who won at the circuit three times, most famously in the wet in 1968, agreed with him and said, "I was always afraid. When I left home to race in the German Grand Prix, I always used to pause at the end of the driveway and take a long look back. I was never sure that I would come home again."

The danger levels were so high that at a drivers' meeting in early 1976, Lauda proposed that the German Grand Prix be moved away from the Nürburgring on safety grounds. He was hoping for a driver boycott of the circuit with immediate effect, but he was voted down, as a considerable amount of money had been spent on safety precautions.

That vote was to change Lauda's life and the course of Formula One history. If it had gone the other way, James Hunt would never have been world champion and Lauda would have become the greatest driver the sport had ever seen. After the vote, Lauda was heavily criticized, which led to the television documentary.

Before Nürburgring, Lauda had been on top of the world. Comfortably leading the world championship, he looked certain to win again in 1976. It would have made him one of the few men to win back-to-back titles and to successfully defend a title. He had already amassed 58 points, while James Hunt had only 35.

He had other reasons to be pleased: The Ferrari management had not collapsed, as he had expected it to, after the departure of Luca di Montezemolo and the arrival of Daniele Audetto. Audetto was slowly improving as he learned the lessons of Formula One the hard way. Lauda was feeling better about the situation anyway, as he had just signed a brand-new and highly lucrative contract with Ferrari for the 1977 season. The contract was worth six times the money his chief rival, James Hunt, was being paid by Marlboro-McLaren.

With his personal deals, he would earn over half a million dollars in 1977, guaranteed.

So it was little wonder he was starting to think more deeply about the dangers of racing at Nürburgring. Now he had far more to lose than when he was a penniless, struggling 19-year-old. For the first time, he admitted he was scared of racing at the circuit: "I'm glad to see the finish line every lap. I'm frightened, I don't mind telling you." But he added, "You either don't come or you get on with the job of racing. So I've got on with the job and I've wound up on pole position again." But not quite this time.

Despite all of the obvious fear and trepidation, Lauda was a racing driver, and like all racing drivers, deep down he always thought it would happen to the other fellow. So qualifying got under way as usual, just as it always did, regardless of the obvious dangers. But it was clear that with safety on his mind, Lauda, as he readily admitted, was not driving as fast as he could.

Otherwise, qualifying was uneventful at the front of the grid, with the now-familiar cars of Hunt and Lauda occupying the front row. When the two days ended, on Saturday afternoon, James Hunt was on pole position.

Lauda was second on the grid and only a second slower than Hunt. Over a seven-minute lap, it was ridiculously close. Afterwards, Lauda summed it up: "My personal opinion is that the Nürburgring is just too dangerous to drive on nowadays."

Behind them was a mixed-up bunch of drivers, which reflected the way the season was panning out. There was Lauda and Hunt, and then there were the rest. Apart from the obvious tail-enders, it seemed that all the rest had been in contention at some point during the season. This time it was Hans Stuck's turn to shine, and he claimed fourth spot on the grid in a March-Ford.

On race morning the weather was unpredictable, and Lauda received some bad news from home, from his friend the Austrian journalist Helmut Zwickl. That morning the Reichsbrüke, the largest bridge in Austria, had collapsed into the Danube in the early hours, resulting in the loss of one life. At any other time of the day, hundreds of people would have been killed. Lauda was stunned by the news, and he wondered if this was another omen. He didn't like omens.

Because of the circuit's length, the race was only 14 laps and the average speed was expected to be close to 120 miles per hour. On the starting grid, it started to rain. Every driver except Jochen Mass chose to start on wet-weather grooved tires. Mass was totally familiar with the meteorological conditions at his home circuit, and believed the track would soon be clear. When a stiff wind rose up and quickly blew the circuit dry, his instincts were proved right.

Straightaway, Mass, who started from row five, was contesting the lead as Lauda and Hunt slithered away from the start. Lauda had a terrible start and seemed to be racing in reverse, dropping as low as 20th place on the unsuitable tires.

By the end of the first lap, Mass was in the lead, followed by Hunt and Ronnie Peterson's March-Ford. Everyone stopped on lap two for dry tires.

Everyone, that is, except Peterson, who was fooled by Hunt into thinking he was going to do another lap on the wet tires and so followed suit. Hunt slowed down and let the Swede by before suddenly diving into the pits.

After changing tires, Hunt's McLaren-Ford rejoined the race in second place, but already 45 seconds behind Mass.

And then Lauda had his accident, which stopped the race. By this time the red flag had been shown to the rest of the field, and there was a loudspeaker announcement in the pit lane that a serious accident had blocked the track at Bergwerk, the most northerly corner of the circuit. The leading cars came round and parked in front of the pits, ready for the restart.

Only the seven drivers who had witnessed the accident and its aftermath knew the extent of Lauda's injuries. The accident had happened a mile or so behind the front of the pack, and the drivers had been behind Lauda before the accident. Although both tail-end drivers, Guy Edwards and Arturo Merzario, had witnessed the horror of the accident, they got back to the start line just in time for the restart and did not speak to any of the other drivers. Neither did John Watson, Emerson Fittipaldi, nor Hans Stuck.

The only news that reached the pits was that Lauda had been walking around after the crash. As he got back in his car for the restart, James Hunt believed that Lauda had escaped serious injury. He said, "He was taken off to hospital and obviously wouldn't be racing again that day, but we thought he'd have his burns patched up and we'd see him at the next race in Austria. That was what we felt then; there were no alarm stories, so one was able to get into the car and go racing again with no qualms."

All except Chris Amon, the 33-year-old veteran driver, had arrived at the accident just after it happened, and when he stopped his Ensign-Ford and saw Lauda lying by the side of the track, he was horrified. According to Amon, he didn't think the Austrian would survive. He drove back to the pit lane and threatened to retire on the spot, saying he was finished with Formula One. Amon had also been witness to how slowly emergency services had responded to Lauda's accident. He spoke to no one and left the circuit.

The biggest loser from the restart was Jochen Mass. Mass had made the right choice of tires, had established a big lead, and was certain to win the race. Now it was all for nothing; as Hunt said, "Fate intervened and ruined it for him."

James Hunt cleared his mind of everything but the task at hand and streaked into a lead that remained unthreatened. He called that first lap "probably the most aggressive piece of driving I did all year. I was absolutely determined to get as big a lead as possible, and everything turned out right."

It was dry, and this time there was no uncertainty about tires. Hunt was 10 seconds clear at the end of the first restarted lap. As he remembered: "I put in a blinding first lap and the others were spinning and falling about all over the place, which helped me, so I virtually had the race won by the end of the first lap. It was only a matter of controlling things from the front."

Hunt was followed home by Jody Scheckter's Tyrrell-Ford, with teammate Jochen Mass coming in third. By the time he finished, he was half a minute ahead of Scheckter. He would later call the victory one of his most satisfying drives. But his abiding memory of the day was seeing Teddy Mayer's reaction: "McLaren had never won at the ring, and it was tremendously gratifying to me to see him so happy."

With no competition from Lauda, the victory had suddenly brought James Hunt to within 14 points of his rival. It was a dramatic turnaround from a seemingly hopeless position just a few weeks before.

CHAPTER 20

Near-Death Experience

Niki Lauda Nearly Dies

August 1976

Niki Lauda started the first lap of the German Grand Prix from the front row of the grid, and like everyone else in the race, he was on wet-weather tires. He made a poor start, which was out of character for him. Later he explained that because of the damp track, he elected to get off the line in second gear instead of first. But he miscalculated, and there was more traction and the track was dryer than he thought, and eight cars powered past him. He remembered: "I accelerated too much. The wheels rotated too fast, which is even worse in second gear. With a higher gear, you practically stop still if the wheels start to spin. That's what happened to me."

The track dried very quickly, and like every other driver, Lauda went for slick tires. As he explained, "As it got more and more dry, I went into the pits for a tire change—a good quick change."

Lauda changed from grooved wet to dry slick tires and drove out of the pits. Speeding away on the new tires, he tried to make up lost time on a mostly dry track that was still damp in places. But straightaway he misjudged the conditions, and his Ferrari mounted a curb with the left front wheel. The shock of the impact went right through the car and caused a tie-rod in the suspension to loosen. Unaware of what had happened, Lauda thought nothing of it. But Ferrari had had problems before with tie-rods failing; it was one of the car's principal weaknesses and had not been fixed.

As he approached Bergwerk Corner, the magnesium tie-rod (one of the components that secured the suspension to the engine block where it was mounted) completely broke and detached from the engine. As a result, the rear wheel mountings collapsed straightaway and the car lurched to the right. Lauda was traveling at more than 130 miles per hour when the component failed.

The car went sideways into the catch fencing just before Bergwerk on the outside of the corner, but it lost hardly any speed at all. With the fencing unable to contain it, the car slammed into the embankment behind and was airborne. It bounced back onto the track with Lauda helpless at the wheel. The car slammed down hard on the track, and the fuel tank became detached and flew through the air, spilling lighted fuel on the track. The stunned Lauda was stationary in the middle of the racing line and looked around, wondering what would happen next. It was too dangerous to move. The next car through was Guy Edwards's Hesketh-Ford. He managed to avoid the Ferrari and stopped beyond it when he saw the burning fuel and realized that Lauda was still in his car. Then the Surtees-Ford car of Brett Lunger came through. Lunger was completely unsighted and smashed straight into the Ferrari with Lauda still inside. The Ferrari burst into flames, and the two cars traveled at least 90 meters (295 feet) down the track from the force of the impact. Harald Ertl's Hesketh-Ford then piled into the wreckage of both cars.

Amazingly, Lunger and Ertl were unhurt, and they leapt from their cars to help Lauda, who was now in serious trouble from three impacts. His car was a fireball, and Lauda was waving his arms in front of his helmet to ward the flames away from his face. His helmet was askew and had been half wrenched off his head in the accident.

Now all the cars behind Lauda stopped. Because the track was so long, the fire marshals were nowhere nearby, and it was up to the drivers to rescue Lauda.

Arturo Merzario in a Williams-Ford was the last to stop, and by then some marshals had arrived. But they had no fireproof clothing. Edwards,

Lunger, and Ertl were doing their best but couldn't get Lauda out of the flames. Merzario rushed along the road, and without thinking dived straight into the flames with only his overalls and flameproof balaclava to protect him. In a moment of incredible foolhardiness, the Italian went in with total disregard for his own life. As quick as a flash, Merzario unbuckled Lauda's seatbelts. However, as he did so, Lauda's helmet came off and the flames licked his face.

Meanwhile, Harald Ertl had found a fire extinguisher and had no choice but to squirt it straight at Lauda to put out the flames. It was then that Lauda breathed in some of the toxic fumes. With the fire temporarily out, Lunger leaped onto the top of the car and lifted Lauda out. Amazingly, Lauda stayed on his feet and staggered around in great pain. Meanwhile, John Watson, Emerson Fittipaldi, and Hans Stuck, all of whom had been behind the accident, stopped their cars and ran down the road to help. Finding Lauda lying on the dirty track, Watson walked him to a dry area by the side of the track and lay him down.

It was clear to Watson that Lauda had suffered bad burns to his head and face, but it was inexplicable that Lauda's helmet had come off without killing him. It later emerged that Lauda was wearing a specially modified AGV helmet with extra foam padding to make it more comfortable to wear. The extra foam had compressed when pressure was put on the helmet, and it had easily slid off his head after the accident. The modified helmet, almost certainly not legal, left his face exposed to the fire.

Max Mosley stamped on this practice when he became president of the FIA and remains convinced that drivers are their own worst enemies when it comes to safety. As he said, "When the crash happened, it just came off. And of course that was the attitude in those days."

Bizarrely, David Benson wrote in the *Daily Express:* "In the force of the impact, Lauda's head had momentarily shrunk and his crash helmet had briefly expanded."

That was one way of putting it, but of course it was total nonsense, and Benson was probably part of a cover-up to hide what had really happened. The fact was that Lauda should never have been allowed to compete with that helmet and in many ways was totally responsible for the injuries he received as a result of his helmet coming off.

As Lauda lay by the side of the track, all the drivers who had been behind him on the track stopped their cars and gathered round him for support. Watson put Lauda's head between his own thighs and cradled it. The other drivers carefully removed his flameproof balaclava but could see he was badly burned. Although still conscious, Lauda remembered nothing of the accident itself. He continued speaking—in Italian to Merzario and in English to Watson. He asked Watson how his face was. He replied in a noncommittal way—this was not the time to tell Lauda the truth.

An ambulance was on the scene in less than three minutes, and Lauda was taken away. Luckily there had been an ambulance stationed at Adenau Bridge, near where the accident had happened.

At the medical station, Lauda spoke to Daniele Audetto and told him in detail where his road car was parked in the paddock. Lauda asked Audetto to telephone his wife and tell her he was all right and to ask her to find him a good hospital. Audetto told Lauda that he should go to Ludwigshafen Hospital, about 45 minutes away, where they had a specialist burns unit. Audetto was superb in this situation and knew exactly what to do.

No more than 40 minutes after the accident, Lauda was transferred to the circuit helicopter and airlifted off the track. Upon seeing the extent of his injuries, doctors anesthetized him in the helicopter and he gradually lost consciousness. Lauda had endured his injuries incredibly bravely and had been fully conscious for over three-quarters of an hour. As he drifted off, the last thing he would remember was the clatter of the helicopter blades as they took off. He recalled: "The first thing I remember is the sound of the helicopter engine starting up. I asked the pilot where we were and where we were going."

As he watched the helicopter take off, it was a moment that Lauda's personal airplane pilot, Hans Klemitinger, had always dreaded. He had long rehearsed in his own mind what he would do if his boss was ever injured and taken to hospital. He knew immediately that his duty would be to go to Marlene Lauda's side. So anticipating events, he decided to fly to Salzburg the moment he saw the helicopter go off. He took off in Lauda's Cessna Golden Eagle airplane as quickly as he could. Klemitinger knew Marlene would want to be at her husband's side as quickly as possible.

Marlene was still recovering from the miscarriage she had endured in May and was now suffering from low blood pressure. But she put that to one side, and immediately upon hearing about the accident, she also anticipated Klemitinger's actions and got in her car and drove the 10 kilometers (6.2 miles) to Salzburg airport to await the plane landing.

So she was already at the airport when Klemitinger landed, and they were at the hospital within hours of her husband's arrival there. Marlene said later: "At the time I had no idea how badly injured he would be. I was told he was all right, but that he was in hospital. It was not until I spoke to the doctors and was allowed to see him that the shock hit me."

As the helicopter landed at Ludwigshafen, Lauda's luck was in. As he explained: "From that moment, all the bad luck turned to good luck. They sent me to the best hospital in Germany. Remember that it was a Sunday afternoon, but when I got to Ludwigshafen burns unit, the boss of the whole place just happened to be there at the time. He took one look at me and immediately decided that the burns on my face were secondary to the burns in the lungs. So he sent me to the intensive care unit in Manheim. There my luck was still good. The youngest professor in Germany just happened to be working that Sunday. His name is Professor Peter, and I owe him my life. He did everything absolutely right and never made a wrong move." And the one thing he did right in particular was to not give Lauda oxygen. As he ruefully recalled to *Daily Express* motoring editor David Benson a few weeks later: "You must realize that the medical knowledge about treating lung damage is not as great as in some other areas. If, for example, I had been given oxygen—which would seem logical for someone with damaged lungs—I would have been dead immediately."

A team of six dedicated doctors and 34 nurses tended to Lauda. His injuries were diagnosed as first- to third-degree burns on his head and wrists, several broken ribs, and a broken collarbone and cheekbone. But as the doctors at Ludwigshafen Hospital had observed, of much more serious concern were the poisonous fumes and toxic gases he had inhaled. His windpipe and lungs were scorched, and the subsequent build-up of fluid in his lungs was already life threatening.

That night the doctors thought he was going to die as they battled to drain the fluids in his lungs through that first 24 hours. While there had been no single great injury, serious damage had been done to his lungs and to his bloodstream, which was poisoned as a result of inhaling the fire extinguisher fumes, smoke, and petrol vapor. The burns on his face, head, and hands were severe, although not critical. And, crucially, there was no impairment to his mental capacity.

Lauda later recalled that first night and his fight to survive: "On the Sunday night, they put a tube down my throat into the lungs and connected it to a vacuum pump to drain off the liquid and the infections. This was critical, because if the pump was used too much, it would destroy the lungs. From the Sunday night, my brain was always functioning, but I felt that my body was giving up. I could just hear voices very far away and a little out of reach. I concentrated on these voices to stop myself becoming completely unconscious."

The world woke up on Monday morning to newspapers full of stories of how Niki Lauda, the world reigning Formula One world champion was clinging on to life and that his doctors did not think he would pull through.

That Monday morning, when James Hunt heard that Lauda was fighting for his life, he was devastated. Although they were rivals and their friendship had suffered as a result, he said, "It was suddenly very important for me that Niki should live, in a way I hadn't realized. And I felt awful because there was nothing I could do about it. There I was, sitting at home, enjoying life when I didn't even particularly want to; I wanted to go and help or do something, and I couldn't."

Lauda's lungs were in a terrible state, and when they X-rayed him on Tuesday, the X-rays revealed they were getting worse. The oxygen count in his blood, which was below the life-maintaining level of a figure of 8, went down to 6.8, an extremely dangerous level.

Marlene Lauda was entirely unprepared for the ordeal she faced but has never spoken of the moment she was told her husband would certainly die. As Lauda recalled: "The doctors told my wife that there was no hope that I would survive."

For four long days and nights, Marlene Lauda watched as her husband's life hung by a thread. She moved into a hotel near the hospital, visiting her husband for only an hour at a time. Each visit to the hospital was accompanied by a barrage of flashbulbs and journalists looking for answers to questions and hoping to record her anguish. She said, "I was deeply shocked by the accident, but it gave me my first real understanding of motor racing. Before that, I had no idea of the dangers of the racetrack. I used to smoke maybe one or two cigarettes a day, but from the time of the accident, I have become a chain-smoker. I know that this is not good for my health, but it helps me through the crisis."

Lauda said of that period: "All the time, I was listening to the doctors and trying to cooperate as much as possible—no matter what personal pain it would cost. For example, they could only use the vacuum pump to my lungs for about an hour at a time. But when I felt the lungs filling up, then I called for them to switch it on, even though the pain was enormous. The doctors told me that it was the first time that anyone had asked for the pump to be switched on himself. But I knew that I could only survive if I followed every instruction of the doctors."

Lauda recalled: "My wife, Marlene, was marvelous. It was very shocking for her, but never once did I feel what she was going through when she was with me at the hospital. She would hold my hand and keep on telling me that I was going to get well again. She must have been terrified by my face, but she only made me feel that I was a great man and gave me the will to get well. So many women would have cried or have become hysterical. I discovered that there was a much greater depth to Marlene than even I had realized."

On Wednesday, as he deteriorated further, a priest was brought into Lauda's room to give him the last rites. Wavering in and out of consciousness, it was clear that Lauda did not like the intervention of the priest. As he admitted: "At one point I was asked if I wanted to see a priest. So I said, 'OK.' He came in and gave me the last rites, crossed my shoulder, and said, 'Goodbye my friend.' I nearly had a heart attack! I wanted someone to help me to live in this world not pass into the next. So I clung on to the voices and to my wife's strength. I would not let myself become unconscious, because I was afraid that I would die. I wanted to keep my mind awake to start the body working again. I knew that if I gave up mentally, then I would be dead. My life was also saved because I was very fit before the accident. And as I have never smoked in my life, my lungs had maybe an extra percent capacity, which helped me work against the infection."

Lauda survived by sheer force of will, although some people did suggest that the reading of the last rites was a ruse by Lauda to mislead Hunt about the extent of his injuries. Lauda admitted, "I do not believe in a personal God, but I believe that there is something more than this life. And I live by the rules. My strength to live after the accident came from this, from my own mind. And from my wife."

But after only four days in intensive care, there started to emerge hope that he would pull through, although from reading newspapers no one would have been aware of that. Lauda remembered that moment well: "Three days after the accident, the lungs began to get better. My blood count though was still bad, with the oxygen at the 6.8 level. This stayed the same for a week. "Nobody knew if my system would start working again and produce enough oxygen for the blood. If it didn't restart, then they could have changed my blood every so often, but they knew that I would then only have one or two years in which to live. So they put new blood into me and waited to see the reactions. After four days it slowly improved, and they changed the blood again. By now my system was working and I was back to normal with the right amount of oxygen in my blood. They did not have to change it anymore."

Immediately after the accident, newspapers, especially in Germany, began writing tasteless articles speculating on the extent of Lauda's facial burns, relying on very sketchy information that had been ferreted from hospital staff. Journalists at the German newspaper *Bild* were particularly shameless. In an article with the headline "My God, where is his face?" one journalist wrote: "Niki Lauda, the world's fastest racing driver, no longer has a face. It is no more than raw flesh with eyes oozing out of it. Niki Lauda has survived . . . but how can a man exist without a face?"The story went on to forecast what life would be like for Lauda, continuing: "Horrible as it may sound, even if his body recovers completely, he will not venture into public for six months at least. It will be 1979 before they can build him a new face. By then, nose, eyelids and lips will have been refashioned. But the new face will not bear the slightest resemblance to the one he had before. Lauda the racing driver will only be recognizable to his friends through his voice and his gestures."

Indeed, when Lauda was first given a mirror to see the extent of his facial injuries, he recoiled. As he so colorfully described: "They showed me my face in a mirror. I looked at myself and I could not believe it. I looked like some grotesque animal, because my whole head and neck were swollen to three times the normal size. You would not believe it could be a human being. I'm told that this is because I had been in 800 degrees of heat in the fire and the body had pumped excessive liquid to the burned areas. I was swelling up even as I looked in the mirror, and then my eyes closed and I was blind for five days. Everything was a big mass of nothing."

Although the newspaper account was all third-hand speculative non-sense, it sold a lot of newspapers that week. True to form, Enzo Ferrari believed everything he read in the newspapers. It was his driver's second major injury of the year, and this time it was not only Italian journalists who were saying Lauda was finished. Enzo entered into panic negotiations with disaffected Brabham driver Carlos Reutemann to replace Lauda immediately. But a few days later, Lauda had recovered sufficiently to be airlifted to Salzburg Hospital, nearer to his home. There he would begin his astoundingly quick recovery on his way to the starting grid at Monza.

CHAPTER 21

Watson Denies Hunt the Advantage

Lauda Watches from His Hospital Bed

Austria: August 13–15, 1976

Niki Lauda's accident and the Ferrari team's absence from the 1976 Austrian Grand Prix was the worst possible news for the organizers and promoters of the race. Lauda and the Ferrari team were its biggest draw, and their absence cost the promoters hundreds of thousands of dollars in lost ticket income. Enthusiastic Italians had always poured over the borders between Austria and Italy to support the Ferrari team. Now they didn't come.

The promoters were very surprised when Daniele Audetto withdrew the entire Ferrari team; they had been expecting a replacement driver in Lauda's car at the very least. The damage was compounded by the loss of Clay Regazzoni, which also decimated the Swiss fan contingent, who usually traveled to Austria to see him race. Tens of thousands of them who normally flocked over the Swiss border stayed away.

In the days after Lauda's accident, Audetto had argued strongly that the Grand Prix at the Österreichring should be canceled altogether out of respect for Niki Lauda. It would have suited Ferrari perfectly had that happened. But the campaign to cancel the race incensed the organizers, and the compassionate plea was greeted with cynicism by those accustomed to Ferrari's reputation for manipulating situations to the team's advantage. There was no possible reason to cancel the race, and Audetto knew it. But it was his job to try.

With that route exhausted, and against Audetto's advice, Enzo Ferrari withdrew his cars from the Austrian event, ostensibly as a mark of respect for Lauda. But the decision demonstrated that at 78 years old, he seemed incapable of rational decision making. But there was now no doubt that he was back in charge and calling the shots after the departure of Luca di Montezemolo.

Enzo announced he felt cheated by what had happened at the Appeal Court in Paris and at Brands Hatch in the British Grand Prix. Enzo threatened to boycott Formula One until such a time when "the rules were enforced and justice prevailed." Bizarrely, Enzo also blamed Lauda personally for causing the crash at the Nürburgring, thereby absolving his own engineers of any blame for the mechanical failure that was known to have caused the accident. James Hunt felt very sorry for Lauda and what was happening in his absence. Speaking to reporters, he called Enzo Ferrari "an old man behaving like a child."

Lauda certainly didn't want the race canceled or for Ferrari to withdraw. He told reporters what he wanted more than anything at that moment was "a feeling of continuity and trust." He said he was "troubled" by what Audetto had said. But that was nothing compared to the anger he felt when he heard that Audetto had announced the withdrawal of the Ferraris from the race altogether. He instantly realized that this decision would severely harm his world championship chances and aid Hunt's significantly. He rang Luca di Montezemolo to try and get the decision reversed, but Montezemolo felt powerless to intervene after finding out it was a direct order from Enzo Ferrari.

The withdrawal of Ferrari was celebrated back at the McLaren factory in Colnbrook. McLaren had been careful not to express any view or to make any comment on Lauda's accident, but the withdrawal of the whole Ferrari team from a crucial race at a crucial point in the championship was a gift from heaven for the British team.

Going into early August, McLaren was at the height of its powers. After Hunt's victory in Germany, the team was a genuine championship contender, and James Hunt had all the momentum of a successful challenger. Hunt had won the last three grand prix races on the trot—four, if the reinstated Spanish win was counted. He was now a firm second in the world championship with 47 points; within 11 points of Lauda's score of 58. A championship bid that had looked impossible just four weeks ago now looked highly plausible.

In the process, Hunt had become one of the most famous sportsmen in the world. His marriage, divorce, and succession of girlfriends, combined with his extraordinary success on the track, had made him a national hero in Britain. It was enhanced even more by the fact that he had taken on and beaten the "German" enemy, Lauda—even though Lauda was Austrian. Although the Second World War had ended 31 years earlier, it was still very fresh in the minds of the many 50-plus-year-olds who had fought in it. They were rooting for Hunt with the same enthusiasm as if the war was being fought all over again. Without question, Hunt was more popular than any Formula·One driver in history.

There was also renewed harmony within the McLaren team. Mutual respect had broken out, and Hunt was now at one with the McLaren team management. The attitude of Teddy Mayer and Alastair Caldwell had totally changed. They now loved him and issued a press release saying as much; Hunt was delighted at finally being accepted by Mayer and Caldwell.

In a prepared statement issued to the press, Caldwell said, "I think Britain now has another Jimmy Clark situation with James Hunt. He is a super driver." Hunt was extremely flattered by the comparison with Clark. Teddy Mayer was even more effusive toward Hunt. He had never been known to praise a driver before, not even Fittipaldi, but now Mayer went so far as to say that Hunt was the best driver the team had ever employed: "Of all the drivers we've had, James has the greatest talent by far, in fact. He possibly makes more mistakes than, say, Emerson Fittipaldi, but he is certainly quicker than Emerson ever was when he drove for us. I think James is as consistently fast a driver as anyone I've ever seen."

Mayer wasn't finished and went on to compare Hunt with yet another of his heroes: "I would begin to compare his talent with Jackie Stewart's in his ability to win races driving a car that, in my opinion, is about the same as many others. Drivers like Jimmy Clark generally won races because they had superior cars. I think James's car is good, but I don't think it's any better than several other cars. Possibly it's more reliable, but it's quick because James is quick."

The setting for the Austrian Grand Prix was the 3.67-mile Österreichring circuit, a magnificent venue located 60 miles from Graz and laid out on the foothill slopes of the Alps in beautiful countryside. Österreichring was arguably the most beautiful circuit on the Formula One calendar.

The race was preceded by a week of private testing at Österreichring with Goodyear. Hunt dominated the testing, which was cut short by rain showers. Interestingly, the rest of Europe was enjoying an unprecedented heat wave that summer, with over 60 days of unbroken sunshine since late May. The only place it rained that summer was Austria.

McLaren had its new McLaren-Ford M26 car in Austria but kept it under a canvas sheet. It had been used by Hunt in the private testing session but had proved to be half a second slower. The car's designer, Gordon Coppuck, said, "Testing a new car is a little difficult when the old one happens to be going so well."

The new M26 was an advanced design with an aluminum and Nomex honeycomb chassis. It had a foil cell structure sandwiched between the aluminum panels, a design taken from the airplane industry. But it had inherent problems, not least with its fuel system, which couldn't suck up the last few gallons in the tank. This indicated a design fault, and one not easily rectified.

Coppuck was the first of a new breed of race car designers. His pedigree was unmatched, and he had joined McLaren from the National Gas Turbine Establishment and was appointed chief designer in 1968. As well as the M23 and the M26, he had designed the legendary M8 series of McLaren Can-Am cars, arguably the single most successful car in motor racing history. The M8 dominated the American sports car series for over five years, winning virtually every race held in that time. But the M23 was destined to become his most successful car, with a five-year lifespan and two world championships in that time. Its secret was being kept right down to the weight limit throughout its life, as well as some clever under-floor aerodynamics that created extra downforce.

The M26 car was his first failure, although everyone expected he would eventually turn it into a race-winning car given time. The continued success of the M23 had given him that time.

When Hunt arrived in Austria for the eleventh race of the 1976 Formula One world championship, despite the disappointing M26 testing, he couldn't have been on a greater high. No drink or drugs were needed to sustain him that golden weekend in the middle of August. It seemed as if the sun was shining on him. What's more, he was about to race on Lauda's home territory in his rival's absence.

Lauda had been knocked out of the championship, and no one at that stage thought he would return before the end of the season. So at that moment, with six races still to run, Hunt looked almost certain to be world champion in 1976.

Hunt's joy was compounded that weekend because it was now clear that Lauda had survived his accident and would not die.

There had also been some doubt about the seriousness of his internal injuries when it emerged that a Catholic priest had administered the last rites. But the suspicions of insiders were raised because Lauda was a confirmed atheist, and apparently apart from when forced by his wife Marlene (for christenings, wedding, and funerals), he had never been known to step inside a church in his life.

It had been suggested by those who knew him that he was perhaps playing mind games with Hunt. Wanting Hunt to believe he would not be returning, he might have been trying to convince people he was more seriously injured than he really was. Certainly, while his outwards burns were horrific and disfiguring, they were not life threatening. And when, two weeks after the accident, it leaked out that Lauda was sitting up in his hospital bed, signing autographs for the nurses, and watching the Austrian Grand Prix on television, it didn't square with the administration of last rites by a priest just a few days earlier.

But Hunt put all that out of his mind as he got on with the serious business of trying to win the race and, failing that, scoring as many points as possible while Lauda was away. Despite the heat elsewhere in Europe, it rained for both qualifying days, and because the land was so dry from the heat wave, the water rolled off the hills and gathered in pools behind the circuit. But none of it really affected Hunt, who, with the Ferraris absent, could afford to take it easy. He turned in a time that gave him his easiest pole position yet. The fast circuit suited him and his car perfectly. He would later set a new lap record at an average speed of 137.83 miles per hour.

With Lauda gone, Hunt looked around and found an unfamiliar bearded face alongside him on the front row. Ulsterman John Watson had put his Penske-Ford car on the front row of the grid. It was Watson's best moment in a stop-start career that had seen him drive for five different teams in three years with no noticeable success—apart from having an obvious talent for driving a car fast. In 30 races in the previous three years, he had scored points only twice: the highlight being a fourth place in Austria in 1974, driving a Brabham.

But he had come good in 1976, signing on as number one driver for the Penske team. Since then he had visited the podium twice already. Penske was a well-managed team, run by American auto industry entrepreneur Roger Penske and managed by Heinz Hofer, a very precise Swiss German. It was a poignant race for the team, as a year earlier Penske's partner and number one driver, Mark Donohue, had crashed on the morning of the race. The victim of a tire failure, he was critically injured and died later that day in the hospital.

Watson had taken Donohue's place in the team, and it had been his big break. Although he was on the front row, however, he must have been dispirited when he came in a whole second slower than Hunt. Hunt attempted to excuse the Ulsterman for being so much slower, saying, "I knew that Watson was quite capable of going as fast. It was just that I'd got organized, had a new set of tires fitted, and gone quick before he had a chance to build up speed."

Amazingly, rain threatened again on race day, slightly delaying the race start. But as the dark skies turned blue, the cars lined up on the grid. Frightened of the consequences of running cars in the rain, the organizers informed the drivers that the race would be stopped if it rained suddenly.

The high-speed circuit when wet was too dangerous for cars on slick tires, which were designed for dry running.

From the start line, Hunt got away first for a change and led Watson. It was the briefest of leads, as Watson quickly passed him and the cars swept down the long straight from the top of the hill.

For two laps, Watson, Hunt, Ronnie Peterson in his March-Ford, and Jody Scheckter's Tyrrell-Ford all diced for the lead. It was the closest racing Formula One had seen for years. Scheckter took the lead for one lap until a pattern formed with Watson, Peterson, and Swedish driver Gunnar Nilsson's Lotus-Ford ahead of Scheckter and Hunt.

It soon became apparent that there was a problem with Hunt's McLaren. It was understeering on full tanks. Hunt recalled: "I was having a real struggle to stay on the road." Then Scheckter had an enormous accident at the top of the hill on the 14th lap, as the front suspension broke on his car. The Tyrrell-Ford comprehensively destroyed itself, luckily without injury to the driver. Hunt put his head down and proceeded to wring the maximum performance out of his badly handling car. He set his fastest lap of the race, indicating just how hard he had tried.

The understeering problem was due to a damaged front wing, and Hunt could do nothing to stop John Watson winning his first Grand Prix. Hunt was fourth behind Laffite and Nilsson.

The real drama followed the podium ceremony, as Watson, complying with the terms of a bet, shaved off his perennial beard in public to reveal a clean-shaven look, which he was to keep from then on.

Hunt was less than delighted with his fourth place, although Niki Lauda, sitting up in his hospital bed, reportedly whooped and hollered as the checkered flag fell. The score, he quickly worked out, was Lauda 58, Hunt 47. Later that week, Lauda spoke to John Watson on the telephone from his hospital bed and thanked him personally for beating Hunt. He told him: "Anything to stop Hunt getting points."

CHAPTER 22

Hunt States Serious Intent

Gap Closes Dramatically

Holland: August 27–29, 1976

Back in Vienna, Niki Lauda was making a remarkable recovery from his injuries and called up James Hunt on the telephone from his hospital bed to wish him a happy birthday for the following Sunday. Hunt's 29th birthday fell on August 29, which was the Sunday of the Dutch Grand Prix, and the two men chatted for a long time.

When people heard about the phone call, it surprised everyone as word quickly got round the paddock. They automatically assumed that the wily Lauda was playing mind games with Hunt, and he probably was. But the assumption made Hunt angry, and he told people it was nothing of the sort and that, despite their rivalry, he felt a growing emotional bond with the Austrian as he fought back to health after his accident. But that feeling didn't stop him taking full advantage of Lauda's absence to narrow the points gap in the world championship table.

The Hunt family, including his brother Peter, his mother, Sue, and younger brother, David, journeyed to Holland for Hunt's birthday and watched all three days of qualifying and racing from the grandstands.

They had been there a year earlier at Zandvoort; Hunt had won his first grand prix driving the Hesketh, a masterful performance during which he was chased hard by Lauda, who was then on his way to winning the world title with the Ferrari.

That race had marked Hunt's coming of age as a driver. Then winning had been a fresh concept to him in Formula One, and he slowly became confident about leading and winning a grand prix under pressure. Now, a year later, the situation was different: Hunt was expected to win.

But with Lauda absent, Hunt was finding a new rival at every race. In Holland it was a resurgent Ronnie Peterson, who was finally finding his form in the works March-Ford car. Many observers still regarded Peterson as the fastest man in grand prix racing, and had done so since Jackie Stewart retired at the end of 1973.

After Peterson walked out of Lotus, it had taken him a long time to get up to speed with March, and Holland was the first race where he was back in serious contention. Peterson and Hunt were old friends and took the opportunity to spend time together in Holland. Hunt listened to Peterson talk about his problems with Lotus at the beginning of the year. Hunt was just thankful that he had not signed with Lotus for 1976 as he so easily might have done.

Ferrari returned to Formula One in Holland after a one-race absence with just a single car for Clay Regazzoni. Lauda was disgusted that he had not been replaced so that Ferrari could field two cars to help stop Hunt from scoring points. He felt it was another stupid decision by Enzo Ferrari. Ferrari bought two cars for Regazzoni. Worse still, Regazzoni was in pain, as he had broken a rib playing tennis a few days earlier and was not on form all weekend, despite the obvious superiority of the Ferrari 312T2 chassis. Regazzoni had another advantage: Ferrari had brought some Goodyear tires from Nürburgring, and these were softer than those Goodyear was supplying to the other teams.

Ronnie Peterson proved to be in scintillating form and was never really challenged for pole position. In the end, his March-Ford was eight one-hundredths of a second faster than Hunt's McLaren-Ford in second place. Hunt had endured handling problems in qualifying, with a severe lack of traction and understeer due to a tire problem. But his problems were small compared to that of his teammate, Jochen Mass, who was a very unhappy driver. He was forced to drive the new M26 and it proved to be a dog, and he could only qualify 15th on the eighth row of the grid.

Tom Pryce was the sensation of qualifying, in third place in his Shadow-Ford. John Watson was fourth, with Clay Regazzoni and Mario Andretti fifth and sixth.

After qualifying on Saturday afternoon, there was a bizarre scene in the pit lane when Hunt tried to keep the peace after his close friend Jody Scheckter got into a vicious argument with his team principal, Ken Tyrrell. Hunt's sponsor, Marlboro, organized a pit stop competition whereby two cars would come into a simulated pit area, change all four wheels, and then go around the circuit. The winner got $500 provided he lapped within 10 percent of the fastest qualifying time.

Scheckter looked set to win, but because of a crowded pit lane, he had to slow down and could not complete his lap within the 10 percent time limit and forfeited the $500, even though he had won on the road. Tyrrell thought Scheckter should have ignored the people in the pit lane and completed the lap in time. There was an ugly scene in the pits as the two men yelled at each other. Hunt intervened to separate the two men. He took Scheckter's side in the argument and was stunned by Tyrrell's attitude. That day Hunt began a personal feud with Ken Tyrrell that would last the rest of his life. The row had immediate consequences. On race morning Scheckter took Hunt to one side and confided that he would be leaving the Tyrrell team at the end of the year.

When Hunt looked around on the front row of the grid in Holland, he saw Peterson's familiar blue-and-yellow helmet and felt somewhat reassured; it was a feeling he had never felt with Lauda. In the race, Hunt botched his start as usual, spinning his wheels and letting Peterson pull away in front. To add to the ignominy, John Watson came through from the second row and overtook Hunt at the end of the pit straight in full view of everyone.

Hunt bided his time in third as Peterson and Watson scrapped for the lead. His McLaren was understeering again as a braking air scoop worked loose. Despite that, Hunt overtook Watson on lap seven and Peterson for the lead on lap 12. Afterwards he said he simply took advantage of mistakes by both drivers.

Hunt said, "I didn't really do any serious passing of anyone during the whole race, but it put me in the lead, which was the best place to be because I had a real problem with the understeer. It meant that the onus was now on Watson to get past me if he could. I think if he had got past me, he would have left me."

In fact, Hunt had to drive as hard as ever to block Watson from getting past. In terms of car handling, the Ulsterman was easily faster, but Hunt was simply better at blocking than Watson was at overtaking. In the end it didn't matter, as Watson coasted to a halt on lap 47 when his gearbox broke. Watson's demise was a signal for Clay Regazzoni, in the lone Ferrari entered in the race, to take up the chase. Hunt got in a panic, because he feared Regazzoni might have instructions to punt him off if he couldn't get past. Hunt recalled: "Boy, was I in a panic. I was something like 10 seconds ahead of Clay, and I didn't want him to get within reach."

But, tellingly, Regazzoni was just not up to it, and by the end, Hunt won the race barely a car's length ahead of the Ferrari—too close for comfort. Hunt was absolutely elated and threw both arms aloft as he had the previous year, and nearly put his car straight into the barriers as a result. In the grandstands opposite the pits, anxiety gave way to relief and delight for his family when they belatedly realized he had won the race.

John Watson remembers it as a classic race: "I had a car which was quicker over a whole lap, but he had a car which was fractionally quicker down the straight because we were running different levels of downforce. He successfully defended his position with a fair degree of firmness. It was a classic duel of two Brits in Formula One."

Hunt's victory was a disaster for Lauda; there would be no more whooping and hollering or congratulatory phone calls. Regazzoni's failure to overtake Hunt was telling, and Enzo Ferrari was said to have decided on the basis of that performance alone to sack the Swiss driver as soon as he found a replacement. The championship score now read Lauda 58, Hunt 56.

Aside from the motor racing, there was plenty of drama off-track in Holland after the race.

As Hunt closed the gap on Lauda and started winning races regularly, he felt he deserved an increase in salary. He was being paid a basic salary of a paltry $50,000 a year, which was a quarter of what other top drivers were getting. Hunt became more and more disgusted with the money

McLaren was paying him. He was actually earning much less than he had at Hesketh the year before, when the team had been on the breadline. At Hesketh he had been paid extra by sponsors for every promotional day. But at McLaren they were all gratis as part of his retainer. He had picked up around $70,000 from such promotional outings in 1975 but hardly anything in 1976. With his share of prize money, he looked set to earn $100,000, exactly the same as he had at Hesketh in 1975.

Before the race, Hunt had appointed his brother Peter as his new business manager. He had previously been managed by a combination of Mark McCormack's American IMG agency and Barrie Gill and Andrew Marriott's British CSS operation. IMG and CSS split the duties between them, but it meant Hunt paid double commission on many of his deals. Marlboro's John Hogan recalled: "For James, it meant that he was able to be freed from the high-pressure American business approach and to operate more easily with his brother."

IMG and CSS agreed to withdraw gradually and to let Peter Hunt take over. But his brother did not want to become his full-time manager and abandon his accounting practice. Hogan recalled: "The brothers eventually decided on a compromise whereby Peter stayed with his firm in London and handled James's affairs from there."

With his new management arrangements in place, an emboldened Hunt decided to confront Teddy Mayer straight after the podium celebrations. They had a brief but furious row, with Mayer telling Hunt to "fuck off" and Hunt saying, "I might just do that." Of course neither man meant it, but Mayer was sticking to his contract. As Alastair Caldwell remembered: "James and Teddy were always on about money. It got to the stage where James decided we weren't paying him enough, although he'd been only too happy to come and drive for us for nothing at the beginning of the year. By now, of course, he'd decided he was a superstar who needed paying a lot of money. That became a constant source of friction."

Hunt stormed out of the pits after his row with Mayer and joined his friends and family waiting outside to celebrate his birthday. They built a huge campfire in the sand dunes of Zandvoort. They celebrated into the night and passed out on the sand, incoherent with drink. His need to celebrate his birthday, along with the anniversary of his first win and his latest victory, all inevitably took their toll. John Hugenholz, the Zandvoort circuit manager, presented Hunt with a giant birthday cake in the shape of the track. It was meant as a token to mark his birthday and as a celebration of his win the year before, but it now became an ever more poignant and appropriate symbol of all he had achieved.

CHAPTER 23

Lauda Returns from the Dead

Monza Rising Stuns Hunt

Italy: September 10–12, 1976

There was plenty of activity for both James Hunt and Niki Lauda in the fortnight between the Dutch and Italian Grand Prix races. There was also plenty of speculation about how the Italians would try and thwart the British at their home race in Italy. There was lots of incentive to do so, as the Italians certainly thought they had been cheated at Brands Hatch and seemed determined to return the compliment.

It started at the beginning of September; news items appeared in Italian newspapers speculating that the Texaco fuel used by the McLaren team was illegal. The stories were baseless, but still, Texaco engineers examined the stories and immediately took precautions and double-checked that its fuel was within the regulations.

The differences were all about octane ratings: a gray area at the best of times and open to much subjective interpretation. The maximum octane allowance was 102. However, the rules were vague and allowed teams to use the octane rating of the best available fuel in their country of origin plus one octane. The best available in Britain was 101 octane, which meant 102 octane would be the maximum allowed. But Ferrari was subject to other measurements prevailing in Italy, as were Ligier in France. In those countries the top grade of fuel available was only 100 octane, so Ferrari was limited to 101 octane. The rules' variance didn't matter, because higher octane levels made no difference to performance in normal circumstances.

But James Hunt realized that it would be a difficult time and decided to get himself out of the way. He agreed to go to North America for a week. He had been offered $10,000 to race in the Formula Atlantic series, which was the North American equivalent of Formula Two. Three fellow Formula One drivers, Patrick Depailler, Vittorio Brambilla, and Alan Jones, also made the trip for the race in the quaint town of Trois-Rivières near Quebec in Canada. It was there that Hunt met the young Canadian driver Gilles Villeneuve for the first time. Villeneuve won the race and Hunt was third, but Hunt was mightily impressed with the skills of the young Canadian. So much so that after the race, Hunt called Teddy Mayer and John Hogan in England and recommended they sign him before anyone else did.

After his Formula Atlantic experience, Hunt traveled south to the Michigan International Speedway to take part in an IROC saloon car race on an oval track and earn himself another $10,000.

The IROC series used identical, modified Chevrolet Camaros that were regularly raced by top American drivers in something akin to a celebrity series. Hunt managed to qualify his Camaro on pole at an average speed of nearly 150 miles per hour. It was his first experience of driving on an oval, and he found he was good at it.

But racing on an oval was altogether a different experience, and he couldn't crack it. As a result of trying too hard, he crashed into a concrete wall at 150 miles per hour and had a very narrow escape from serious injury when a piece of metal guardrail pierced the cockpit of his car. Hunt was shaken by his inability to race other cars on an oval track. He said, "I got in the race and didn't have a clue because of all the high-speed drafting. I was right out of my depth. To tell you the truth, I was scared shitless." After berating the organizers of IROC about safety, it was with some relief that he boarded an airplane to return to Europe.

Meanwhile, Niki Lauda was preparing to come back from the dead. After three weeks, he was discharged from the hospital and went to the island of Ibiza to recuperate, taking with him Willie Dungl, the physiotherapist who had helped him when he broke his ribs. Under Dungl's supervision, Lauda began taking physical exercises for 12 hours a day. Lauda wanted to return to Formula One as soon as he could properly hold a wheel, and he believed that lying in bed thinking about the accident was counterproductive. He said, "I wanted to get back to work as soon as I possibly could." Dungl believed as much physical exercise as he could stand was the secret to Lauda's quick recovery. Just as when Lauda broke his ribs, Dungl set out to perform a miracle so Lauda could race again. Whereas a serious rib injury recuperation was shortened from six weeks to two weeks, Dungl now set out to shorten a year's recovery process to just six weeks.

Dungl was with Lauda 24 hours a day, and when they weren't exercising, he was massaging his body. Lauda also hired a doctor who worked with Dungl to look after every detail of his day, including rest, diet and, crucially, how much exercise he could tolerate. Soon his lungs and physical fitness were certified as being back to normal.

The treatment regime was so successful that he said, "My training program is entirely up to me and my own willpower. I feel better now than I was before. That was when I took the decision to go to Monza."

In the intervening period, it seemed that Lauda had reappraised his whole attitude to motor racing. As he explained: "The problem I have had to face since the accident is whether I would enjoy my motor racing again and what effect it would have on me. No one can discover this until they have been through an experience like mine. I have found that I love the positive side of motor racing. So why should I give it up?"

On September 6, exactly 38 days after the accident, he reported to the Ferrari factory at Maranello and told Daniele Audetto he was fit again and would be able to race at Monza.

Audetto and Enzo Ferrari were shocked to see Lauda. They did not believe he would be returning in 1976 and did not think he would race for Ferrari again. In his absence they had hired Carlos Reutemann as his replacement. Reutemann had fallen out with Bernie Ecclestone and had abruptly left the Brabham team, probably sensing that a more competitive Ferrari drive might be available after Lauda's accident.

It was the news of Reutemann's appointment that inspired Lauda to return quickly. Lauda did not like Reutemann; as he confessed, "We never could stand each other, and instead of taking pressure off me, they put on even more by bringing Carlos Reutemann into the team."

Reutemann's premature signing had been fueled by all the hysteria in the Italian press. Its timing was a huge error and caused immediate problems in the team.

Audetto, who couldn't believe Lauda was fit enough to race, ordered him to test the Ferrari at nearby Fiorano to see if he could drive competitively. Lauda was as fast as he had ever been. With that, Audetto had no choice under the terms of his contract but to make a car available for him and to enter a third car for Reutemann at Monza.

But it was not as easy as that for Audetto. Entering a third car breached Lauda's new contract, and as a result, Audetto had to ask Lauda to waive the clause for Monza. Lauda agreed, but only for one race, believing he would soon see the back of Reutemann. Inwardly Lauda was furious with both Enzo Ferrari and Audetto. As he said later, "To the outside world, Enzo Ferrari and his company were standing by their slightly singed world champion, but from the inside, the pitiful insecurity of each and every one of them was palpable. Tactics took precedence over trust. Ferrari kept telling the world how solidly they were behind me, but in private they were at sixes and sevens."

It was clear that the Ferrari team didn't want Lauda back. They thought he was finished and wanted him gone. As Lauda recalled: "They didn't know what to make of a defending champion with a disfigured face who carried on as if everything was quite normal."

The fact that Lauda had signed a new contract for 1977 before his accident put him in a much stronger position than he might have been otherwise. As he admitted: "If I hadn't had that contract, they could have ground me down mentally and turned me out to pasture. It was my one piece of good fortune that [Enzo] Ferrari had been so anxious to get me under contract for the following season."

After the test, Lauda departed from Maranello that night and returned to Austria, leaving a stunned Daniele Audetto and Enzo Ferrari behind him. That evening, as soon as his plans were confirmed, Lauda called up his trusted friend, the motoring editor of the *Daily Express*, David Benson. He told Benson he had an exclusive for him. And what an exclusive that was.

On Wednesday September 8, Benson flew into Salzburg airport to meet up with Lauda. From Salzburg he flew with him on Lauda's private plane to Milan airport and on to the Monza circuit for the Italian Grand Prix. Also on the plane were Willie Dungl and Marlene.

Lauda had chosen Benson to tell his story to the world, and the writer got an exclusive interview with Lauda on the flight and scooped the rest of the world's press. It was an amazing coup for the *Daily Express* newspaper, and it became the first and last time Lauda ever talked intimately about the accident and his recovery.

He told Benson during that flight: "A lot of people have said that they think I am crazy to go back to racing so quickly. They say that a man with a face that is not like that of a human being but like a dead man's skull should want to give up immediately. People who think like that are those who would probably be very happy to be ill and stay at home and not have to go out to work. This is not my attitude to life.

"I do not enjoy life unless I am active and have something to do and look forward to. I must work. If I have an accident in my work, then my aim must be to recover as soon as possible with all the help of modern medicine. Once I had decided to go on, then I had to make a comeback as quickly as possible. That is why I am here at Monza.

"I have not raced for over a month, and when I climb into my car, there will be enormous pressure on me because it is Italy, and Ferrari is the 'king,' and we have three cars entered for the race. But I will not let this pressure affect me. I may only finish in 15th place, but now I know that I am ahead of my programs, and when we go to Canada and North America, I'll be in a position to win and to keep my world championship."

The interview appeared almost verbatim in the *Daily Express* of Friday, September 10, the day Niki Lauda reappeared at the Monza track; it had been less than six weeks since he had crashed out of the German Grand Prix and been airlifted to the hospital. His return to the paddock at Monza was only 41 days after the accident. He had missed two races and ceded 21 world championship points of his lead over Hunt.

Statistically, the two rivals were now even, as both drivers had now completed exactly the same number of races during the season. Lauda and Hunt were within two points of each other in the championship table.

Lauda's arrival in Monza was greeted with pure amazement by the rest of the Formula One fraternity. As for James Hunt, he was just as stunned as everyone else at Lauda's quick return to racing. In fact, when he analyzed it, he found Lauda's story of his recovery all rather unconvincing, saying, "I know that little fucker. Only Niki could take the last rites and come back at the Italian Grand Prix." John Hogan, who sponsored both Hunt and Lauda and was very close to both of them, agreed: "Niki, who'd never been to a church in his life, wouldn't know what the last rites were if they hit him in the head."

Hogan now believes that Lauda overstated his injuries in order to get a psychological advantage over Hunt and to lull him into false sense of security. Whether that was true or not, no one will ever know, but the fact was that Lauda was there and he was going to race.

When he finally emerged, it was clear that Lauda was making a supreme effort. He was obviously very frail and weak, and it was clear he should not have been there. In today's strict medical environment, he would not have been allowed to race. Although hidden by bandages, his face and head were still noticeably disfigured. He kept his cap firmly planted on his face, but the disguise wasn't enough to allay the serious doubts about his fitness to race—doubts being expressed even within his own team. Hogan said, "He looked horrible: blood and pus all over him."

It could not have been lost on Lauda that donning a racing helmet so soon after the accident would make the scars on his face ultimately much worse and more visible for the rest of his life. Lauda admitted: "My matter-of-factness in automatically resuming my career as soon as all systems were go was disconcerting. Some thought it betrayed a lack of dignity; others found it downright unappetizing."

In the pits, Lauda's wife, Marlene, kept attending to her husband's face and stroking it to give him reassurance. She had her sewing kit and was constantly modifying Lauda's new flameproof balaclava for maximum comfort. She wanted to be certain that there was no irritation to the sensitive new skin grafted around his eyes. Everyone was deeply impressed by Marlene's devotion. David Benson wrote in Saturday's *Daily Express:* "I am conquered by her courage. Here is a woman truly worthy of a very great sportsman." He added: "Marlene is a delightfully warm person. Her handshake is firm. Her eyes are steady and constant. They are the eyes of a woman who could inspire a man to great things."

And that is exactly what she did that weekend.

Besides worrying about Lauda's return, the McLaren team had problems of its own to worry about. At Monza, McLaren was not only fighting Ferrari for the world title but was battling the entire Italian nation. In a fair fight, there was no doubt that Hunt could beat Lauda. But Teddy Mayer knew that the Italian Grand Prix was unlikely to be a fair fight. He knew the Italians would try do anything they could to handicap the team. The fuel octane scare stories in the press had been an early warning.

It started almost immediately. As the McLaren team's trucks reached the Italian border, the Italian border guards decided to take a long time signing off on the customs paperwork. There was nothing wrong with the paperwork or the trucks, but the trucks were effectively detained for a day and a half. The time that was lost at the border ate into precious time at the track to prepare the cars.

When the McLaren trucks finally did pull into the Monza paddock, they found a hostile reception. As they entered Monza park, they saw fans holding up banners that read *"Basta con la Mafia Inglese."* Translated, they said "Away with the English Mafia." And whenever James Hunt appeared in public, he was loudly booed.

But all this was nothing compared to what would happen in scrutineering, which was outright Italian chicanery. The CSI officials present seemed powerless to intervene as the Italian scrutineers pored over Hunt's car. It seemed they had already decided how to hinder him. But even they had no idea how effective they were to be as the rains fell on the track, rather conveniently for Ferrari.

The first qualifying session on Friday was wet, and Hunt spun off and damaged the nose of his car. When he walked back to the pits, the Italian fans erupted in the grandstands with joy. It was unseemly as they spat on him from the stands. He had to put his helmet back on to avoid being soaked in saliva.

Meanwhile, Niki Lauda, with the Italian crowd right behind him and willing him on, got back into a car for the first time since his accident. On Friday he had employed his normal mental preparation tactics, which included an objective review of his emotions to ensure he was mentally "well primed" before going out to qualify.

But then it all changed. As Lauda recalled: "When I climbed into the cockpit at Monza, fear hit me so hard that all self-motivation theories flew out the window." Lauda's lap times were poor, and he admitted later that he had lied to journalists, including David Benson, whose interview had been published only that morning, about his state of mind. Truthfully, he had been "rigid with fear" during qualifying, and in particular he found the rain had been "terrifying."

Lauda explained later: "I had to play the hero to buy myself enough time to sort things out. The fact is you have to play the hard man on occasions, whether you actually feel like one or not. It is really all a game of mental hide-and-seek; you would never be forgiven if you blurted out the truth at an inopportune moment. You would be finished."

That night, alone in the quiet cocoon of his hotel room, Lauda reviewed his performance and tried to identify what had gone wrong. He had been trying to drive as he had before the accident, and it wasn't working. Feeling insecure, he said, "I had got myself into a stupid tangle."

His overnight analysis helped him, as he put it, "reprogram his brain for the following day" and to eliminate all the pressure he felt. Managing to repress his anxiety somehow, Lauda told himself to "drive more slowly." He said later: "And that's what I did. I started slowly, then gradually built up speed until, suddenly, I was the fastest of the Ferraris—faster than Regazzoni and the newcomer Reutemann. I had managed to prove in practice what I knew in theory: I could drive as well now as before the accident."

Sunday, August 1, 1976

Niki Lauda was wearing a specially designed helmet made for him by AGV during the 1976 racing season. As can be clearly seen in this photograph, it had extra-thick foam padding for greater comfort. During his accident in Germany, the foam compressed, enabling the helmet to slip off his head and exposing Lauda to the full force of the flames. The helmet was illegal and contributed greatly to the nature of the burns on Lauda's face. If the helmet had stayed on, he probably would have emerged with only minor facial damage. The situation was eerily similar to events 18 years later, when Ayrton Senna was wearing an illegal lightweight helmet that greatly contributed to the head injuries that caused his death.

James Hunt ponders the next 90 minutes of the German Grand Prix before the restart. He knew Niki Lauda was out of the race but at this stage did not know he had been so badly injured. Note that his helmet was completely legal and he was far better protected in case of an accident.

Mariella von Reininghaus started going out with Niki Lauda in 1968 when she was just 18, and the two were inseparable after their first date at the Vienna hunt ball. But she wanted him to retire after he had won his first world championship and to devote himself to a family and what she called a "proper career." When Lauda was an upcoming and struggling driver, he went along with that, but as soon as he was successful, he wanted more glory.

The inaugural US West Grand Prix around the streets of Long Beach, California, went off surprisingly well. After a straight two wins, Lauda was obliged to let his teammate Clay Regazzoni have his victory. In truth, Regazzoni would have won anyway after Lauda had car troubles.

In the autumn of 1975, Niki Lauda coldly dumped his fiancée, Mariella von Reininghaus, after eight years together. After returning from the US Grand Prix at Watkins Glen, he walked into their apartment and walked straight out again—and into the arms of his new girlfriend, Marlene Knaus. He told Mariella he had fallen out of love with her but did not tell her about Marlene.

Up to the US West Grand Prix, Niki Lauda and Clay Regazzoni had been very close friends. However, a schism opened up between them after team orders were brought into play at Long Beach. In this event it did not matter, as fate dictated Regazzoni would win the race anyway.

Marlene Knaus was the girlfriend of Austrian actor Curt Jurgens when she first set eyes on Niki Lauda in the summer of 1975. But from that moment, she only had eyes for him, and they were soon engaged and then married, shocking the whole of Europe with their swiftness and Lauda's cold dismissal of his longtime love, Mariella von Reininghaus.

Niki Lauda was somewhat bemused in Long Beach by the strange orders of his team manager, Daniele Audetto. Audetto told him he had done too much winning and to let his teammate, Clay Regazzoni, take victory this time. Lauda was completely shocked and said to Audetto, "Are you mad? These points will be needed to win the world championship."

At the Spanish Grand Prix, Niki Lauda put on a very brave face but was wracked with pain from a set of badly broken ribs. He was pumped full of painkilling drugs to enable him to compete.

Niki Lauda felt a real affinity with five-time world champion Juan Manuel Fangio. In America Lauda tried out one of the Mercedes Silver Arrow cars driven by Fangio in his heyday.

James Hunt was recognized as a genuine Formula One star by midseason in 1976. His off-track earnings were growing and overseen by his accountant brother, Peter (left).

Jochen Mass (left) thought he would be team leader of the Marlboro McLaren team in 1976, and so did everyone else. But from the very first race in Brazil, he was blown away by James Hunt, and any such notions were quickly laid to rest.

The McLaren-Ford M23 was magnificently dominant at Jarama in Spain for the 1976 Spanish Grand Prix, with Niki Lauda trailing round in second place. Hunt won on the road and stood on the podium and sprayed the champagne, but he also had to win again in the appeals courtrooms of Paris.

Niki Lauda was the king of Monte Carlo, while James Hunt languished in the also-rans. The new Ferrari 312T2 was an absolutely magnificent car, especially in baking-hot weather, such as at Monaco that year. The temperature seemed to make huge difference in how the car performed. During the heat wave in Europe in 1976 it over-performed. But in the coolness of the autumn in North America and Asia, i wasn't so successful.

James Hunt was a sponsor's dream, and he did more for the Marlboro cigarette brand than any other individual in history. Out of the car, he always had a cigarette in his mouth. Interestingly, he did not smoke Marlboros. Every night he emptied cartons of Rothmans cigarettes into Marlboro packets to keep his sponsors happy.

By midseason, high airboxes had been banned, and Alastair Caldwell came up with a novel twin-intake airbox that met the letter of the regulations.

The Ferrari 312T2 was designed by Mauro Forghieri, who had returned to Ferrari in 1974 to form a triumvirate with Lauda and Luca di Montezemolo to restore Ferrari to the top of Formula One. It was wildly successful and yielded two world championships, which could easily have been four with better luck.

The chaotic scenes in the pit lanes as the British Grand Prix forms up the grid again after its aborted false start. But it would be a good 90 minutes before a restart.

The start of the British Grand Prix at Brands Hatch, with Niki Lauda on pole and James Hunt beside him. The serene start was soon disrupted by Clay Regazzoni, behind on the second row.

Jody Scheckter (left) and Roger Penske (right) were great friends with James Hunt during his championship season. The friendships lasted for the whole of Hunt's life.

On the grid again for the restart of the British Grand Prix. A hostile crowd would not allow the race to be restarted without its hero, James Hunt. The crowd got its way.

Luca di Montezemolo (middle) and Piero Ferrari (right) both came to Brands Hatch to give Niki Lauda moral support at the British Grand Prix. But the politics of the team saw them take very little part in what went on.

Niki Lauda was dominant during the first half of the 1976 Formula One season and very fast at Brands Hatch. But at the British Grand Prix, he ran into James Hunt at his very best.

The Ferrari 312T2 as driven by Niki Lauda in 1976 is one of the most valuable cars in the world. If one were to come up for sale, the asking price would be $20 million plus.

Bernie Ecclestone and Max Mosley were both great friends of James Hunt in 1976. Mosley in particular was very close to him, and the two had come to motor sport through very different routes. Ecclestone's interest was, as ever, fiduciary. He saw Hunt as the key to Formula One's television future, and so it proved.

Niki Lauda had a shock at the French Grand Prix. Expecting to sweep James Hunt aside, he found a newly competitive McLaren team and then ran into severe engine problems, forcing a rare retirement.

Teddy Mayer sits on a wheel guarding James Hunt's McLaren-Ford M23 on the grid of the British Grand Prix at Brands Hatch. Mayer had to stop the stewards from wheeling the car off the grid, which they wanted to do.

Niki Lauda looks on in bemusement as James Hunt stands bolt upright on the podium for the playing of the national anthem at Brands Hatch after he had won the British Grand Prix.

James Hunt celebrates his British Grand Prix victory by showering the crowd with Moët & Chandon champagne.

The last photographs taken of Niki Lauda, conferring with Clay Regazzoni, in the Ferrari 312T2 before his accident at the German Grand Prix. It could clearly be seen that Lauda was not happy competing on the Nürburgring. He did not think it was safe.

Niki Lauda had few doubts that he would be world champion racing driver again in 1976. He was at the top of his form, and his Ferrari 312T2 car was one of the greatest cars ever built in Formula One. But he suffered from management problems in the team, which disturbed his happiness and caused him periods of great self-doubt.

Danielle Audetto (center) talks to Niki Lauda before he goes out to race in the German Grand Prix. Lauda had just signed a lucrative new contract for the 1977 season and didn't have much time for Audetto's management and motivation methods.

Niki Lauda, from second on the grid, makes a bad start at the German Grand Prix and falls farther behind the Tyrrell of Jody Scheckter.

Niki Lauda did not compete at the Austrian Grand Prix because of injuries received at the previous race in Germany. However, his presence was everywhere in big posters erected by the organizers to celebrate their national hero, including a big one opposite the Tyrrell-Ford pit area at the Österreichring.

James Hunt tried his best to take full advantage of Niki Lauda's absence from his home race in Austria, but he could not stop a resurgent John Watson from scoring his first victory.

John Watson tried desperately to win two grand prix on the trot in the Netherlands. But unreliability stopped him in his tracks as he chased down James Hunt's McLaren in Holland before retiring.

James Hunt with a local journalist in the pit lane at the Austrian Grand Prix.

James Hunt wins the Dutch Grand Prix at Zandvoort on his birthday weekend, on Sunday, August 29, 1976. The celebrations in the sand dunes followed.

James Hunt gets offline and onto the dirt as he drives
to victory at the Dutch Grand Prix at Zandvoort.

Niki Lauda, the reigning champion, led the world championship from the first race to the last, until almost the very last lap of the season. But "almost" became the crucial word in the Austrian's dictionary.

Niki Lauda led the world championships for 274 days. It was not until the very final few minutes of that 10-month period that James Hunt moved ahead of him and won the world title by a single championship point.

Lauda was fifth fastest by the end of the session. For some reason, both the Ferraris and the McLarens had been slow, but Lauda was fastest of the five. He had outqualified both his Ferrari teammates, causing Reutemann and Clay Regazzoni considerable embarrassment, not to mention James Hunt, who could only manage ninth place on the grid. There was also no excuse for Hunt, as Monza was a fast circuit that suited the characteristics of his car. Lauda's returning performance simply stunned everyone. Psychologically, he had struck an enormous blow on his rivals, including those in his own team.

Jacques Laffite put his Ligier on pole, followed by Jody Scheckter's Tyrrell-Ford, Carlos Pace's Brabham-Alfa Romeo, and Patrick Depailler's Tyrrell-Ford.

During the Saturday session, fuel checks were made by the scrutineers in the pits. Forewarned, Texaco had made absolutely certain that the McLaren's fuel was legal, measuring at 101.2 octane. But overnight the Italian stewards analyzed the McLaren's fuel and found it was 101.6 octane, not 101.2, but they seemed to confirm it was within the allowed limits. Then, feigning ignorance of the rules, the Italians telexed the CSI, the FIA's sporting division in Paris, and asked the governing body for clarification of its own ruling. The message in the telex was vague in the sending, which was deliberate, and even vaguer in the reply. The secretary of the CSI replied and said the maximum allowed was 101.

So on Sunday morning, the Italian stewards announced that Hunt's and his teammate Jochen Mass' fuel was illegal and that their Saturday times would be disallowed. Only their Friday qualifying times, run in the wet, would count. The cars were sent to the back of the grid. They also disqualified Saturday times for John Watson's Penske car. The Penske team had no argument, as their fuel was almost certainly over the allowed maximum. They had pushed the rules to the limit and imported special fuel from the United States.

The organizers' clear intention had been to put the McLaren cars out of the race completely, thereby thwarting Hunt. The disallowed times effectively meant that Hunt, Mass, and Watson would not be allowed to start; their sub-two-minute, rain-affected qualifying times on Friday were not fast enough to get in the race.

But even before all this happened, there was an even more bizarre incident—Italian policemen came to the McLaren pit and took Alastair Caldwell away. They told him they were arresting him on suspicion of importing illegal fuel into Italy. It was a trumped-up charge, and Caldwell's theory was that Ferrari wanted him out of the way when the stewards made their fuel announcement.

Caldwell believed that Enzo Ferrari had been able to manipulate the situation by calling a friend in the local police station. He explained: "[Enzo] Ferrari had obviously said, 'We need to get rid of Caldwell completely because he'll go bananas. He's the man to worry about. What can we do? We'll pretend that the fuel has been illegally imported; we'll tell him that and have him arrested on this basis.' We had Texaco fuel, which had been brought in a truck from Belgium, certainly imported correctly with the right paperwork, but that didn't matter. They had an excuse to lock me up."

Caldwell was put in a cell at Monza police station and was held incommunicado for over two hours until a Texaco technician brought the customs paperwork that proved the fuel had been correctly imported. Caldwell emerged from incarceration only to be surprised with the news that Hunt was out of the race.

In the absence of Caldwell, Mayer had gone to the stewards' office with Texaco's analysis in his hand, demanding to know what was going on. The Italians showed him the telex they had received from the CSI in Paris to explain why they had acted as they had. But crucially, they showed him only the reply and not their original message. It was deliberate, underhanded skulduggery, as the scrutineers had always known exactly what the rules were. If they hadn't, they had the very articulate Teddy Mayer on hand to remind them. Waving the CSI telex in his hand, the Italian chief scrutineer confidently sent Mayer away. But he was a dishonest individual, and for once Mayer had not asked the right questions, and lacking much Italian, he had been fobbed off with much gesticulations and mock indignation. Mayer lacked Caldwell's technical knowledge to make an argument and couldn't understand the paperwork in front of him as Caldwell would have been able to do. Enzo Ferrari had been very clever in removing Caldwell from the scene.

Meanwhile, Hunt, also lacking Caldwell's guidance and the requisite technical knowledge about fuel chemistry, was in high dudgeon and prepared to believe that his fuel was illegal. The Italians had done their job so well, they convinced Hunt the fuel was illegal. He was furious with John Goosens, who headed up Texaco's racing effort in Europe. Goosens was adamant that Texaco had done all it could, but Hunt was having none of it.

Hunt was apoplectic, not so much because of his exclusion but by the scrutineers' assertion that he was a cheat. The implication of their actions was that the team had not competed fairly throughout 1976. Hunt, on learning the facts, later recalled: "The implication that we had been cheating annoyed me enormously. Not only had we not been cheating but running a high octane fuel would not help unless we had increased the compression ratio of the engine to match the increased octane rating. You have to modify your engine accordingly, and we certainly hadn't done that—we could have run 150 octane petrol and our engine wouldn't have given an ounce more power. Our fuel was totally legal, and we had gone to a lot of trouble before the race to make sure that it was, but to have that understood by the general public was more than one could ask. So this mud had been thrown, and some of it was inevitably sticking."

Meanwhile, Mayer was continually on the telephone to Paris asking the CSI officials exactly what was going on. Mayer effectively wanted to know why the fuel, which was identical to that used throughout the season, had not been declared illegal before. No one had any answer to that. CSI officials were just as confused as Mayer about what was going on in Italy in its name. The Italians had done a lovely number on everyone. Niki Lauda and Daniele Audetto, who despite his many failings was an honorable man, realized exactly what was happening and were embarrassed but could hardly intervene.

Both Mayer and Hunt finally realized exactly what was going on but were powerless to do anything about it. They appealed the decision straightaway, which proved to be a mistake, as the matter then became sub judice in the eyes of the stewards, and they then refused to discuss it further. As Hunt remembered: "Because we appealed, we couldn't discuss it further, so I was stuffed out of the race. You can't run the grand prix a month later; and by putting me on the back of the grid, the argument could only be sorted out later."

And that was the genius of the Italian tactics. It was one thing appealing a result after the event. But a no-result caused by cheating could not be reversed.

The fuel situation was later clarified and corrected by a statement from the CSI, but by then it was too late; the damage had been done. Hunt laughed when he saw the statement and said, "I was frustrated even more when the CSI put out a press release saying that everything was all right and that the McLaren team hadn't been cheating."

Added to what had happened in Spain and Britain, the Italian press ran huge headlines announcing "McLaren cheats," and the coverage was read around the world. Mayer said, "I think Ferrari began to believe that if James could beat them, we must be cheating; and they began to try and find excuses."

It was later found that the Italian fuel checks had been wrongly interpreted by the stewards, an interpretation that would almost cost James Hunt the world championship. He said at the time, "The rules are very complicated and they are difficult to understand, but they state that you can use the top grade of commercially available fuel in the team's country of origin plus a tolerance of one octane."

But at that moment, the Italians believed that Hunt, Mass, and Watson were out. But then something equally bizarre happened. Before the exclusions, three drivers hadn't qualified for the race: Brett Lunger's works Surtees, Arturo Merzario's Williams, and Otto Stuppacher's private Tyrrell. Gradually, all three drivers withdrew to make way for the disqualified drivers, and much to the chagrin of the Italians, Hunt, Mass, and Watson were back in the race.

But Hunt would still have to start the Italian Grand Prix from the second to last row of the starting grid. Hunt was so angry, he even thought about withdrawing. But realizing it would be a fruitless protest, he focused on trying to get some points—although he knew he could no longer win outright.

But his heart was not in it, and by the 11th lap, he was in 12th place when he came together with Tom Pryce's Shadow and went off the road. His McLaren-Ford went into the sand and got beached, with its rear wheels spinning wildly. The sand traps, which were gradually replacing catch fencing, decelerated cars very effectively and slowed the McLaren so that it stopped just in front of the barrier. Hunt jumped out of his car and walked round, checking for damage. Seeing it was intact, he pushed the car out of the hole dug by the spinning tires. But he was then prevented from getting back in the car by the Italian marshals. For once, the Italians were abiding by the rules; although they didn't please Hunt. But the longer time went on, the less relevant it became.

Hunt said, "They wouldn't let me get back in. They pounced on me. But it wasn't really worth making an issue of it because, firstly, the car was stuck in the sand and, secondly, I was now completely out of the race, even if I could have restarted. It was then hopeless trying to gain points as far as I was concerned."

All this was going on against a backdrop of hissing and booing Italians. It was more like feeding time at a zoo than a motor race, and as he was too far away for their spittle to reach him, they started throwing the contents of their picnic baskets at him. Hunt showed his contempt for them by casually picking up an apple that had hit him and starting to chomp on it. He casually waved back in thanks, incensing the Italians in the stand.

In reality, Hunt was stupefied with frustration and seemed to want a fight with the entire Italian nation as he began his long walk back to the pit lane. During that walk he made up his mind that his accident had been the fault of Tom Pryce, so he decided to have it out with the young Welshman after the race. The blame culture and revenge seeking were a throwback to his public school background. When it surfaced, it exhibited the worst elements of his character. The truth about the accident was that Hunt had become distracted when he went into the corner and had braked far too late, with the inevitable result.

Convinced that Pryce had blocked him, however, Hunt stormed up to him after the race and shouted, "You are a brainless moron," adding in for good measure that he was *absolutely* brainless." Almost immediately afterwards, as he cooled off in the motor home, he knew he had been wrong. He went to find Pryce and to apologize. He said later, "I just made a mistake."

His high emotional state after the race had been made worse by his walk back to the pits. He called them "animals" and explained, "They were spitting and hissing. I wanted to confront them but thought better of it." In the end, Hunt confessed, "I must admit I was quite pleased to get out of there unscathed. The propaganda campaign against me in the Italian press was really quite incredible: a very heavy deal. They really hated me in Italy, to an extent that was quite unbelievable. Anybody would think it was I who had caused Niki's accident."

Meanwhile, Lauda, unaware of all the drama, had enjoyed a steady race and managed to finish fourth. It was the bravest driving performance ever seen in Formula One—before or since. When he took off his helmet after the race, his fireproof balaclava was soaked in blood; his head and face wounds had opened up. The repercussions for the scarring on his face would be enormous. But he had done what he came to do; he had increased his championship lead. Hunt's failure to finish had also been a huge bonus. Lauda's courageous comeback had exceeded all expectations, not least those of his English rival.

Lauda said, "I did what I could. On the last lap, the oil pressure dropped and I took my foot off the gas a bit, as I wanted to finish at all costs. In the circumstances, fourth place was not bad at all for me."

Hunt was full of praise, and any ill feelings toward Lauda from the past were genuinely put aside as the two men became temporary friends again and started speaking every day on the telephone. Hunt said, "To virtually step out of the grave and, six weeks later, to come fourth in a grand prix is a truly amazing achievement." He added, "Niki drove a typical Niki race: well contained within himself and within his new limitations."

The race was won by Ronnie Peterson in the March-Ford. It was the first win by March in almost five years and the first for Peterson since he left Lotus. Regazzoni was second and Jacques Laffite third in his Ligier. The three points Lauda won for finishing fourth in Italy gave him a five-point lead over Hunt, with Lauda on 61 points and Hunt on 56.

When the race was over, Ferrari team manager Daniele Audetto was very embarrassed by what had gone on that day. Audetto may have been overbearing at times, but he was fundamentally an honest man who believed in playing by the rules. He knew his countrymen had not been playing by the rules. He confessed admiration for Hunt, saying that the crowd's hatred had been directed at the McLaren team and not at Hunt personally.

With that off his chest, Audetto then decided to make some bizarre and seemingly unprompted predictions about what would happen in the last three races. He predicted Hunt would win the United States Grand Prix at Watkins Glen, finish second in Canada, and third in Japan. Lauda, he said, would win the Canadian Grand Prix, finish second at the Japanese, and not score at all at Watkins Glen. How he knew all this was beyond anyone's guess, but his predictions were widely reported around the world and taken seriously by many, especially Italian journalists.

Audetto also praised Lauda's teammate, Regazzoni, predicting he would finish third, second, and first in the remaining three races. Again, no one really understood what he meant or how he could make such accurate predictions. But they also received wide publicity in Italian newspapers. But it was all typical Italian false praise, as Enzo Ferrari had already decided to fire Regazzoni and to replace him permanently with Reutemann after Monza.

Audetto's ultimate prophecy was that Lauda would take the championship by one point from Hunt, 76 to 75. But interestingly, Audetto's prediction took no account of the outcome of Ferrari's protest against the British Grand Prix and the mountain that Hunt still had to climb to win.

For Hunt, things could only get better. But first they would have to get much worse.

CHAPTER 24

Hunt Loses British Win

McLaren Mess Up the Hearing

Paris: September 24, 1976

As the hoo-ha at Monza died down, James Hunt made a critical decision not to appear at an appeals court hearing in Paris that would either confirm or cancel his win at the British Grand Prix. The FIA Court of Appeal in Paris was convened to consider an appeal by the Ferrari team as to whether Hunt's McLaren-Ford should have been disqualified from the results of the British Grand Prix. Ferrari had appealed the result, but James Hunt didn't think they had a chance of success. Instead of planning a schedule that included going to the hearing in the three-week gap between Italy and Canada, he embarked on an alternative schedule of his own choosing—one that combined spending money and having a good time. He opted to ignore Paris and leave it all to team boss Teddy Mayer.

Astonishingly, Mayer told Hunt he could handle it. But the truth was that he couldn't.

McLaren was very confident that it would defeat the appeal, and Hunt was simply too lazy to go and was overconfident about the result. As he said, "I didn't see how they could possibly throw us out because it was an open-and-shut case as far as the legalities were concerned." But, he admitted later, "I was a little nervous of the outcome."

Much of the blame for Hunt's absence at the hearing lay at the feet of Teddy Mayer. Mayer was a trained lawyer and must have known how important Hunt's testimony would be, but he still wasn't able to exert his authority over the driver and make him attend. Hunt was the principal witness and, arguably, the only witness who mattered. His nonappearance was inexplicable and fatal to McLaren's defense.

So as soon as the Italian Grand Prix was over, Hunt hotfooted it back to London's Heathrow Airport and hopped straight onto a flight to New York that Sunday night, where he would earn $10,000 competing in an IROC saloon car race the following weekend. He then flew straight to Toronto in Canada and drove in a test session at Mosport, the venue for the Canadian Grand Prix.

When he finally got there, Hunt was looking forward to having a marvelous time in Canada enjoying the country's many attractions. His libido seemed to be at its highest, as he had a different woman on his arm every evening and was even indulging during the day where he could.

There was an embarrassing moment at the Mosport track during testing when he seduced the Mosport circuit manager's wife while her husband was standing nearby. Getting on very well with the woman, Hunt spotted an empty ambulance by the pits with the doors unlocked and invited her inside. Meanwhile, her husband strolled up the McLaren pit to have a word with Alastair Caldwell just as the ambulance was rocking on its shock absorbers in the background. Back at the hotel in the evenings, Hunt was also busy seducing the singer of the band that was entertaining in the hotel lounge.

After an incident-packed few days of testing, Hunt flew back to London and then straight onto Malaga and home. After a few days at home in the sun, he flew back to Toronto on September 23 to get ready for the race at the Mosport track on October 3. It was an extraordinary schedule, motivated by his desire to earn some extra money and spend a few days at home in peace before the end of the summer and the run-in to the championship-deciding races.

But Hunt never should have been in Canada at all. In going so early and not attending the upcoming FIA Court of Appeal in Paris, he made a catastrophic error of judgment that would cost him dear.

On September 26 the FIA hearing got under way in Paris. The issue at stake was simple: Ferrari appealed Hunt's win at the British Grand Prix, arguing he should have been disqualified after the race was restarted. Ferrari was seeking to have the stewards' decision, which had declared Hunt the winner of the race, overturned.

The hearing was in front of a six-member panel of judges composed of FIA delegates from France, Germany, Spain, Brazil, Switzerland, and the United States.

Ferrari's case was presented by its team manager, Daniele Audetto, accompanied by two lawyers. Audetto stated that after the accident at the start of the race, Hunt's car had been abandoned by the driver and was being pushed by the McLaren mechanics while the race was still in progress and was therefore incapable of completing the first lap.

McLaren's defense, presented by Teddy Mayer and a lawyer representing the British Royal Automobile Club, stated that Hunt stopped only when he saw the red flag being displayed and that the car was only pushed after the race had been officially halted. Hunt, they maintained, could and would have completed the lap had he felt it necessary.

Teddy Mayer brought with him to the proceedings a videocassette machine and a recording of the race. The videotape, he thought, substantiated McLaren's claim beyond doubt. Caldwell agreed: "We had clear video evidence of him driving the car; the video was taken to Paris, and a CSS producer swore that this was untouched film."

But without Hunt, much of McLaren's evidence was still all hearsay, and the team effectively had no case. His absence annoyed the six judges immensely; it smacked of arrogance.

In contrast, Ferrari made no such mistake, and there was never any doubt that Niki Lauda would show up to give evidence. Although Lauda had not really been directly involved, he was an eyewitness and he was present to give what evidence he could. His appearance gave Ferrari a tremendous tactical advantage, which it fully exploited.

Mayer couldn't believe it when Lauda made his appearance. Immediately upon seeing Lauda, he realized that McLaren had made a mistake not having Hunt present, and he hoped it would not be fatal—although from that moment, he feared it would be.

Lauda had flown in from Salzburg to Paris for the hearing and arrived at the FIA's headquarters with a blood-soaked bandage on his head. Since his wounds had healed by then, it was thought by many to be pure Italian theatrics to gain the court's sympathy. Lauda's appearance was an emotional moment, and the judges were visibly moved when he entered the room. They were honored that he had taken the time and trouble to come.

They listened carefully to every word he had to say and, astonishingly, appeared to view him as an independent and uninterested witness, so convincing was he.

In top form, Lauda was very persuasive and visibly swayed the judges. Alastair Caldwell recalled: "Niki was the living saint, and the silly old sod who did the deciding decided that it was unfair on poor Niki."

Additionally, Lauda was portrayed very effectively by Ferrari's lawyers as a victim. If Hunt had been there, he might have countered the argument. But he wasn't, so he couldn't.

The hearing took 11 hours, completed in one session, and the next day the secretary of the FIA delivered the verdict. It was simple: Hunt was disqualified from the results of the British Grand Prix and would lose nine points. To make matters worse, Lauda was promoted to winner and gained three points.

All in all, Hunt had effectively lost 12 points. The points score now stood at Lauda 64 and Hunt 47, a 17-point difference. And it was all the English driver's own fault.

Hunt was playing squash in Toronto on the afternoon of Tuesday, September 28, when he heard the result of the appeal. A call from a Canadian journalist got through to the club where he was playing, and he was handed a piece of paper by a club staffer that read: "Call me back and be prepared for bad news."

Hunt knew exactly what that meant. As he said, "News is only good or bad, and it was going to be a black-or-white answer anyway." With that, he effectively knew the result and didn't immediately return the call. Taking his cue from Sir Francis Drake, he decided to finish his game of squash first. As he said, "I wanted to think about it a bit, so I went to the changing rooms and straight down to the court. I'm pretty tough professionally, and it's difficult to move me because I've trained myself to be hard—there's no mileage in letting things upset you. But boy, I couldn't hit that squash ball and I couldn't concentrate on the game at all."

By the time Hunt finished his game, word had traveled around and he had been joined at the squash club by a horde of journalists telling him more about what had happened. He was very upset but still spoke to them. He described the decision as "a very heavy deal."

Hunt was never given the real reason for being thrown out of the results. He said, "They never said why. In appeals prior to this, they had always stated the findings of the court and their reasons for finding it, but in this case all they did was issue a result."

There was only one possible reason in Hunt's mind: the FIA had simply chosen to disbelieve the witnesses, including the clerk of the course and the marshals. Hunt never considered his own absence to have been the reason. He said, "The fact was that my car was running and hadn't retired, and I can't see how anyone can talk about a driver's intentions, because not even I knew then whether I intended to retire or not—it was totally irrelevant." But he had not been there to tell them that, and now, 3,500 miles away, it was too late.

Later, he did admit that when he heard the result, it occurred to him that perhaps he had been wrong not to go to the hearing.

Years later, he tried to rewrite history by saying the hearing took place a week after it did: "I was already in Canada waiting, ready to race. I have to say it was a supreme shock to me to get the news from Paris two days before practice for the Canadian Grand Prix started." But his protestations were undone by Lauda's appearance in Paris at the hearing.

Later Hunt blamed Ferrari for having brought such an unnecessary appeal. Hunt said, "I happened to be the guy who was beating the great Ferrari machine, and they didn't like it. They've done a lot of work to make sure I didn't succeed, starting with the fuel business at Monza and, now, this. Combining this news with the Italian fiasco, I felt really cheated—yes, cheated. Here I was in a position to win the world championship after 10 years of effort, and here I was being politically assassinated, being cheated by events over which I had no control whatsoever. It was downright wrong, and there was just nothing I could do about it."

Afterwards, Teddy Mayer was totally shocked by the result and said, "James won the race fair and square; there was no question about that, there was no question of his car being illegal."

Later Hunt would admit he and the team were somewhat at fault in not preparing for the hearing thoroughly enough: "Quite honestly, neither I nor McLaren took it particularly seriously because there was nothing in the rulebook, no grounds in the rules, that could possibly suggest that I was going to be disqualified or that it was going to be a problem. As a result, I think McLaren and Teddy Mayer didn't set up a proper defense when they went to Paris in September."

Alastair Caldwell summed it all up: "We were never any good at politics at McLaren. We got done."

Meanwhile, Niki Lauda was ecstatic and was quoted widely as being "delighted at the outcome—madly delighted." To journalists who contacted him at his home in Austria, he said it was a "proper thing" that the FIA court had done and that "at last, a positive decision had been taken."

Lauda laid it on thick for the press, and Hunt got very worked up when he read it.

Hunt accepted any television interview offered to him to attack Lauda and Ferrari, and Lauda responded in kind. Hunt said, "We all live in glass houses, and I don't understand the self-righteousness that was shown by Ferrari saying that they never broke rules. It's all right to say those things, but to say them and believe them is something else. To display the sort of self-righteousness that Ferrari did seems to me childish."

Lauda felt that Hunt was overreacting and being malicious: "When I was robbed of the Spanish Grand Prix, James did not say anything to me or tell me that it was a bad decision. So why should I say anything to him about the decision at Brands Hatch? Sure it was a surprise to me; I did not think that the FIA would cancel his Brands Hatch win, but they took the evidence and they decided that it should be canceled. It is very tough luck on James; he drove a very good race that day. But the decision has been made and we must accept it. We must not go on shouting about it in public."

Many years later, Hunt tried to explain why he hadn't gone to Paris. He said the reason was simple: that he didn't want anything negative distracting him from the last two races in North America. He was in a very confident mood and was totally focused on the world championship. He wasn't sure he could beat Lauda for the title, but he believed he would run him close.

As everyone assembled in Canada, Lauda and the whole Ferrari team was exultant about the result of the appeal, and some gloating in the press was inevitable. It stirred up tremendous resentment between Hunt and Lauda, and any notions of friendship or rapprochement apparent after the Italian Grand Prix were long gone. But Hunt was up for the fight with three races to go. He said, "I was all set to give it a go. I was fired up and wanted to drive, and the only place I could be on my own to get on with the job was in the car. So I enjoyed my driving there more than ever because it was such a relief. The rest of it I hated."

CHAPTER 25

Hunt's Faint Chance

Only Winning Would Suffice

Canada: October 1–3, 1976

Perhaps unsurprisingly, Niki Lauda was intensely safety-conscious after his accident, and as soon as he arrived in Canada, he went to war with the organizers of the Canadian Grand Prix, due to be held over the first weekend of October.

The 2.1-mile Mosport circuit is situated in an idyllic and magical lake land surrounded by a wilderness of trees that are beautifully red-brown in the early autumn. But it suffered for being under snow for most of the winter, which caused considerable damage to the circuit, exacerbated by the fact that it was not well maintained.

The state of the track was atrocious and a serious safety hazard. So the stage was set for a nasty confrontation as the teams checked into the Flying Dutchmen Motel near Bowmanville, 45 miles from Toronto. James Hunt described the atmosphere as "tightrope tension," saying, "I eventually got so depressed by the whole scene that I locked myself in my room on the Thursday night and waited for Friday's official practice and the opportunity to get back to the sanity of the cockpit of my car. Once I was in the car, all the aggravation, all the pressure, disappeared and I concentrated on driving. It was beautiful."

The Grand Prix Drivers' Association safety committee, led by Lauda, remonstrated with the organizers over the condition of the track. Finding no satisfaction, a meeting was scheduled to discuss it. When he was asked by Lauda to attend the circuit safety meeting, Hunt apparently shouted at him, reportedly saying, "To hell with safety. All I want to do is race."

It was the last thing Hunt wanted to say to the injured Lauda, but his reaction was the fallout from the British Grand Prix appeal and what had happened at Monza. Lauda understood and remained reasonably philosophical about it: "We have been friends, but James broke the rules in England. If you break the rules, you are out. No argument. Now he shouts at me. This is not right. He should respect me as a driver. We have a job to do. Bad feeling only makes it more difficult."

Hunt didn't attend the official safety committee meeting and made his excuses. His absence severely weakened the drivers' position. The other drivers were furious, and some questioned Hunt's motives. The truth was that there was a real danger of the race being canceled, which was not in Hunt's interests at all. With one less race, he had no chance of winning the championship. Alastair Caldwell probably advised him not to go, but of course Hunt wasn't about to admit that. Drivers always maintain that safety is paramount. But on this occasion, as far as James Hunt was concerned, it wasn't.

His behavior completely disrupted the post-Monza harmony between the two drivers. Much later, Hunt admitted that for tactical reasons he had been keen to inflame the situation rather than cool it down: "I was deliberately trying to make Niki think that I was freaked out by what was happening so he would steer clear of me on the track. It was purely a professional piece of gamesmanship. If you can psych out another driver and make him frightened of you, then he's much easier to pass. I certainly wasn't about to shove him off the track, but I wanted him to think I was in that frame of mind."

Tossing aside their ethics, journalists also began to fuel the anger between the two drivers. Hunt, thinking that Lauda had tried to psyche him out earlier in the year by revealing that he had had the last rites administered to make him think he was out of the title race altogether, retaliated. Realizing he could intimidate Lauda to the point where he would let him pass on the track rather than risk a confrontation that might put both of them out, he added: "I had cultivated the idea with Niki that I was worked up and, without ever saying it, made him think that."

The feud was intense, and everyone knew what was happening. John Hogan, whose Marlboro cigarette brand sponsored both drivers, felt it more than most. He described one incident when he arrived: "I'd just got off the plane in Toronto, and I walked into the huge dining room at Mosport. Niki was sitting over there with the Ferrari guys, and James was sitting over there with the McLaren guys. And I walk in and Niki says, 'Hogan, come sit here.' Then James shouts, 'Hogie, over here.' So I started with McLaren, then moved over to Ferrari." Hogan, who was close to both drivers and could take an objective view, mostly blamed Lauda for the trouble and believed he was guilty of exploiting his injuries to get an advantage. The disputes, he maintained, were not of Hunt's making: "Niki was being a little bit the Austrian brat. Throughout that year, James had had sort of a testy relationship with Niki."

Hunt was walking around the motel like a bear with a sore head. On the following night he got into a furious row with Daniele Audetto in the restaurant. Teddy Mayer stood by while it raged on. It had all started when Audetto, a courteous man, attempted to convey his apologies to Hunt about losing the appeal. Hunt replied with two words: "Get lost." Or at least these were the words reported in the Canadian newspapers. Audetto told him he was only doing his job. The fuse was lit, and Ferrari and McLaren personnel joined in until Hunt got bored and went to bed. He said the next day: "I thought Audetto's apology was slightly gross. He didn't have to apologize because he need not have protested my win at Brands Hatch in the first place. So I explained to him in a rather terse way that I wasn't interested in his apologies."

It was Ferrari's turn to be at a disadvantage, and the following day Audetto got a shock when the Canadian scrutineers told him that the Ferrari gearbox oil cooler was mounted in an illegal position, and it transpired that it had been in this position ever since the Spanish Grand Prix. As soon as it was pointed out, there was no arguing. Audetto could see it was illegal.

Ferrari hadn't been trying to cheat, as there was no performance advantage, but it was a mistake and it had not been spotted until Canada. The team simply had not understood the rulebook properly, nor had eight sets of previous scrutineers.

Audetto was hugely embarrassed, and the team quickly repositioned the coolers. It left Teddy Mayer and Alastair Caldwell with a huge decision to make—whether or not to appeal the results that were clearly achieved with an illegal car. After a great deal of discussion, they decided not to protest. If they had, arguably Ferrari could have been disqualified from every race since Spain.

When all the drama died down, the action on the track began.

Ferrari brought 312T2 chassis numbers 26 and 27 for Lauda and Regazzoni, and chassis number 28, which was brand new, was kept under covers in reserve. The car had been built for Carlos Reutemann, but Lauda had enforced the terms of his contract and Reutemann was out in the cold. Audetto and Enzo Ferrari had wanted to replace Regazzoni with Reutemann, but Lauda had blocked that as well. He just didn't like the man. The new Ferrari engine design was now sorted out, and the power advantage, especially at the lower end, was very noticeable.

As soon as the race weekend got started, most of the differences between the drivers were forgotten. For the first time, it was apparent that Niki Lauda's face was badly damaged by the burns he had suffered in the accident. Hunt was deeply sorry about Lauda's disfigurement, which caused anguish to everybody in the Formula One paddock. Hunt knew life would never be the same for Lauda, and he could not help but confront the thoughts of his own mortality when confronted with Lauda's visible injuries every day. Everyone seemed bothered except Lauda himself. The change in his appearance didn't seem to bother Lauda at all. And if it did, he would never admit it. It did bother him that others were disturbed, but he realized he could do nothing about that and simply got on with his life with the cards that he had been dealt.

McLaren had given up with its new M26 car, and Jochen Mass would not have to drive it again in 1976. Officially Caldwell told people that the team did not want to bring two sets of spares to the flyaway races. The trio of M23s sufficed, and Hunt had to use the spare car when his engine blew on the first day of qualifying. For both days, Hunt was easily the fastest man on the track, and he was never seriously challenged by Lauda or Regazzoni, despite their powerful engines. Qualifying was fought out between Hunt and Ronnie Peterson's resurgent March-Ford. Peterson was now back on top form. But he wasn't strong enough to stop Hunt taking pole position four-tenths of a second clear: a huge margin. Vittorio Brambilla, also in a March-Ford, and Patrick Depailler's Tyrrell-Ford were on the second row. Lauda was only sixth fastest alongside an increasingly in-form Mario Andretti in his Lotus-Ford. No one could explain Lauda's tardiness, but as Regazzoni could only manage 12th, it was assumed the car was not suited to the circuit's characteristics.

For Ferrari it was its worst overall qualifying performance of the year, and Lauda had no chance of winning the race. If Regazzoni had not been so slow, people would have blamed Lauda's injuries. Lauda had a technical explanation of his own: "Cold weather brought out one of Ferrari's weaknesses. When the camber of a wheel changes dramatically as it raises or droops on its suspension, it causes heat in the tires; and the ideal temperature of a racing car tire is a little over 100 degrees centigrade. The cars of most of the teams have suspensions that do a lot of the work, while the play in our cars is almost nil. In consequence, when the days were hot, we had the advantage. But at Mosport, it worked against us."

As had become, for him, depressingly normal, James Hunt made a very poor start to his race and was left behind on the grid by Ronnie Peterson. For eight laps he trailed the Swede before his superior speed got him past. A few laps later, Depailler in the six-wheeled Tyrrell nosed through into second place and moved closer to the McLaren. Hunt scythed through the back markers majestically. As he recalled: "They all gave way to me beautifully." His tactics, intended to intimidate Lauda, had clearly worked on everyone else as well.

The grand prix had been enlivened by the duel between Hunt and Depailler, who was a very strong challenger. But in the closing laps, Depailler began to drop back inexplicably, and there were six seconds between them at the finish as Hunt took the checkered flag to win, with Mario Andretti finishing third.

Niki Lauda, who had had a very poor start, could not even finish in the points and came home a lowly eighth: easily his worst race performance of the year.

He said later, by way of excuse, "A rear suspension component snapped and threw me right back." Teammate Regazzoni beat him in the end to get a single point. Regazzoni could not move over and give Lauda the point, because Carlos Pace's Brabham-Alfa Romeo was between them. Lauda simply could not get past him. Lauda had fought an ill-handling car with a rear suspension problem for the entire race. He had scored no points: a disaster for him.

Afterwards, the Ferrari mechanics discovered that a rear suspension mounting had failed. At the time Lauda said, "About halfway, it started to oversteer very badly. I don't know why."

Patrick Depailler was bemused as he stood on the podium; he believed he could have won the race. But it turned out that petrol fumes had been leaking into his Tyrrell cockpit, leaving Depailler feeling intoxicated in the last few laps. He said he felt as though he had drunk a bottle of whisky. When he removed his helmet, the padded lining was wet with fuel. Second place had become his specialty; he was to finish second five times in 1976.

Hunt admitted that his victory had not been a formality: "Depailler was really giving me a hard time, keeping the pressure on, and if he had got past, he was probably capable of running a bit quicker than I was. But he wasn't quite quick enough to attack me. My main worries in Canada were the back markers trailing the field when we came through to lap them, because you only need to do that wrong once and the guy trailing you is through and gone. The back marker moves the wrong way at the wrong moment, you have to brake and there is a big gap on the other side of the road. So I took great precautions not to let that situation arise. I started playing the back markers against Patrick. I'd cruise, as it were, between groups of back markers because I obviously wasn't going to get away from him, so there was no hurry. Then, when we got near the back markers, I'd put on a real spurt to get as much air between him and me and to give myself a bit of maneuvering room. Soon I was timing my arrival with the back markers so that I was ready to pass them at the right part of the circuit. I was giving it real thought and I was managing to get through better than he was, but you need a bit of luck there as well."

Hunt was ecstatic when he passed the finish line. He had done what he had come to Canada to do. All thoughts of the Brands Hatch disqualification disappointment were banished from his mind. After the race, Hunt and Lauda got together to resolve their differences. Hunt consciously may have been playing up the much-publicized rift between himself and Lauda to his advantage, but there comes a point in any psychological confrontation when it is difficult to isolate the truth from the tactics. Hunt realized that this point had come and that the so-called feud needed to be laid to rest permanently.

Hunt was tired of what had happened in Italy and Canada and wanted a fair fight to the finish in an atmosphere of good sportsmanship. He genuinely didn't want to win in a state of gladiatorial confrontation with Lauda, especially after the Nürburgring accident.

After Canada, with two races to go, the points gap had opened up to eight.

CHAPTER 26

Fate Intervenes in New York

Hunt Victory Takes Championship to the Wire

Watkins Glen: October 8–10, 1976

A week after scoring no points in Canada, Niki Lauda took the short trip to New York fully expecting to wrap up the world championship.

He had scheduled a major facial reconstruction operation for the following week and did not even intend to travel to Japan for the final race of the season—when Carlos Reutemann, who he now accepted would be his new teammate in 1977, would stand in. But those plans were soon to change when fate intervened at Watkins Glen.

Watkins Glen is a small tourist town situated on Seneca Lake in New York State, around 120 miles from the Canadian border. No one would know about it were it not for the race circuit that had hosted the US Grand Prix ever since it was inaugurated in 1961. The focus of the Formula One circus was the intimate Glen Motor Inn hotel. Almost all of the Formula One drivers stayed at the Glen Motor Inn, with the mechanics staying at the nearby Seneca Lodge.

The Franzese family managed the Glen Motor Inn at the time and were familiar with all the Formula One drivers. The Franzeses gave the race a real family feel, and the drivers loved it. So the Glen Motor Inn was an ideal venue for a rapprochement between Niki Lauda and James Hunt. A rapprochement sorely needed after the bitter disputes in Canada that had broken out over Ferrari's Brands Hatch appeal and the safety issues at the Mosport circuit.

In order to talk through their differences, the two men sat down for dinner in a quiet corner of the Glen's dining room, surrounded by the giant picture windows overlooking the lakes. The scene could not have been more tranquil. At any one time, the whole of the Formula One community could be sitting down for a meal in the restaurant. They both realized it would be better if they discussed their differences before things got completely out of hand. Lauda insisted that he had never said the things he'd been quoted as saying after the announcement from Paris. He also said his derogatory remarks about Hunt at Mosport were a case of "flagrant misreporting" by a "vicious journalist."

Hunt also denied the quotes about Lauda that had been attributed to him. He was adamant his anti-Lauda comments had been instances of fabrication and misquotation. After they had talked, the two shook hands and the feud was buried forever. The meal had broken the ice, and the two drivers subsequently spent a lot of time together smoothing over their differences and renewing their friendship, which had been fractured temporarily by the events in Canada.

Hunt said afterwards, "The press was winding up both of us badly, and we got a bit irritated. For a few hours we hated each other, but after we got it sorted out, our good relationship continued."

After that, they arranged to move to adjoining hotel rooms, where they kept their doors open and socialized together as much as possible. At the time, *Fawlty Towers* was Europe's top comedy TV show, so Lauda used to wake Hunt in the morning with practical jokes and hilarious *Fawlty Towers*–type John Cleese impressions.

But others do not remember the relationship being anywhere near so congenial—especially not John Hogan, who was secretly working behind the scenes to get Lauda to leave Ferrari and join McLaren to create a dream team for 1977. Hogan had sensed his chance after Lauda's accident and Reutemann's recruitment to Ferrari. Hunt was all for it, but Hogan says that Lauda balked at the idea of being Hunt's teammate. As he remembered: "James had no problem at all. He said, 'You gotta look at it this way,' thinking about the game again, 'you gotta put the competitors somewhere, so it might as well be in the same car.' But Niki was: 'ooooough.'"

On track, qualifying was mostly uneventful round the 3.3-mile circuit save for the weather, which kept interfering. The first half of Friday was written off by torrential rain, but it cleared up in the afternoon. There was a very nasty incident when the air bottle that was used to pneumatically start the car fell off Hunt's McLaren and was run over by Patrick Depailler and Emerson Fittipaldi's cars. There was major damage to Depailler's Tyrrell-Ford and some damage to Fittipaldi's Copersucar. It was an extremely worrying moment.

Friday afternoon was to prove the only dry period of the two qualifying days, when the fastest times were set.

The weather seemed a minor irritation for Hunt, who, for the eighth time in the season, seized pole position. This time he had Jody Scheckter alongside him in the six-wheel Tyrrell-Ford, which was proving very effective in its debut season. Scheckter was improving race by race. But he had no future with the Tyrrell team after the Zandvoort incident. It was announced he was leaving Tyrrell to drive for Walter Wolf's team. Wolf had paid him $250,000 just as a signing-on fee to persuade him to make the move.

But Scheckter's new turn of speed was not Hunt's problem; his problem was Lauda's performance. He realized that the odds were on Lauda retaining his title and said, "I hadn't given up completely because where there's life, there's hope. I could only knuckle down and go after each race as it came and try to win it. If I couldn't win, I had to finish as high as I could."

Hunt was aided by another indifferent qualifying performance by Lauda. He could only manage fifth, and the critics would have been all over him but for the fact that his teammate Regazzoni was way back in 14th place, beaten even by rookie driver Larry Perkins in the second Brabham-Alfa Romeo. Something had happened to the Ferrari's speed at a crucial point in the season, but no one knew what. Lauda kept insisting it was the cold weather, but this was a concept Mauro Forghieri could not understand.

Saturday's qualifying day was completely written off by torrential rain virtually all day. At one point the circuit was flooded, threatening the race.

During qualifying, Hunt aggravated an inflamed nerve in his left elbow, and the pain became worse overnight. A doctor was called, and he was given painkilling injections before he got in the car.

The race-day weather dawned bright and sunny, with no rain threatened at all. Hunt may have been on pole eight times during 1976, but he had only led one first lap, and this day would prove no exception.

This time Hunt made a good start, but it was still not good enough to prevent Jody Scheckter from taking the lead. And that is how it stayed for many laps, with Hunt in station some three seconds behind Scheckter. Behind them was third-place man, Niki Lauda, five seconds back. But Hunt knew he had to win and started focusing hard on the physical act of driving the car, something which he confessed afterwards he did not do often. It usually all came so naturally to him, and that was often good enough. But that day, it wasn't. His McLaren-Ford was oversteering alarmingly round Watkins Glen's many corners. He remembered he spent 20 laps concentrating and working out a technique to go faster. He called it a "self-administered driving lesson."

He admitted afterwards that the exercise had given him huge personal satisfaction: "I got myself together. It is very important in all walks of life to be able to catch yourself when you're doing something badly and to make sure you improve." That day he was able to do it. Hunt gritted his teeth, gripped the McLaren's steering wheel more firmly, and zeroed his mind in on Scheckter, who stood between him and the victory. Hunt was determined to get him. As he bore down on Scheckter, leaving Lauda farther and farther behind, he planned ahead, looking for likely passing places and opportunities to outmaneuver the leader.

On lap 36 Scheckter was delayed by another car slowing for a tight corner, and Hunt tucked his McLaren in behind the Tyrrell's rear wing. As they accelerated down the straight, Hunt darted out of Scheckter's slipstream and took the lead.

But four laps later, Scheckter got in front again as they were lapping back markers. Hunt was furious with himself, losing the lead after all that work. As he said afterwards: "Jody blasted past me on the straight. I really thought I'd blown it."

Hunt's adrenaline level was high and he pressed on, determined to win. Adrenaline levels were always a Hunt problem. As Alastair Caldwell recalled: "He put a tremendous amount of effort into racing, and he had the biggest adrenalin pump of any racing driver I've ever known. He was so excited in the car before a race that if you sat on the side of it, you'd think the motor was running."

One advantage was that Niki Lauda was trailing around a few places behind. He was not even on for a podium finish, and all the action was at the front between Scheckter and Hunt.

Within a lap, Hunt was again within striking range. For several laps he waited to pounce, testing Scheckter's reaction when he moved to the left and right sides of the track behind him. Finally, with 12 laps to go, Hunt forced his way alongside the Tyrrell coming into a slow corner. The two cars went round the bend side by side, and on the straight, Hunt got past. This time he drove like a demon to put air between him and Scheckter, who he realized was a master at negotiating slower back markers.

Hunt reeled off a succession of quick laps and eventually smashed the record with a lap that was an astonishing one second faster than his pole position. That sort of performance is rarely achieved in Formula One, and spectators that day got a master class in fast driving.

Hunt went across the line eight seconds ahead of Scheckter, and Lauda came in a minute behind in third. He got out of his car, exhausted and soaked in sweat from an outstanding drive. Hunt had closed the gap to within three points of Lauda, and there was one race remaining. On the podium he downed a bottle of cold Miller beer instead of the traditional champagne.

As Hunt stood on the podium, he told journalists, "It was as tough a race as I ever had to drive. For the first 20 laps, I drove like an old grandmother and just couldn't adapt to my car. Both Jody and I were making mistakes in those opening laps. Then I got it together and I chased Jody and passed him fairly easily. I missed my gear change and got a fistful of neutrals, and by the time I had found a gear, Jody was past again. But I was quicker on the straight and hauled him in."

The victory sent the whole circuit wild as they sensed the historic moment and the showdown to come in Japan. Hunt was cheered in the pressroom by the normally cynical journalists. He left the pressroom in company with David Benson, and the two men were mobbed as they walked to the Goodyear hospitality marquee for a champagne-fueled post-race party. Benson recalls: "It was an intoxicating, exciting scene. At that moment, I really believed that James was at last going to win the world championship. I wanted him to win. My emotions told me that he deserved to win."

Between gulping down champagne, Hunt said, "This was the most important race of my life. I simply had to win. Thank God, Jody was second. That puts Niki only three points in front of me for Japan. If I win there and he comes second, I could still win the championship. We would have equal points, but I would have more grand prix wins."

A disappointed Niki Lauda had genuinely expected to clinch the championship at Watkins Glen but was left empty-handed save for the four points earned by coming third. Lauda said of his race: "It was okay at the beginning. After all, I had 44 gallons of fuel aboard, putting a useful extra load on the tires. But the lighter my car became, the more critical the tire adhesion, as they just never reached their optimum working temperature. I had to be pleased that I came third."

After the race he went directly by helicopter from the circuit to the airport for his home in Salzburg. When he got there, he discussed with his surgeons whether he could delay his facial operation. The skin grafts around his brow and cheeks were so tight that he couldn't close his right eye properly, and it was becoming inflamed. An immediate eye operation was deemed necessary, but Lauda insisted it could not happen until after the Japanese Grand Prix. He had no choice but to travel to Tokyo without having had the operation. Fate had marked Niki Lauda's card.

Hunt had no such worries, and later that evening he partied like never before at the Glen Motor Inn. Going back past a construction site, he stole a road worker's yellow hard hat with a flashing orange light on it. In the bar, with the flashing hat perched on his head, a cigarette dangling from his mouth, and a beer in one hand, he cavorted with the many adoring girls in the bar that night. Also at that party were Caldwell, Mayer, and John Hogan. And it was there, in that bar, that these three men conversed, plotted, and came up with a plan that would make James Hunt world champion. The plan would be decisive over the course of the next two weeks.

Before the Canadian Grand Prix, Hunt had only been five points behind Lauda, which meant that he had only to take six points from the final three grand prix races without Lauda scoring to be champion. But his disqualification from Brands Hatch had turned that into a 17-point deficit. Somehow he had now reduced that to three and the score was Lauda 68, Hunt 65, with one race left.

The math was relatively simple: To be champion, Hunt needed to finish first outright, and he would be world champion no matter what Lauda did. If he was second, Lauda needed to be fourth or lower for him to win. If he was third, he needed Lauda to be sixth or lower. If he was fourth or under, then Lauda would be champion.

And Lauda was not the only one with medical problems. The next day, Hunt went for an examination of his left arm. He had been suffering from inflamed ligaments and had had cortisone injections earlier that week. A cure before Tokyo was vital.

A showdown loomed in Japan at the eponymous Mount Fuji track.

CHAPTER 27

Caldwell Outsmarts Audetto

Hunt Drives 12 Vital Laps

Tokyo: October 11–16

B y any measure, Niki Lauda should have been crowned world champion in North America. In that event, Ferrari would have traveled to Japan and entered cars for Carlos Reutemann and Clay Regazzoni. Lauda had no intention of going to Japan, nor would he have needed to.

As it was, Daniele Audetto accepted the situation, and Ferrari packed up its cars as usual, ready to put them on the Formula One charter jumbo jet to Japan. He telephoned Reutemann, who was in Italy, and told him his services would not be required until the following season. Audetto's sense of sangfroid was astonishing, and despite having been thoroughly trounced at Watkins Glen, Ferrari's complacency after the race defied explanation. Audetto made no attempt to change his plans or do anything special to prepare for the last race on which the championship would depend.

By comparison, on the evening of Sunday, October 10, 1976, Teddy Mayer, Alastair Caldwell, and John Hogan sat quietly in the lounge of the Glen Motor Inn contemplating their next move. Caldwell and Hogan were staying in America and flying straight onto Japan, while Mayer was returning to London.

Before that, Mayer, Caldwell, and Hogan joined in a deadly serious conversation. They were in a place in time they had never expected to be.

With one race left, McLaren could win the Formula One world championship. James Hunt's victory that day, and Niki Lauda's fourth place, meant there were only three points between them. It was suddenly all up for grabs in Japan. As usual, Hogan summed up the situation succinctly: "James knew it was just there, and he was kind of standing on Niki's throat."

This was the kind of situation in which Alastair Caldwell was at his best. A tremendously competitive man, he had a brain that worked in a certain way, different from that of most people. Sometimes he was stubborn and hopeless, but other times, brilliant and untouchable. Sometimes it was pure genius, although sometimes his ideas turned out to be the opposite. But when Caldwell was right, he was very right. It was the reason that Bruce McLaren had liked him so much and that Teddy Mayer put up with his idiosyncrasies. Hogan agreed with that analysis and said, "James always said Alastair Caldwell won the championship, not him."

This time Caldwell's plan was brilliant, even if Mayer did not think so. And indeed, what happened next probably dictated the eventual outcome of the championship.

Caldwell had been brooding about the task in hand since the checkered flag had fallen on Hunt's victory, trying to see where McLaren could get an edge on Ferrari. Finally, he turned to Mayer and barked out an order to his boss: "Teddy, go ring Fuji and tell them we want to be testing there on Monday, i.e., tomorrow." He told Mayer, "We'll put the car on a plane, and we'll go to Fuji tomorrow morning."

Mayer stared at Caldwell as if he was crazy; the cars and equipment were already packed and ready to go the airport for the Formula One charter flight. Mayer was also worried about the cost and tried to talk Caldwell out of it. The charter was already paid for, as were the airfares for all the team personnel. What Caldwell proposed would cost at least an additional $15,000, and it wasn't budgeted for. Mayer was also uncertain about track availability, getting the car through customs, and having enough spares on hand in case the car broke down. There was also the little matter that the teams had already agreed beforehand between them, on grounds of cost, not to test in advance at Mount Fuji.

But Caldwell knew that was an informal, nonbinding agreement that he could easily get round.

Thinking the whole scheme foolhardy, Mayer told Caldwell to forget the idea: "No way; we're not going testing in Japan. It isn't feasible." And Mayer thought that was that. He had no notion that Caldwell would defy a direct order from his boss.

But Caldwell was exasperated with Mayer's attitude. He excused himself and got straight on the phone to an airfreight agency in New York. The agency's night desk informed him of a flight leaving for Tokyo late the next day. It was an important flight to catch, as it was the only outbound-scheduled plane that week with big enough cargo doors to take a Formula One car on a pallet. Caldwell said he would ring back to confirm the booking. But in his head, he already had.

As soon as he put down the phone to the freight agency, he rang the Watkins Glen circuit, where his mechanics had just finished the packing. He informed the mechanics of the new plan and told them to pack the spare car separately in a crate with enough tools and kit for a two-day test session. The car would have to be ready to go to the airport on Monday morning. The mechanics got straight down to work. Crucially, they asked Caldwell how many spares they should pack. Remembering Mayer's warnings about cost, Caldwell replied, "the minimum." Caldwell returned to the lounge and mentioned not a word of his phone calls. Mayer was none the wiser.

Back at the circuit, the Ferrari mechanics watched the McLaren men unpack a car and immediately guessed what was going on. Chief mechanic Ermanno Cuoghi telephoned Daniele Audetto back at the hotel and told him. Audetto immediately put in a call to the Ferrari factory in Maranello for permission to do the same. If Caldwell was testing, he was going to test as well. But there lay the crucial difference in the two men's characters. Unlike Caldwell, Audetto wasn't willing to take responsibility for the extra cost on his own head.

Meanwhile, Alastair Caldwell dropped Teddy Mayer at the local heliport on his way to New York's JFK airport to catch his plane back to London that night. On the journey, Mayer thought Caldwell too chirpy, and he thought he smelled a rat. His last words to him over the clatter of the helicopter blades were "Don't send that car to Japan; it's a waste of time and money."As the helicopter took off for New York, Caldwell shouted out, "Well, stuff you."

Mayer's comments simply galvanized Caldwell and made him even more determined to do it. As soon as he returned to the hotel, he rang the shipping agent and told him the crate would be ready first thing in the morning. The agency was keen to help out the famous racing driver James Hunt anyway it could and was only too pleased to send a truck over to Watkins Glen from New York to pick it up.

While all this was going on, Ermanno Cuoghi had also telephoned the same shipping agency to ask if Ferrari could get a car on the flight as well. The shippers answered that a truck was already arranged to pick up the McLaren and that the Ferrari crate could go on as well. But Cuoghi, like Audetto, didn't have the nerve to authorize the cost himself. Cuoghi sought out Audetto and told him what he proposed. But Audetto told him he must first get permission from Enzo Ferrari to spend the $15,000. When Audetto finally spoke to Maranello, they promised to get authority from Enzo. But Enzo Ferrari couldn't be contacted until Monday morning, with the time difference giving them just enough time to meet the truck and load the car.

Without thinking, the shipping agency then telephoned Caldwell at the Glen Motor Inn and told him the Ferrari would be on the same flight but that they were waiting for authorization from Italy.

On Monday morning, Enzo Ferrari gave his blessing straightaway, and his secretary called the track to let Audetto know he could send the car. But strangely, she couldn't get through to him.

But there was nothing strange about it. By then, back at the circuit, the wily Caldwell had noticed the to-ing and fro-ing from the pit lane telephone, and understanding just enough Italian, he had worked out what was happening and resolved to try and intercept the call in order to stall Ferrari. He knew if Audetto and Cuoghi couldn't get permission to spend the money, they wouldn't risk sending the cars.

There was only one telephone in the pit lane at the time, and it was right next to McLaren's garage. Cuoghi told the security guard, who was stationed near the phone and generally answered it, that Ferrari was expecting a call and asked him to come find him when it arrived. Caldwell, overhearing this, went over and told the unsuspecting guard to shout for him first if there were any calls, as he too was expecting one.

Caldwell recalled the story to writer Christopher Hilton many years later: "He'd get a call and shout: 'Hey Alastair, telephone.' I'd go over and say, 'Hello.' The Italian voice said, 'This is Italy, this is Ferrari; we wish to talk to our team manager.' I said, 'Hang on a minute, we'll see if we can find him.'"

Caldwell could see Audetto and Cuoghi in the Italian pit, but instead of calling him over to take the call, he waited a few minutes and then picked up the phone again and said, "No, we can't find him; he's playing golf." The Italian voice said, "Can you tell us where?" to which he replied, "Watkins Glen Golf Course. We'll get you the number."

Having provided the number for the golf course, Caldwell put down the phone. Ten minutes later, the phone rang again. The same routine followed, with the security guard handing Caldwell the telephone. The voice said, "This is Italy, this is Ferrari; we can't find our team manager at the golf course." Caldwell replied, "Perhaps he's gone to the Seneca Lodge hotel. We'll get you the number." It went on in a similar vein for the entire morning, and Caldwell managed to prevent people from the Ferrari factory in Maranello from ever speaking to Audetto. Audetto could only assume that they had had difficulty in locating Enzo to get authorization. It was no surprise, as he was an old man and often slept late. So when the shipper's truck arrived, only the McLaren was loaded onto it. Caldwell, Hunt, and two mechanics followed on a flight to Tokyo the next morning.

When Audetto finally spoke to Maranello, he realized immediately what Caldwell must have done, but by then it was too late. Ferrari's cars had already been loaded onto the charter flight truck and had left for the airport.

However, when Caldwell got to Japan, he quickly realized that he may have been too clever for his own good. Initially, it did occur to Caldwell that perhaps Mayer had been right about what a waste of time it was. He spent a very frustrating week trying to get the car out of Japanese customs. The customs service in Japan was notoriously difficult, and it had a particularly difficult import policy that was carried out with the utmost rigor. This became a problem because the CSI regulations were very clear—that teams were not allowed to test at a circuit in the same week as the race. Caldwell remembers: "Because you weren't allowed to test on the week of the race, we had to do it all by the Saturday."

In the end, the car was released on Friday afternoon and taken straight over to the Mount Fuji circuit. But after less than a dozen laps, the gearbox seized up. It had been assembled incorrectly in England, and there was no spare gearbox in the crate. But those completed laps proved incredibly important, as Hunt learned the track and acclimatized himself to Japan. After the car failed, Hunt donned his running gear and ran round the track a few times; noting all the corners and circuit characteristics. It was the first time the Mount Fuji track had hosted the Japanese Grand Prix, and it would now work to Hunt's advantage.

CHAPTER 28

Hedonism at the Hilton

On a High and a Low

Tokyo: October 17–21

T he intensity and closeness of the battle for the world championship between James Hunt and Niki Lauda had made front-page news all over the world and propelled Formula One into the global spotlight. Because of them, Formula One was now one of the top sports in the world, and every major country decided to broadcast the Japanese Grand Prix live. Formula One had never before received such exposure, and it was to mark a big sea change in attitudes toward the sport.

In the process, James Hunt had also become a global celebrity and was now more famous than any previous Formula One world champion. Hunt enjoyed pop star status globally. The spin-offs were huge. From having had virtually zero interest in Formula One, the world's major broadcasting companies were now cajoling Bernie Ecclestone to grant them broadcast rights for the Japanese Grand Prix in their respective countries. In the end, Ecclestone sold the broadcast rights to virtually every territory, and it was the first time he had experienced any real demand. Up until then, Ecclestone had not even been able to give the rights away gratis. What's more, the TV companies were opening negotiations to take on Formula One for a longer-term basis, and it was all down to James Hunt and Niki Lauda.

The TV companies had 14 days to prepare for the showdown, and all the satellites that transmitted TV pictures were quickly booked up. And so too were all the airline seats to Tokyo.

But there was a downside for the man at the center of it all. Suddenly James Hunt became bothered by all the attention he was getting. Overnight, it seemed everyone wanted a piece of him, and it spooked him. All the pressure was on him, as Niki Lauda was now virtually a recluse as a result of his facial injuries. Hunt found it all rather overwhelming, and his new fame did not rest easily on his shoulders.

Uncomfortable with the attention, Hunt wondered whether it was going to his head. As he said, he was worried he might start believing his own press: "People spend a lot of time telling you how clever you are, and it's very easy to believe. I've seen too many people become victims of such flattery and start taking themselves too seriously. That's when they destroy themselves and their personalities."

In truth, things became so extreme in Japan that, for the first time, Hunt found he was not enjoying his racing. As he said, "I try to be myself, but I worry that I've lost the ability to enjoy life. I'm a tax exile, but England is where my heart is and where my friends are. And everywhere, the demands on my time are so great that already my private life is shot to hell, and I feel the loss of close friends. The main problem in this business is that you lose your individuality. Whatever you do or say is watched. You are used as evidence against yourself." There were signs of paranoia setting in, but there is no question it was a difficult time.

Luckily, Hunt found his oasis just in time. The McLaren team was booked into the luxurious Tokyo Hilton in downtown Tokyo. Japanese hotels were then the very best in the world. The rooms were loaded with gadgetry unknown in the West and the decor was minimalist. As soon as he arrived in Tokyo, he checked in and found the Hilton was a giant playground for someone like himself. Once in the confines of the hotel, he was unmolested, and so he set out to have a good time in the few days before the race. With his privacy guarded by the hotel staff, he tried to distract himself by stepping up his physical fitness routine to new levels. He was constantly in the Hilton's state-of-the-art gym: running, swimming, and playing squash every day. In the evening he was flexing his mental skills by playing backgammon with anyone who was around, and he won over $1,000 that week.

But the hotel's headwaiter blanched when Hunt wanted to play backgammon in the main restaurant during dinner. He had already made an exception and let the famous racing driver into the restaurant with no shoes on. When the backgammon board appeared, he told Hunt the restaurant was not a "playhouse." Hunt reportedly responded, "The whole world is a playhouse" and carried on playing. The headwaiter was overruled by the hotel's manager, anxious to do anything to please the eccentric famous young Englishman who was spending (Teddy Mayer's) money like water.

Then Hunt really got lucky. He discovered that British Airways, then called the British Overseas Airways Corporation (BOAC), used the hotel for its flight crew layovers and that a new batch of stewardesses were arriving fresh every day. He couldn't believe his luck and sought out their timetables for flights. He got to know exactly when they would arrive and began greeting the arriving stewardesses in the hotel lobby each morning. He would tell them his room number and invite them to a party that night, to which they would all dutifully turn up. Hunt particularly enjoyed these sex sessions, and many of the stewardesses were up for it, with Hunt bedding as many as four of them every night. He thought that very novel. The girls were generally staying for one night, as they rested up and caught flights out the following day. At night it was just sexual mayhem, compliments of BOAC. It was the perfect situation, as the girls were straight in-an-out with no repercussions, and any potential problems took care of themselves.

Also staying in the hotel was another world-class playboy named Barry Sheene, the motorcycle world champion. Hunt and Sheene had become good friends, and Sheene had traveled to Japan to give Hunt moral support. He also came without his girlfriend, the model Stephanie McLean, whom he would later marry.

McLean was a stunning woman and *Penthouse* Pet of the Year in 1971. But that didn't stop Sheene partying with the same fervor as Hunt and sharing the stewardesses with him. The then 27-year-old motor-cycle racer regarded the trip as his last fling before getting married to Stephanie. Sheene admitted: "We were both sportsmen, and we drank and smoked and chased women, went to places you shouldn't go, and did things you shouldn't do." Hunt was also, by then, officially going out with Jane Birbeck and in some ways also regarded it as his last fling.

Sheene remembered that Hunt was never out of his T-shirt and shorts, even at formal occasions: "I loved going somewhere with James, because he always made me look well dressed." In turn, Hunt took to calling Sheene "Mr. Sheen" after the spray-on furniture polish popular in England and chortled merrily every time he did. Sheene was not particu-larly amused, especially when the stewardesses he was wooing also began addressing him as such.

By contrast with Hunt's early arrival, Niki Lauda arrived in Tokyo at the last possible moment. After Watkins Glen he had flown straight home to Austria, and he rested up at home in Salzburg as long as he could, mainly to rest his eyes, which he knew would cause him problems in the race. Lauda was not interested in girls, nor was he interested in the casual sex that was so readily available around the circuits. In direct con-trast to Hunt, he was enjoying married life with his wife, Marlene. She had adapted magnificently to his injuries and greatly assisted his recovery.

At the last minute, Marlene decided to accompany Lauda to Tokyo. She realized her husband was in no shape for the task in hand, and she resolved to give him all the support he needed. It was not a happy time for him.

As soon as they checked into his hotel room, Lauda was feeling rather down and depressed. He really did not want to be in Tokyo and longed to be home in Austria. Constantly in the back of his mind was the fact that he should not have been there at all. He had been absolutely sure he would win the championship in Watkins Glen and then be able to recu-perate at home from his much-needed eye operation.

In truth, the euphoria of his comeback had worn off, and he admitted the physical and mental trauma of Nürburgring was suddenly getting to him. Lauda was clearly tired and jet-lagged. Hunt's two weeks in Japan, on the other hand, meant that he was totally acclimatized.

Lauda rued the day he had missed his chance to have the corrective operation on his eyes. It was a legacy of the accident in which both his eyelids had been burned away. He had sought the advice of six different specialist eye surgeons on how best to proceed. Eventually, a Swiss surgeon had taken skin from behind Lauda's ears to graft on as new eyelids. But they weren't perfect, and the right eye in particular was a problem. The skin grafts were so tight he could hardly close his right eye. His doctors advised him not to race in Japan, telling him he needed an urgent operation on his right eye and that it would close properly only after further skin grafts. He was reluctant to bring the problem with his eyes to anyone's attention lest he should fail a medical inspection and be stopped from racing altogether.

Lauda was desperately worried by the weather forecast and knew the Fuji weekend would be stressful and inevitably full of drama. But even he had no idea just how stressful and dramatic it would turn out to be. He had heard that Hunt had been testing at Mount Fuji the week before and knew what a huge advantage this would be when qualifying began. Lauda constantly tried to play the situation down and told journalists who pestered him: "Of course I want to win the championship, but you must remember the Japanese Grand Prix is not the biggest battle I have had this year: That was the fight for my life after the accident. I'm just very happy to be alive and still racing."

Far from being the favorite to win the world championship, Lauda felt like the underdog.

CHAPTER 29

Showdown in Japan

One Point Becomes the Difference

Mount Fuji: October 22–24

T he 12,389-foot Mount Fuji is a volcano that last erupted in 1707. On a clear day, Japan's tallest mountain and its snowcapped peaks are easily visible from many of the high-rise Tokyo hotel bedrooms. The 2.7-mile Mount Fuji circuit, which was built in its shadow, is situated in the Shizuoka Prefecture, 60 miles west of Tokyo and an hour and a half, by car from the Japanese capital.

The circuit was built in the early 1960s, originally to host Nascar racing, and to that it owed its very long main straight, measuring 1.5 kilometers (0.93 mile). The long straight dictated the design and meant the circuit was devoid of any character and was never particularly challenging to drivers.

As a result of Alastair Caldwell's efforts, James Hunt was the first man to drive a Formula One car on the circuit. Hunt didn't share the general view and found that he liked it straightaway and that it suited his style.

So it was a confident James Hunt who drove into the circuit on the first day of qualifying, and he couldn't help but reflect on what an extraordinary season it had been. He and Niki Lauda had dominated the season and won 11 of the 15 grand prix races held so far. But this was the showdown, where two hours would decide the outcome of the 1976 Formula One world championship. Winning and becoming world champion obviously meant far more to Hunt than it did to Lauda. Lauda had already done it once and tasted success. It was different for Hunt, who had fought his way from relative obscurity in just a few short years. From being over 50 points behind, he had fought back and become the man of the moment in Formula One: the man who would take Niki Lauda down to the wire in the battle for the title. The Austrian had overcome the horrific injuries he had sustained in the Nürburgring accident, had heroically returned to racing, scored points, and was now hanging on to his lead in the world championship.

Now it had come down to the wire, and although Lauda held the mathematical advantage, either of them could be world champion on Sunday night.

But as Niki Lauda knew, the result would be more dictated by their cars and their teams than by the drivers. Lauda now knew that his Ferrari was hopeless in colder weather conditions. The last three races of the year were held in cool conditions, and the weakness of the Ferrari 312T2 had only just become apparent. Weather forecasts indicated the Japanese Grand Prix track conditions would not be good.

However, if the weather stayed fine, Lauda believed he would do well. As he said, "It was a track particularly suited to the Ferrari. The practice laps were also encouraging."

Aside from his car, Lauda had also realized that McLaren's management team, consisting of Teddy Mayer and Alastair Caldwell, was vastly superior to his own combination of Enzo Ferrari and Daniele Audetto. Lauda had no regard for either of his own managers. Although Lauda didn't particularly like Alastair Caldwell personally, he knew how effective he could be when the chips were down. That weekend, Lauda wished that Caldwell was on Ferrari's team and not McLaren's. Caldwell was determined to win and thought about nothing else. As far as he was concerned, the contest with Ferrari was a battle with no rules. His attitude was completely different from that of Audetto, who seemingly treated Mount Fuji just like he would any other race. But Caldwell knew this was the battle of his life, and there was a world of difference in the two men's attitudes toward what had to be done.

As usual, Lauda had read the situation correctly, and Caldwell struck two early blows: the first by arranging private testing and the second by a clever trick he pulled even before qualifying had begun. Caldwell believed he could outsmart Ferrari for a second time, and he decided to start spreading disinformation about McLaren's race tactics. He was the only team manager who had seen the track under racing conditions, and he knew people would believe what he said. He told some journalists that he thought the tarmac surface was brittle and that it could break up when the cars took to the track on Friday. In various discussions, he laid it on really thick. Hunt also joined in and misled even his old friends among the journalists, including David Benson, to whom he said, "I went just seven laps here, and even on a wet day, parts of the track started to break up. It could prove to be a real nightmare on Sunday."

Benson and his colleagues spread the news around, and seeing the worried faces, Caldwell instructed the McLaren mechanics to make up dummy metal gauge screens for all the air intakes on the team's spare car. Caldwell then had all the brake ducts, radiators, and air intakes covered by these screens, and a tarpaulin was placed over the car as it was held under close security by guards on shift both day and night. All this activity interested Audetto and particularly intrigued Lauda when he arrived in the McLaren pit garage to greet Hunt. But Lauda's pit visit was no accident. He had been sent down by Audetto to find out what he could, and Caldwell made sure he was successful.

When he saw Lauda in the McLaren pit on Friday morning, Caldwell casually slipped off the covers, pretending he hadn't noticed the Austrian. When Lauda saw what they had done, he also pretended not to notice but immediately rushed back to the Ferrari pit with the news. Audetto immediately instigated a crash program to do the same for all three Ferraris in the garage. Friday morning was entirely taken up with the modifications, and every open orifice on the three Ferraris was covered up with fine mesh grilles.

Just before qualifying, Caldwell removed all the screens on the spare McLaren and took the covers off, prominently displaying it in the pits. Immediately Lauda and Audetto realized they had been fooled. But the damage was done; Audetto had wasted a lot of his team's valuable preparation time reacting to a load of concocted nonsense.

The two qualifying days were entirely uneventful, with neither Ferrari nor McLaren dominating. Lotus proved to be the most-improved team of the year, with Mario Andretti taking pole and Hunt managing second-fastest time alongside the American. Lauda was third, and the two main protagonists were very close, separated by only 0.28 second. The qualifying sessions were exciting as the three men battled for supremacy. Andretti achieved his time by flattening the rear wing and making the car as slippery as possible. It worked.

Hunt had all sorts of varying problems with tires and understeer, but the McLaren was fundamentally suited to the Fuji circuit, so the problems were all relative. Surprisingly Lauda seemed to have the same problems as Hunt, saying, "Fight oversteer, change tires, fight understeer—the more laps, the more understeer—so I stop." Lauda asked for an engine change prior to the race, saying his engine was tired. He also admitted that he was very tired himself, and he was undoubtedly feeling the strain. Mentally, Lauda was well below par. To one journalist he confessed himself to be "tired; tired and confused." It was an extraordinary admission for a racing driver to make.

John Watson's Penske-Ford was next to Lauda on the second row. Jody Scheckter's Tyrrell-Ford was fifth, and Carlos Pace was sixth. It was one of his best showings of the year, in what had been an otherwise disastrous 1976 for the Brabham team with its thirsty Alfa Romeo engine. Clay Regazzoni was seventh in what would be his last race for Ferrari.

There was a brief row between all the teams over tires when the rest of the grid realized that Hunt and Lauda had been given priority and extra-sticky tires. But it blew over after a Goodyear spokesman said, "I've got to give my tires to the men I think are going to get the job done for me. It's as simple as that."

There was also drama late on Saturday when Alastair Caldwell's rumormongering became a self-fulfilling prophecy as the track did start to break up in places. Large chunks of the 15-centimeter-wide bordering strip also began to come loose. Lauda described the track as being "as worn out as the average German autobahn." Audetto was probably cursing his mechanics for throwing all the metal gauge away. The wily Caldwell of course had kept his and wondered whether to reinstall it back on Hunt's car. In the end, the problem was found to be on just one particular part of the track, and the organizers sorted it out by calling in motorway experts who worked all night to fix it.

Daniele Audetto had been seething all weekend about Caldwell's tricky behavior, and he put in an official request for practice periods to be extended on Saturday. The reason he stated for it was that Hunt's pre-race testing had been unfair, and the other teams needed more time to compensate for it. Audetto said, "It is manifestly unfair that Hunt came to test last week. In Mosport we made an agreement that no one comes to Japan for testing before, but McLaren broke the agreement." The organizers turned him down, unaware of any agreement.

Having Mario Andretti on pole was good for Ferrari. Andretti, who was half Italian, felt the need to tell journalists that—despite his origins—he was neutral and would do nothing to influence the outcome of the race either way. But he also pointed out: "Hunt's got everything to lose. You don't have to be a mathematician to work it out. Lauda just has to beat Hunt, but Hunt's got to beat him—and all the rest of us. He's got to win." But Andretti's comments were the least of Hunt's problems. The poor weather forecast for Sunday was becoming one of his primary concerns.

Up until then, the weather had been relatively good and the only drama had been caused by the sheer number of journalists—print and broadcast—demanding interviews. Such was the interest in the Hunt-Lauda showdown that the media contingent was nearly eight times the normal number. Nearly 1,000 media personnel crowded into Mount Fuji, and everyone wanted to talk to Lauda and Hunt. They weren't interested in any of the other drivers.

As predicted, race day brought dramatically different weather. It had been raining all night. As the drivers looked out of their hotel bedroom windows in Tokyo, it was hard to imagine a worse storm. The weather had closed in, and Mount Fuji was completely obscured by low clouds. The whole of the surrounding countryside was shrouded in thick drifting fog.

Niki Lauda immediately knew his car would perform badly in the prevailing weather conditions and that nature had handed James Hunt a big advantage.

The organizers responded by hiring dozens of laborers, whom they kitted out with cagoules (lightweight hooded, weatherproof jackets) and wide brooms. These men started sweeping water off the track all around its length. As the fog rolled in, no one could see the circuit sweepers in their gray-colored cagoules.

In the morning warm-up session, several cars crashed and one aquaplaned off the main straight. When Lauda took out his car, he knew he was in deep trouble. Not only was his car useless in the conditions, he was very worried about his eyes in the wet conditions and his reduced visibility. He said, "Rivers course down across the circuit. Doing no more than 20 miles per hour in a warm-up lap, you are simply flushed away at corners because the tires cannot cope with that volume of water." For him the rain was an absolute disaster, and he knew it would probably cost him the world championship. He said, "In the wet you have to call on additional reserves of motivation and endurance. I have no such reserves. I am finished. The rain has totally destroyed me."

But there was still a chance that the race would be canceled or postponed to the following day and to better weather conditions. Hunt was a member of the drivers' safety committee with Lauda, and the two now joined forces to tell the organizers that there couldn't be a Japanese Grand Prix, as it was far too dangerous for the drivers. With the exception of Brambilla and Regazzoni, all the drivers voted against racing.

But Hunt's attitude incensed Alastair Caldwell. He was absolutely adamant that Hunt drive, saying to him, "James, don't be an idiot. You can't win the championship unless there is a race." James simply responded by saying that safety came first and that he and Lauda would not race. Jochen Mass agreed with Hunt.

Hunt had become so friendly with Lauda after Canada that he was now in his camp where safety was concerned. In fact, Hunt was so adamant he would not race in the conditions that he said, "I would rather give Niki the title than race in these conditions."

The team managers usually took little notice of the drivers, but this time they were worried. In normal circumstances, as the weather was so bad, the race almost certainly would have been abandoned. But these were not normal circumstances. The organizers had spent over $1 million to stage the event and would have to refund the spectators who had paid high ticket prices. The circuit was full of television crews from all over the world who had booked expensive satellite time to broadcast the race live. From a financial point of view, there had to be a race. There were nearly 80,000 people rammed into the circuit, and the world championship had to be decided. There had never been so much pressure to hold a sporting event to schedule.

As the day wore on, however, the race was not canceled, so Hunt told Lauda they should try to have the race postponed. However, postponement didn't appear to be an option the organizers were willing to entertain. Slowly the drivers' moods began to change, and Ronnie Peterson, Tom Pryce, Vittorio Brambilla, Clay Regazzoni, Alan Jones, and Hans Stuck all fancied their chances on a wet track and decided they should get on with it. When Hunt heard this, he knew he was fighting a lost cause; once a few drivers lined up on the grid, others would surely follow—especially as their team managers were threatening to fire them if they didn't race.

Meanwhile, with the race still in doubt, Hunt was behaving very bizarrely. At one point he came out, jumped over the pit lane counter, dropped his overalls to his ankles, and proceeded to urinate in full view of the crowds in the grandstand. The spectators, many of whom had high-powered binoculars trained on him, applauded him after he finished. He waved back.

As the Formula One cars remained motionless, covered in tarpaulins in front of the pits, the team managers huddled with organizers and race officials in the first floor of the race control tower. It was plain to everyone that it was too dangerous to race. The time scheduled for the race start came and went. The pressure from the television crews was relentless.

The pressure on organizers was immense. They sought the opinions of both Hunt and Lauda, asking them if they wanted to race. Lauda didn't want to race. Hunt was now ambivalent, although he still agreed with Lauda. Hunt had decided to defer to Lauda and told him that he personally felt they should wait and race the next day. But he told Lauda he would participate if the race was held, saying, "Everyone was still arguing and expressing their point of view. Mine was to not race, to have it another day or something like that. But you get a few weak people to break the strike and then everybody's at it."

After further discussions, Hunt changed his mind again and told Alastair Caldwell that he and Lauda were withdrawing from the race, whatever decision the organizers made.

Meanwhile, Bernie Ecclestone was frantic. He had sold the broadcast rights for large sums of money, and if there was no race, he faced having to give it all back. He was not sure where he stood if the race was postponed to Monday.

The grandstands, which ran the whole length of the main Fuji straight, were packed with fans sitting silently beneath a sea of umbrellas. The crowd sat motionless and in absolute quiet, a perfect demonstration of Japanese reserve. There was none of the Brands Hatch mayhem; it was a different world.

Caldwell thought them too quiet and, remembering what had happened at Brands Hatch, decided to get the crowd agitated. He got one of the McLaren mechanics, Lance Gibbs, to stand and blow his whistle to get them roused. Caldwell knew that most of the Japanese carried whistles. The gesture worked, and they all brought out their whistles and started blowing to put pressure on the organizers. With Gibbs's encouragement, they also started shouting.

As the crowd became increasingly roused, the organizers became more and more nervous. Bernie Ecclestone also frightened the organizers by telling them they could have a riot on their hands if there was no race. Ecclestone, by now frantic with worry, told them, "You've got to hold the race. You'll have a riot. They'll tear down the stands."

Caldwell believed that the fans and their increasing agitation, admittedly stirred up by him, was a strong factor in eventually getting the race started.

Lauda remembered: "We all refused to drive in the prevailing conditions. We sat in the race officials' trailer and told him 'no go.' At that point the organizers had decided there would be no race. But they were being stalled from making an announcement by Bernie Ecclestone and others."

At four o'clock in Fuji, it started to get really dark. Ecclestone told them, "The race must start."

Caldwell had noticed Lauda's demeanor and guessed there might be a problem with his eyes in the wet. He knew it was now or never, and if the race was canceled or abandoned, then McLaren might lose the title race by default. Caldwell literally grabbed Hunt by his overall lapels and told him that if the race was on, he would drive. A shocked Hunt agreed. Lauda was now in a difficult position, saying, "It was barely credible as it was now raining harder than ever."

The race should have started an hour and a half earlier, and in another two or three hours, the Mount Fuji circuit would be in darkness. Finally a decision was made and announced over the loudspeakers; the Japanese Grand Prix would begin in five minutes. Vittorio Brambilla led the drivers out to their cars.

But James Hunt was missing. And at the precise moment the start was confirmed, he was elsewhere according to Patrick Head, then technical director of the Walter Wolf racing team. Head had accidentally walked into a pit garage that was empty—but not quite empty. He was surprised to find Hunt inside, with his racing overalls down around his ankles and a young Japanese girl kneeling in front of him with his penis in her mouth. Hunt laughed when he saw him, but Head hemmed and hawed and quickly left in a daze, not quite believing what he had seen. He was clearly disturbed by having witnessed such antics from a leading participant so near to the start of an important race. When Head recounted the story at dinner later in Tokyo, he found that no one was shocked at the story and said they had seen him do far worse before a race.

When Hunt emerged from the garage, he rushed to get into his car. Lauda, Emerson Fittipaldi, and Carlos Pace were all determined not to race and would do just a few laps to please their team owners. Lauda said,

"We went to the start so that our respective teams could pick up their starting money, but then we would pack it in because nothing changed. Everything was just as dangerous as before, and the fact that it was getting dark could hardly help matters."

The drivers went out and did some exploratory laps and then came back in to vote again. Another drivers' meeting voted by a substantial majority that the circuit was too dangerous, but the organizers overruled them and decided to hold their motor race. But the new worry was the light and the deteriorating visibility.

They opened the pits, and the cars trickled out one by one to take up their positions on the grid. Hunt again told Caldwell that he wasn't driving, and, again, Caldwell told him he was. Hunt said to Caldwell, "Alastair, fuck this, I'm getting out." Caldwell retorted, "Get out of that car and I'll break your fucking neck." John Hogan witnessed this and remembers: "James replied, 'Oh, all right.' And that was it." But Caldwell wasn't completely reckless and did recognize the dangers. He told Hunt that if he wasn't happy after the warm-up lap, he could come into the pits and retire without consequences, but he warned him that his championship bid would be over.

So the race officials took the decision away from the drivers, and the showdown in Japan finally got under way. Niki Lauda would start the race and see how conditions were. He said, "At the start, the feeling was absolutely unbearable. I was sitting there, panic-stricken, rain lashing down, seeing nothing, just hunched down in the cockpit, shoulders tense, waiting for someone to run into me."

In the gloom, the cars were pushed out to the starting grid. Lance Gibbs drilled holes in the visor of Hunt's helmet to stop it fogging. He placed down a plank of wood on the tarmac so Hunt could walk to his car with dry shoes.

Once Hunt was in the cockpit, it felt damp, and he wiped water off his steering wheel. There was a warm-up lap, and straightaway Lauda had a fright as John Watson's Penske-Ford car span out of control right alongside Lauda and tobogganed off into the grass runoff area, just missing ramming Lauda's Ferrari.

Hunt started as favorite to win the race as the in-form driver with a high grid position. From the start he went straight into the lead and, with a clear track in front of him, sped away easily. Hunt had made the best start of his life, and his McLaren's heavy spray covered everyone in his wake. The other drivers all had to contend with spray and fell farther back. As only he could see where he was going and the other 24 drivers were navigating blind, Hunt sought to maximize the advantage he had earned.

Lauda was losing positions on every lap and was clearly in some sort of trouble. As Caldwell had suspected, his eyes were not up to it. There was so much standing water on the track that Lauda could hardly control his Ferrari; he simply couldn't see through his damaged eyelids. He couldn't have continued even if he had wanted to. He said, "Everybody was skating and spinning; it was crazy. Looking at it this way, it seemed only sensible to drive into the pits and give up."

After two laps, he stopped. He had been unable to see and couldn't blink his eyes, which ruined his focus. It was too dangerous to continue. As he pulled to a halt, his four mechanics shielded the cockpit and he told them he had decided to retire from the race. Cuoghi said they could blame engine failure, but Lauda wanted none of it, and he'd tell the truth to whoever asked—but of course not the whole truth. Without making excuses or offering explanations, as he didn't want the trouble with his eyes to stop him from racing in the future, Lauda said, "The rain has totally destroyed me." He added, "I regard the men who allowed the race in Japan to proceed as absolute lunatics."

The truth was that he should never have come back that season. His right eye was very poor and he was mentally unfit to compete, but he would never admit he was unable to cope with the conditions that prevailed at the start of the race. Later, as the track dried, he rapidly began to change his mind, but by then it was too late.

Lauda sat on the pit counter, cross-legged next to Daniele Audetto, watching events unfurl. As he remembered later: "It was a miracle; after 12 hours of solid downpour, the rain stopped, about a quarter of the way into the race. If I had only held out that long, driven slowly, and avoided being hit, there would have been no problem putting my foot down, which was necessary to clinch the title. As it turned out, fifth place would have been enough. Sadly, hanging on patiently was more that I could manage that day."

Three other drivers—Emerson Fittipaldi, Carlos Pace, and Larry Perkins—also withdrew after a couple of laps.

As Hunt sped past the finish line for the third lap, he was shown the McLaren board, which read: NIKI OUT. Straightaway he knew why, but Hunt took no pleasure in his rival's demise. Lauda's behavior that season had earned his total respect.

Hunt maintained his lead, and surprisingly Vittorio Brambilla was now in second place in his March-Ford. On lap 22, Brambilla actually tried an overtaking maneuver on Hunt, but as he drew alongside, he inevitably lost control of his car and missed Hunt's by a few millimeters. He went off the circuit in a shower of mud.

As Brambilla departed into retirement, the conditions started improving with every lap. By lap 23, the two McLaren-Fords led 1-2, with Mass tucked up in second place, guarding Hunt's flank. The cloud cover was lifting, taking with it the rain, and a strong breeze was beginning to dry out the track. Speeds picked up accordingly, and the gaps between cars shrank appreciably.

Lauda was standing in the pits when the rain stopped and was astonished at the rapid change in the conditions. He said, "I don't blame myself; it was the right decision. The rain stopping—unforeseeable—was my personal bad luck. I consider that I had bad luck not that I made a mistake." He believed the organizers had been very wrong to start the race: "It could easily have been fatal in the first laps with dead and injured and the race abandoned. The possibility of catastrophe was just too great."

Lauda now realized that if Hunt finished fourth or above, he would lose the championship. But it was not over yet.

The drying track meant the wet-weather tires were unsuitable for the new conditions and were starting to overheat. As the track dried, Caldwell kept out a permanent pit sign with COOL TYRES written on it. He needed Hunt to drive through the puddles to get the tires home. Jochen Mass immediately understood, and he began searching for the puddles to drive through.

Hunt was so focused and preoccupied with winning the grand prix that he failed to give any consideration to the state of his tires. He either ignored the sign or didn't understand it. With remarkable candor, Caldwell told Hunt's biographer Christopher Hilton: "James handled the race very badly. He disobeyed clear instructions. In previous races we'd suffered the same problem: You went from a wet track to a dry track, and the wet tires overheat. They've so much more rubber on them, and when they begin to slide around in the dry, the rubber boils and starts to rip off. The sign was to get the drivers to drive in puddles on the straight bits of the track. That kept the temperature down, and while you'd get less grip, the tires certainly lasted longer.

"We hung this out to James and Jochen, who were traveling in line astern. Jochen saw the sign and immediately turned right, nearly hitting the pit wall in a big cloud of spray. Then, lap after lap, they came down the straight together: James running clear and open in the dry, Jochen in the wet. In the end, we were waving this sign over the pit wall."

Mass continually sought out the wet areas of the track to keep the tire temperatures down. As the pace of the race dropped dramatically, his tires kept in good condition. Mario Andretti was also searching out the puddles.

While all this was going on, Niki Lauda decided not to wait for the result of the race, and he left the circuit to go to the airport. Win or lose the championship, he did not want to be part of the post-race hoopla, as he called it. He told Marlene he wanted to catch the earlier flight. When Mauro Forghieri realized what Lauda was doing, he said he would come as well. While Lauda walked away to get in the minibus that would take him, his eyes were glued to the track. But as the bus drew out of the circuit, he put it to the back of his mind, closed his eyes, and dreamed he was already home. On the car radio they listened to the Japanese commentator until they approached the terminal. As Lauda remembered: "A quarter of an hour later, the race result was announced, and at that very moment our car went into the underpass near the airport and we couldn't hear."

Meanwhile, Jochen Mass was getting frustrated because, having preserved his tires, he caught up with Hunt and could easily have passed him and won the race. But he knew he couldn't win the world championship with what was at stake, although Hunt still could have been champion from second place. In the end, it didn't matter; a frustrated Mass lost concentration on lap 35 and glanced a barrier, bending his front suspension and being forced to retire.

So by two-thirds of the race distance, Hunt was still the comfortable leader. But his tires were degrading fast and he was slowing. Patrick Depailler's six-wheeled Tyrrell-Ford started to catch him up. The six-wheeler's tires were coping well as Hunt's rubber deteriorated rapidly. Depailler soon passed Hunt, and so did Andretti.

Andretti's tires were in great shape, as the wily American kept them cool by driving through the standing water. Like Hunt, Depailler hadn't done so, and his tires were worn out. Within two laps, his Tyrrell-Ford was forced into a pit stop for six new tires, and Andretti took the lead.

There was now a tricky decision to make, and the McLaren team decided to leave it to Hunt whether or not to pit for new tires. Depailler did pit, and that lifted Hunt to second and Andretti to leader, making his decision even trickier. As Caldwell recalled: "We had two signs for bringing drivers in. The first said IN and was compulsory. The second sign was an arrow offering the opportunity to come in if the driver wanted to. Both signs were well recognized; James knew them, so there was no doubt about what we were doing."

Because of the changing conditions, the arrow was up from lap 25, and the mechanics waited on full alert with four new tires and the jacks primed and ready to lift the car. Mayer said, "Only James knew the true state of his tires. We didn't because we couldn't."

Although Caldwell and Mayer felt Hunt should decide when to stop, Hunt thought the opposite and began gesticulating furiously each time he passed the McLaren pit.

Inevitably, Hunt's front left tire wore through the canvas and began leaking air, slowly deflating. But still Hunt stayed out. A tire change pit stop would have cost at least 35 seconds, and Lauda would win the title by default if Hunt finished fourth or lower.

The call for a tire change could have been made much earlier by the pit crew, but it was now too late.

It was a very tricky situation for team principal Mayer and team manager Caldwell. Whatever they did, it could be the wrong decision. It seemed better not to tempt fate, so they didn't make a decision at all.

Hunt said afterwards: "The team had all the information about the rate of tire wear. They'd seen what happened to other cars, and they should have told me what to do. Instead, in response to my frantic requests for information, they hung out the arrow like a huge bloody question mark."

But fate was to prove kind to James Hunt that day, although he didn't realize it at the time. On lap 68, as he came off the last corner, his left hand front tire blew out the rubber that had finally worn through. It was the perfect position to have a blowout, and Hunt simply turned his car into the pit lane, controlling it masterfully.

The decision had been made for them. The McLaren team mechanics, who had been anxiously waiting lap after lap, were ready. When he stopped, Caldwell and a mechanic didn't bother with a jack—they physically lifted up the car for the tire change. Caldwell played it safe and put four new wet tires on the car instead of slicks. The four new tires went on in 27 seconds, and Hunt spun his wheels and got back in the race. As Hunt drove down the pit lane, the Ferrari mechanics went wild, believing he had lost the race. They waved their arms and cheered with undignified pleasure.

During his stop, Clay Regazzoni passed Hunt to take second, Alan Jones passed to take third, and Depailler passed to be fourth. But Regazzoni and Jones were on old worn tires, and Depailler soon went past both of them to be second.

In his head Hunt knew his pit stop had been too long, and he thought he had lost the championship. Now he would need a miracle to get the third place he needed. A red mist descended, and on fresh tires and with nothing to lose, he drove for his life. From a man pacing himself to the finish, Hunt was now racing to win. He gave it everything he could: "I went out in midfield, but of course everyone was on different laps. It was one of those confusing races. I had flown round the track at huge speeds as one would, as I was on a set of fresh wets and everybody else was on bald wets. And the track was dry, so even those who had changed a few laps earlier were a lot slower because they were already overheating. The only thing I could do was shut my eyes and floor it, and pass as many cars as I could."

Under his helmet, he was silently cursing his tires, his team, his general luck, and, most of all, the weather.

The McLaren pit board told him he had rejoined in sixth place. He needed to make up three places in eight laps. He flung caution to the wind and passed Regazzoni's Ferrari and Jones's Surtees-Ford easily.

As neither had changed tires, they were easy meat for him, just as they had been for Depailler. He swept down the short hill at the back of the pits and simply drove round the outside of both of them on the tight left-hander, the only slow corner on the track. Hunt thought he was fourth but didn't realize that McLaren lap scorers had made a mistake: Hunt had been fifth when he left the pits. He was now third but didn't know it. He then went after Depailler as fast as he could.

The tension in the pits heightened, as the other teams were well aware he was third. To them it seemed impossible that Hunt could have changed his tires and been back in title contention again. McLaren finally worked it out, and on the penultimate lap, the mechanics hoisted the P3 sign over the pit counter. The last lap was a nail-biter for both men. As the checkered flag dropped, Mayer was certain that Hunt had finished third and was the new world champion, but Caldwell still wasn't so sure. In the cockpit, Hunt had no idea.

As the checkered flag came out, three cars flashed past—Andretti, Depailler, and Hunt. Although Depailler and Hunt were both a lap down after their pit stops, it all added to the drama, as at the end Hunt was 100 meters (328 feet) behind the Frenchman's Tyrrell-Ford. There was no doubt as to the winner. Andretti had made it through on one set of tires to win; he had preserved his tires perfectly and proven what a fine driver he was.

Hunt was livid as he drove the slowing-down lap, believing he was fourth and that he had lost the championship by one point. He was furious that Mayer and Caldwell hadn't pulled him in for an earlier pit stop for new tires. He held them entirely responsible for losing the championship.

Hunt came down the pit lane blipping the throttle, furious and ready to vent that fury. He climbed out of the car and made a grab for Mayer, planning to punch him out for his stupidity.

Caldwell could see Hunt was angry, and so he disappeared back to the garage. By this time he was exhausted by the drama and fed up with Hunt and thought: *I'm not putting up with this crap. Why should I get abused?* In truth, Caldwell wasn't sure whether Hunt had finished third or fourth and couldn't bear the tension. He would wait for others to clarify it.

With Caldwell absent, Hunt vented on Mayer. Although Mayer could hear Hunt, Hunt still had his helmet on and his ears were blocked, so he couldn't hear Mayer. Knowing Hunt couldn't hear, Mayer made three-finger gestures at his driver and smiled. Confused by the sight of a team owner who didn't look like he'd just lost the championship, suddenly it dawned on Hunt that he might be champion after all. Mayer stood there shouting, "You're world champion" over and over again.

Behind him, Colin Chapman and the Lotus mechanics were climbing over the pit wall onto the track to congratulate Andretti, who had snatched the lead 10 laps from the end to win the race that he had started from pole position. It was the team's first and only win that season.

A confused Hunt held back any celebrations until it dawned on him that he had indeed finished third and was world champion. As Mayer told him what had happened, Hunt said, "I want proof." Hunt would not allow himself to believe it until he had seen the lap charts and had confirmation from the officials that there were no protests on hand.

By this time, Hunt was engulfed by well-wishers, and no one could see him or his car as people pressed congratulations. But all he wanted was official confirmation that he was third, and he kept shouting, "I want proof; I want proof." His supporters lifted him onto their shoulders but then, in the chaos, promptly dropped him. As Hunt picked himself up from the floor, he demanded a drink and glared at Mayer while he drank it.

Hunt was sick with worry after all the disappointments, protests, changes, and disqualifications during the season. He said afterwards: "I was absolutely determined not to think that I was world champion and then get disappointed, because there were 300 good reasons why something should have gone wrong. It was only really when I checked the laps and when the organizers said I was third—and there were no protests in the wind—that I allowed myself to start half-believing it. "

In fact, later recalling standing on the podium beside Andretti, he said, "I still didn't feel that confident when they put me up on third place on the rostrum, because I wasn't sure I wasn't going to be dragged off there at the last minute, so the championship win came to me slowly."

Long afterwards, while reminiscing with journalist Nigel Roebuck, Hunt said, "The thing was that the pit signals I got were not consistent. Suddenly it said fourth, which wasn't right because I had passed someone for third. But with their track record for handling things in a crisis and a panic, I wasn't prepared to believe them because I had had too many disappointments already that year with things happening after the race. So I basically didn't accept that I was world champion, because everything happened so quickly."

As he got off the podium, Hunt went to the pressroom to chat with the print journalists. Later, as it was getting dark, he said, "When I came out it was pitch black, to see that everybody had gone, organizers and everything; everybody had had enough. When I realized everybody had gone, I realized nobody was going to take it away from me because there was nobody there, nobody was interested. So then I believed it. I thought I must be world champion."

Niki Lauda had no idea what the outcome was until, while waiting for his flight home, he looked at a television at the airport. It confirmed he had lost the world championship. When he saw the result, Forghieri rushed to an airport telephone to phone the Ferrari factory in Maranello. He was put through to Enzo Ferrari. Ferrari asked to speak to Lauda directly. They exchanged a few words, and Lauda told him that it would have been "madness to go on." Lauda described Ferrari's attitude as "heartless." He said Ferrari did not even ask him how he was. With that, Lauda put down the phone and gathered up his wife and rushed for the plane.

For Alastair Caldwell, it was a bittersweet ending to a magnificent season. He was furious with Hunt for what had happened in the closing laps. He was adamant it would not have happened had he obeyed instructions. Caldwell never understood why an intelligent driver like Hunt disobeyed him to his obvious disadvantage. He didn't discuss it with Hunt at the time. With the championship won, it seemed churlish. Ten years afterwards, they had a short conversation in which Hunt dismissed his concerns.

Caldwell later unloaded his frustrations on Christopher Hilton, a patient journalist who liked to listen and who enjoyed a good relationship with Caldwell, saying: "I was irritated, because in books and the media, James said we didn't bring him in for new tires when we should have done, that we were idiots because we didn't run the car properly—we always gave him the wrong pit board and so on. In fact, we gave him exactly the right information all the time. We could never have stopped the car for tires and won the world championship, so it was up to him— and we told him that all the time.

"My opinion is that we handled the race perfectly. There was nothing else we could have done.

"Regazzoni and Jones did the same thing as he'd done and stayed out, and both wore their tires to the air. They came to a walking pace because of that, and James was able to pass them."

Afterwards, Hunt disagreed entirely with Caldwell: "I knew from well before half-distance that there were going to be tire problems later on, and I started asking the McLaren pit as best as I could without a wireless. I had seen plenty of people going in and out of the pits changing tires, so they had all the information, and in a situation like that, you watch the other cars and see how quick they are going on fresh rubber. They had all that information, and I didn't have any. As it was, their response to my frantic request, which they did understand, was to hang out a huge question mark and go: 'What do we do?' So the only thing I could do then was to stay out, and it very nearly cost me the championship because, when I did come in, I already had a blown front but I also had a slow puncture. They couldn't get the jacks under it. It was a huge panic to get me a new set of tires."

In the end it didn't matter. Somehow, after all the drama, Hunt had won it and he wanted to get back to the Tokyo Hilton to really celebrate.

But the narrow roads around the foot of Mount Fuji, some 60 miles from Tokyo, meant that the traffic was jammed solid after the race, so the 300-odd members of the Formula One circus stayed put at the track and began the celebrations with Hunt in a room rented by Marlboro.

John Hogan was exhausted by what he had witnessed. He couldn't believe the lad he had met barely five years earlier had become world champion. Hogan's judgment about Hunt had been finally vindicated.

Hunt's win had meant more exposure for the Marlboro brand than they ever could have dreamed. It was Marlboro's most successful marketing campaign ever, and Hunt was responsible for it all. Marlboro bosses phoning to congratulate him from Lausanne in Switzerland told Hogan that he was not to stint on the celebrations. Hogan would pick up the bills for all the parties, which started that night in Fuji and continued on into Tokyo.

But Hogan didn't party as hard as he might have. He was just glad it was over. He had had a very difficult first season with Hunt. As he later admitted: "It was a bit like having a dog; you think you have just trained it and it's being good, and then it goes and craps on someone else's living room carpet. And that's what he did all the time. Every race there was something."

But it had all come good in the end.

CHAPTER 30

A New British Champion

Two Months of Celebrations

November to December 1976

Niki Lauda caught an earlier flight back to Europe from Tokyo and was very glad he did. For as soon as the checkered flag had dropped, it was all about James Hunt. By finishing third, Hunt had won the world championship by a single point.

After leading the world championship all season until the final race, Niki Lauda left Tokyo with nothing at all. For him there lay ahead some delicate operations and months of recuperation. His aim was to get all the surgical work done and then rest up to the maximum to be fit and ready for 1977.

But the scenario for James Hunt was wholly different. Like all new world champions, he was thrust into a cauldron of celebration and sponsor backslapping. Now that he was champion, suddenly everyone wanted a piece of James Hunt.

The other winner that day was John Hogan, Marlboro's head of motor sport. The championship win was set to deliver Marlboro huge value. Hogan would have been a winner no matter what the outcome in Mount Fuji that day. Obviously he preferred Hunt and his own Marlboro-sponsored McLaren team to win, but if not, it would not have been a complete disaster. Niki Lauda was also a Marlboro-sponsored driver.

Thanks to Hunt's success, sales of Marlboro brand cigarettes were taking off across Europe and the rest of the world. Signing Hunt had proved a coup for Hogan, and it was to make his career.

The sponsorship was incredibly successful; and when Hunt won, he straightaway lit up a Marlboro in the pit lane. It really couldn't get much better—especially for a marketing man like Hogan. For a brief moment, Hunt was the Marlboro man: the perfect example of what smoking could do for you.

As he stood in the pit lane that afternoon in Japan, Hogan knew that reality would go out of the window for the next few days. The parties came first. Hunt led the celebrations from the front, and Hogan paid for everything. Hogan figured the more celebrating and the more publicity generated, the better.

Barry Sheene, the motorcycle world champion, was also in on the act, and together the two world champions partied like never before. Girls were falling at their feet, and it was the start of a magical 48 hours for both men, who had sensibly left their girlfriends at home.

It all started as dusk fell at the Fuji Lodge, a hotel adjacent to the circuit. Hogan had booked the hotel's biggest function room to get the party started, and although the celebration was principally for the McLaren team and Marlboro guests, everyone in the paddock was invited. There was unlimited liquor, and Hogan made sure that the tables were laden with food.

The festivities went on late into the night, then Hogan organized a fleet of cars for everyone to get back to the Tokyo Hilton, where he had booked another huge room for another huge party. Hunt grabbed four hours of sleep, but for the next eight hours, people came and went and partied through to the next day. At around 5 p.m. Hunt and the Marlboro and McLaren executives trooped off to the British embassy. Hunt could hardly stand up, and Hogan just prayed they would get through it. Hunt was unsuitably dressed to enter the British embassy and to be greeted by the ambassador, but the normal protocol was waived for the new British world champion.

Then it was back to another room at the Tokyo Hilton for a very formal Marlboro cocktail party, where all the top executives and staff of the cigarette company's Asian subsidiaries had gathered to congratulate their champion, who looked as though he had just come in from a long day at the beach. Looking back 36 years later, Hogan recalls: "We drank for two days solid." And that is about the extent of his recollection.

Late on Monday evening they all got onboard Japanese Airlines Flight 421 from Tokyo to London. The party continued on the plane, even though everyone was exhausted and urgently needed sleep.

Hunt had been booked into economy, but the airline upgraded him to first class, where he found his boss, Teddy Mayer, in the departure lounge. Mayer sniffed when he saw his driver and gave the impression he didn't much like traveling with the hired help. Nor was he impressed with the commotion Hunt was causing in the first class lounge.

Hunt was playing with a toy gorilla that Alastair Caldwell had given to him to celebrate the championship. The gorilla was called "Smiler" and had cymbals attached to its paws, which Hunt kept bashing together.

Mayer squirmed when Hunt got into a stand-up row with Pierre Ugeux, the new president of FIA, who was also in the first class lounge. Ugeux was concerned that Hunt wouldn't attend the annual FIA prize ceremony in Paris to collect his world championship trophy. Hunt told Ugeux that he would not. Ugeux knew Hunt was upset by CSI rulings at Brands Hatch and Monza but appealed to his better nature to put the past behind him. In the end, Hunt said he would consider it. Mayer was somewhat relieved when the flight was called.

The captain greeted Hunt personally at the top of the aircraft steps and motioned him into the first class cabin. But Hunt wanted to be with his friends and the mechanics and said he would take a seat in economy class. The captain said he would keep Hunt's first class seat free and asked him to join them for dinner. In those days Hunt always traveled economy, and it didn't occur to him to book himself into the first class cabin, although by then he could easily have afforded it. He tended to be anesthetized by alcohol on flights, so he had little need for any pampering. As long as the drink flowed, which it did in those days in the economy cabin, he was happy. *Daily Express* motoring editor David Benson deliberately plopped himself into the seat next to Hunt's in first class.

As Hunt entered the cabin, a huge cheer went up. Within a few hours, the drink ran out and Hunt had to go into first class to top up supplies. The Japanese captain had ordered his crew to let the champion do what he wanted, and so they obliged his every wish.

In the end, as the lights in the cabin were dimmed, everyone fell asleep completely exhausted by the nonstop drinking, which had by then stretched out for nearly 48 hours. Hunt then went up into the first class cabin to take the seat reserved for him for dinner.

He sat next to Benson. During 1976 and through all the drama, Benson had proved himself the most skilled reporter of his day, and his stories had been picked up by newspapers across the globe. That night, he got another exclusive interview.

The captain came by to chat about the race, and the crew served Hunt a special dinner of shrimp to start, followed by Chicken Princess with duchess potatoes. Hunt alternatively slurped beer and red wine with his meal as the stewardesses danced up and down the aisle with constant refills of both glasses.

In those days the Boeing 747 100 series had nowhere near enough fuel capacity to make it in one hop from Asia to Europe, so a midflight stop was necessary. After they had feasted, Hunt got to his feet and did some slapstick comedy routines for Benson and the other first class passengers as the Boeing started to make its descent into Anchorage airport for refueling. The captain let Hunt make the announcement that the plane was beginning its descent, and Hunt put on the best Japanese accent he could muster.

When they took off again, Hunt went into the back of the plane to speak with Max Mosley. He and Mosley looked for empty seats so they could stretch out. Later he went back to his seat in economy, and David Phipps took a photograph of Hunt asleep surrounded by his close friend Chris Jones, along with Alastair Caldwell and John Hogan. The Phipps photograph caught everyone's imagination, and the photo was published around the world.

Barry Sheene didn't get any sleep at all and spent the entire journey trying to persuade women on the flight about the merits of joining the mile-high club, apparently with some success.

John Hogan summed it up: "It wasn't an outrageous flight, and everybody was just very very happy."

As the plane descended into Heathrow, Hunt woke up with the worst hangover of his life, but he had no regrets about what had happened—although it took him some time to remember precisely what had happened.

When the plane landed at around nine o'clock in the morning, Hunt emerged from the Boeing 747 blinking and carrying his toy gorilla. A posse of photographers ambushed him at the foot of the Boeing's steps, but he was rescued by airport staff, who whisked everyone through the VIP disembarkation exit.

A huge crowd of fans had gathered outside the customs hall, and Hunt was greeted by more than 2,000 people waiting to welcome home their champion. Among the fans were his mother and father, Wallis and Sue, who had watched the race live in a TV studio. Hunt had no idea they would be there and was very surprised as they were publicly reunited. All three of them were embarrassed as the flashbulbs went off. After hugging his mother, he hugged Jane Birbeck, now very definitely his official girlfriend. It was a surreal experience. As Hunt recalled: "I hadn't expected my family to be there, and it was the most unnerving thing to have to say 'hello' to them in front of all those people. It was all quite overwhelming."

As Sue Hunt hugged and kissed her son, it was all broadcast on television. She told reporters: "He's done it. He's done it. I'm elated, absolutely elated. It's magnificent." Then she added, "He may be the world champion, but he hasn't changed. He's still my naughty James."

The normally reserved and cautious Hunt family had thrown caution to the wind and had decorated the front of their house in Belmont in a gaudy display of Union Jacks and other patriotic embellishments. His parents just couldn't help being caught up in the emotion of it all.

A press conference followed, and his mother and father sat beside him as scores of journalists shouted questions and flashbulbs went off front of them. Hunt thought he might have been dreaming. As he said, "In most situations I feel in control, but, when I get out of control, I'm not sure whether I'm doing or saying the right thing—not because of what people want to hear so much as the difficulty of what I want to say to them."

When all the brouhaha was over at the airport, Hunt got in a car and was driven back to Jane Birbeck's apartment in central London. When they finally arrived at Birbeck's flat, Hunt longed for some peace and quiet. He was tired out, and only the adrenaline was keeping him awake. But outside they found another throng of reporters and photographers, some of whom had followed them from the airport. When he finally got inside and left the chaos outside, the enormity of what he had achieved still hadn't hit him. All he wanted to do was sit down and have a drink and a smoke with his friends and family.

First the Hunt family ate breakfast while Hunt brought them up to date with all the events of the previous weekend. Around lunchtime, he went off to the bedroom with Jane, and everyone else left to give him some peace and quiet. Wallis and Sue Hunt went home to Belmont to celebrate with their friends and neighbors, and their son went straight to sleep for eight hours. When he woke, he and Jane went out for a quiet dinner.

On Wednesday morning Hunt went to his brother's offices to discuss the multitude of financial offers that had landed on his desk in the few days since he had won the championship. In the afternoon John Hogan had him at work giving interviews to favored journalists and broadcasters.

With that over, Hunt was free to return to Spain for a long weekend and was booked on the nine o'clock flight that Thursday evening. Inevitably, he was running late, but Iberia, the Spanish airline, decided to hold the flight for the new world champion. Hunt found everything was different as world champion. As it happened, the McDonnell-Douglas DC9 was almost completely empty: with only Hunt, two journalists, and three other passengers in an aircraft that could seat 250.

The flight was due to land at 1 a.m. at Malaga airport. Despite that, it seemed that every British expatriate living in the area had decided to welcome him back at the airport. A huge crowd, led by his immediate neighbors, greeted him with champagne at the exit of the customs hall, and there was an impromptu party in the airport. The drive to his house took an hour. When he got there, more neighbors and expats he didn't know were inside, having set up another party. Hunt, by now refreshed and wide awake, loved it and didn't go to bed until well after eight o'clock on Friday evening.

Later, friends from England arrived to continue celebrating over the weekend. After that, it was back to work.

James Hunt found he was now public property, or at least he was Marlboro's property. Marlboro paid him an extra $3,500 a day for promotional work, and he was ready for as many days as it wanted to pay him for.

Hogan remembers: "We went off on a whirlwind tour of Europe, and in those days there used to be a lot of car shows at the end of the season. We bounced around all the car shows. I was in total admiration. We had this and that organized for him, and James's feet didn't touch the ground for a whole month. He behaved impeccably throughout and was a very good boy."

Hogan stage-managed the whole of the next month for the benefit of the world's media. The value to the cigarette company of those few months was immeasurable. It received global publicity that was probably worth around $100 million, completely dwarfing the money it had actually spent that season.

Hunt's first official assignment was at the London Motor Show at Earls Court, where he was mobbed by his British fans. Then he flew to Cologne for another car show and then back to Britain for a planned rendezvous with his fans at Brands Hatch.

At the circuit, Hogan and circuit managing director John Webb got together and organized a celebratory binge for fans at an event Webb called a "Tribute to James" day. Over 15,000 people turned up to celebrate with their world champion. Hogan also asked Niki Lauda to fly in. The meeting of the two rivals on friendlier terms sparked acres of newspaper coverage around the world, not to mention hours upon hours of TV coverage, especially in mainland Europe.

Next Hunt was feted by the city of London. His father used his connections, and he was made a "Freeman of the City of London." The honor was conferred upon him and the chain of office put round his neck in the presence of a beaming Wallis Hunt. Then he was off to Lausanne to the Marlboro European headquarters, where executives thanked him profusely for his contribution to its bottom line. And he was honored in Switzerland by the Lausanne local authority.

The following evening, it was back to London, where Hogan threw an exclusive party for McLaren employees. Patty, Bruce McLaren's widow, was guest of honor.

Hunt also visited the huge General Motors factory in Luton, Bedfordshire. The sprawling plant made Vauxhall cars and Bedford trucks and employed thousands of people. Hunt went for a lap of honor around the site on a Bedford flat truck, as if he had just won a race. He then formally launched an advertising campaign that had been made for him, with the catch line "Take my advice. Test drive a Vauxhall." As a result of that campaign, Vauxhall sold many cars in the last quarter of 1976.

While Hunt was in London, Marlboro arranged to sponsor a party to celebrate the fifth anniversary of the opening of the Ladbroke Club casino in London's Mayfair. Richard Burton was a member of the club and turned up for the event with Suzy. By now, Hunt and Burton had become good friends. But despite the presence of two of the most famous people in the world, it was Suzy who attracted the most media attention and who was asked for the most autographs. Neither man was surprised and gave each other knowing looks; they had long become accustomed to being overshadowed by their beguiling wife.

After that, at the request of Bernie Ecclestone, Hunt flew to Linz in Austria to open the Jochen Rindt Racing Car Show. Hunt wanted to return the favor Ecclestone had done him at the beginning of the season when he was out of a drive. Hogan didn't mind, as it was an excuse for a huge round of promotional events in Austria, Lauda's home country. The crowds were enormous outside every venue, and Austrian newspapers carried little else but news of Hunt's visit to their country. Lauda was at home recuperating after his eye operation and did not particularly enjoy reading wall-to-wall coverage about his rival in Austria's newspapers.

From Austria Hunt flew to Switzerland for a few days in Geneva for Marlboro parties and receptions.

Then he returned to London via Munich and went straight into the judging for the Miss World contest. The Miss World contest was a very big deal in those days and scored the highest audience ratings on ITV every year. The judges were all famous figures, and it was considered a great honor when the promoter, Eric Morley, invited Hunt to be one of them. Hunt couldn't have enjoyed himself more that evening, and the smile never left his face. Photographs of him and the new Miss World appeared in virtually every newspaper in the Western world.

He went straight to Dublin, then Essen and on to Vienna. The Vienna trip was to open the Niki Lauda Racing Car Show at the request of Lauda himself, and the two of them together attracted publicity everywhere. Racing car shows in the '70s were very profitable events, and there were at least a dozen of them held in Europe across November and December. Hunt attended most of them that year. The public flocked to them until they lost popularity in the '80s.

Hunt left Vienna and went straight to Zurich. Much of his schedule was dictated by awards that all sorts of people wanted to bestow on him. So Hogan went with the flow and organized his schedule around the award ceremonies. Hunt was keen to scoop up all of them, especially if Marlboro cigarettes was paying his daily fee of $3,500. He couldn't get enough of the ceremonies, as sometimes the organizers of the events paid him another $5,000 on top of what Marlboro gave him. On one pro-motional day, Hunt was paid by three different companies for effectively attending the same event. Again John Hogan didn't seem to mind, as Marlboro benefited from the publicity each appearance generated.

Back in London, Hunt attended the Royal Automobile Club (RAC) prize-giving lunch. Normally that event would hardly have been noticed. But Hunt decided to thumb his nose at the RAC for past slights. He turned up for its awards ceremony in jeans, a T-shirt, and, on this occasion, sandals. It's impossible for anyone, even tradesmen, to get into the RAC club with-out a jacket and tie. Hunt had decided to leave immediately if he was barred entry, leaving the club's directors to explain his absence at the dinner. But the RAC directors were cleverer than that and, suspecting there might be a confrontation, decided in advance to let him in as if nothing was amiss with his dress and instructed the doormen not to react at all. There would have been difficulty turning him away since the dinner was in his honor. Hunt had calculated he had the advantage and reveled in his revenge, although he was surprised how easily they acquiesced.

The annual British Racing Drivers' Club (BRDC) dinner dance at the Dorchester Hotel was altogether different. The Dorchester had no dress code, so there was no question of him not getting in. Hunt had no grudge against the BRDC but decided that, having got away with it at the RAC, he would again dress in jeans and an open-necked shirt and test the BRDC's resolve. Gerald Lascelles, the Queen's cousin and the president of the BRDC, decided it was all too much and told Hunt exactly what he thought of him. But Hunt was already drunk and didn't even know who Lascelles was. He proceeded to get increasingly drunk, and by the time the Duke of Kent presented him with the BRDC award, he had no idea what was going on.

He went from London to a presentation in Bologna, and after that he opened Giacomo Agostini's motorcycle show, also in Bologna. At every event he attended in Italy, he needed at least 20 policemen on hand to control the crowds. Hunt marveled at the contrast to his last visit in Italy for the Italian Grand Prix, when he had been booed at every opportunity. As he said, "I was the villain at Monza, but when I went back after I had won the championship, you would have thought I was the biggest hero ever to come into Italy."

In the end, the police would only allow him five minutes at each event—such was the frenzy he created. The presence of him and Agostini together in Bologna created a mini-riot, which led the Italian news bulletins that evening and was treated as a national incident.

The show was followed by a round of press interviews in Milan, where Hunt was attending the annual *Autosprint* magazine awards. Hunt, however, was very cross with the hypocritical attitude of the Italian journalists, saying, "They treat racing like a religion, get very passionate, and are fed a complete load of rubbish by their press."

Hunt was exhausted by the nonstop pace. As he said, "I feel like a bloody Ping-Pong ball being bounced all over the place. Everybody is tugging at me from all sides, and I seem to be moving in a world that's gone completely mad." With the frenetic schedule, Hunt was often giving interviews with up to 10 journalists a day and was being shuffled here, there, and everywhere by the very serious Marlboro PR people, who realized they were hot and that this was their one moment to reap the rewards of it. Consequently, a host of exclusive James Hunt interviews began appearing around the world, and his image graced countless magazine covers.

But the big one still awaited Hunt. The one award he wanted to win was the BBC Sports Personality of the Year. Jackie Stewart and Graham Hill had won it before him, and he desperately wanted it too. There was no question of jeans and T-shirt for this one, and he was dressed in a very fetching purple suede jacket and white heavy polo-necked sweater, fashionable at the time.

Hunt was very much the British hero and hot favorite when he took his seat at the BBC Television Centre to hear the results. But just like Lewis Hamilton would be 34 years later, he was visibly shocked when the Olympic skater John Curry's name was called instead of his. He later asked BBC producer Jonathan Martin, "Why didn't I win? I don't understand." Martin said to him, "Well, James, all the women voted for Curry—they like him." Hunt looked at Martin and said, "And they don't like me?" He was affronted and simply didn't understand how a Formula One driver champion could be beaten by a skater.

He had better luck with the Sports Writers' Association, which named him the *Daily Express* Sportsman of the Year, and 300 people cheered him as he arrived to receive the award at the Savoy Hotel. Everyone who was there that night remembered Jane Birbeck dressed to the nines in a stunning gown that left little to the imagination.

By then Hunt was getting very tired, and even his legendary reserves of energy were being depleted. As he said, "My personal freedom is something I had worked for, for so long, and now it seems completely gone. I am simply not my own man anymore."

In mid-December he flew to Paris with John Hogan for the FIA Awards, where the championship trophies were officially bestowed on the winning drivers. And so on December 17, he finally got his hands on the world championship trophy and saw his name engraved upon it, where it would remain for all time.

He was the 37th winner, and he couldn't have loved it more.

CHAPTER 31

Postscript

James Hunt and Niki Lauda

1976–2011

For Niki Lauda, the 1976 season turned out not to be about his close battle with James Hunt for the Formula One world championship, but all about his accident and recovery.

But there was no doubting his disappointment at losing out to Hunt; he felt that, but for the accident, he would have been world champion again.

No official statement was ever released by Ferrari as to the cause of the accident. Only Ermanno Cuoghi, Lauda's chief mechanic, ventured an explanation. As for Lauda, he said, "I recollect nothing. Not a damn thing. Except a big black hole."

After many skin grafts, Lauda's face was made reasonably presentable, and his eyelids were rebuilt with plastic surgery. But angry scars remained, and no attempt was made to replace the missing half of his right ear; he always jested that it made it easier for him to talk on the telephone.

Lauda was always unconcerned with the physical changes to his face and body. As he said, "My talent for overriding my emotions by staying detached and objective served me well. There was really no point in having a complex about losing half an ear. Take a good look at yourself in the mirror—that's you, that's the way you are. And if people don't like you that way, you might as well forget them. I'm not going to have cosmetic surgery. As long as they function unimpaired, I don't feel the need."

The accident seemed to have no lasting effects on him, although he admitted he was unsure of the psychological effects. Since then he has had only one flashback to the accident: in 1984, when he inadvertently smoked a cannabis cigarette, which caused hallucinations and memories of the flames. He then had complete and accurate recall of what had happened after the accident, and he replayed it in his mind. He remembered: "Suddenly it hit me: Nürburgring and the intensive care unit."

For the 1977 season he stayed with Ferrari and won the world championship again, this time with relative ease. But the relationship with Enzo Ferrari was effectively over when Carlos Reutemann was hired after his accident. So when Bernie Ecclestone offered him $1 million to drive for the Brabham-Alfa Romeo team in 1978, he readily accepted.

Apart from flashes of brilliance and the brief appearance of the famous Brabham fan car, it was a career mistake and probably cost him two more world championships, although he became very rich. He lasted two years at Brabham before he became fed up with not winning and abruptly retired in the middle of the Canadian Grand Prix, at the age of 29. Ironically, he left just as Ecclestone dumped the Alfa Romeo engine for a Ford-Cosworth and the Brabham became competitive again.

Lauda needed every dollar he earned in Formula One for when he started his own airline, called Lauda Air. On the day he retired, he flew to California and started negotiations to buy a brand-new McDonnell Douglas DC10.

He expanded the airline, rapidly ordering Boeings as well; by 1982 had spent all his earnings from Formula One and more.

So he sought a comeback at the age of 33 and found some willing takers, notably John Hogan of Marlboro and Ron Dennis, who by then had bought the McLaren team from Teddy Mayer. Hogan and Dennis paid him a reputed $2.4 million a year to reprise his role as team leader, initially partnering John Watson and then Alain Prost.

It was another successful period, and although well past his best, he was good enough to win a third world championship title in 1984. He raced on until 1985, when he finally retired for good.

He went to back to his airline, which was thriving again, and became a consultant for the Ferrari team, which was back in the doldrums. For over 10 years he worked hard and built Lauda Air into a large concern. But in the end it was wracked by internal politics, and he was ousted from his own company as it was taken over by Austrian Airlines in 1999. He sold all his shares in 2000.

All this time, Lauda had been keeping in touch with Formula One by commentating regularly for RTL, the German television station. In 2001 he was surprisingly hired by the Jaguar Formula One team as its team principal, earning $4 million a year, a role that lasted for two years until he was ousted by an internal putsch.

During all these adventures, he gradually grew apart from his wife, Marlene, and split from her in 1991, just as he had from Mariella in 1975. After having had two children, Mathias and Lukas, they too had fallen out of love. Because of the accident, their relationship had been very special, but just as he had with Mariella, Lauda coldly ended it.

Lauda talked openly about the end of his marriage and described how it came to an end after a bizarre conversation with Marlene at the family home in Spain. As he recalled: "I took her [Marlene] out for a walk and I said to her, 'Listen, I think we should get divorced,' and she said, 'I think that's a good idea.'" Having expected a somewhat more robust reaction, Lauda admitted he was taken aback. His attitude to her was, "Oh really?" To which she replied, "I've got my life," and he said, 'Okay, tell me what you want. You can have anything you want.'"

Her demands were modest. She told him: "I want the house, I want the donkey, I want the cat and the dog and the three chickens." By this time Lauda was getting annoyed at how easy it all was. He had expected a fight and outrageous demands. He replied, "Fucking fine, help yourself woman. I couldn't give a shit."

Lauda later confided in John Hogan, the man he had enlisted to help him get married all those years ago: "Well, the dogs, the horses, and cats and the donkey, and all the other shit, that's what drove me mad anyway. Then I realized I'm stuck with two houses in Austria, fucking airplanes, cars, all this fucking shit that I don't want anyway. And she's got the stuff

I want." It was an astonishing reaction to the end of a relationship that had once been his life. But then, it had been the same with Mariella once.

He then took a leaf out of James Hunt's book and became a playboy, chasing girls around the fleshpots of Europe. Lauda spent the next 15 years reliving the youth he never had. He also laid down plans to launch a new airline based on the low-cost Southwestern Airlines model.

In 2003 he acquired the bankrupt airline Aero Lloyd and changed its name to FlyNiki. To finance it he formed a joint venture with Air Berlin, each owning half the shares. It grew quickly, and now the airline flies out of Vienna International Airport and has 14 Airbus jets and 7 Embraer 190s, looked after by 650 full-time staff.

One disappointment lay with his two sons, who tried to establish themselves as racing drivers. But neither proved to be fast enough, and their careers eventually dwindled.

His playboy days ended only when he fell for one of his airline stewardesses, Birgit Wetzinger. She donated him a kidney, which he badly needed as a relic of the accident. In 2008 they had twins—a boy and a girl. They married in 2009.

With his business and personal life back on track, he settled down. Now at 63 years old, his life is lived largely free of drama.

Not so James Hunt, who almost inevitably was not destined to live a life into old age. As soon as his world championship was won, some of the fire seemed to go out of his belly.

Straightaway, the 1977 Formula One season did not start well for him, and the new McLaren-Ford M26 was nowhere as good as the M23. It took six months to turn the M26 into a race winner, and by then the fight for the championship was over. But he had a memorable win at the British Grand Prix at Silverstone in July. By the end of the season, after a season in the doldrums, he had reestablished himself as the quickest man on the track. He won two of the last three races in America and Japan and finished fifth in the championship. But if the world championship had been decided on the results in the latter half of the season, he would have been champion again. As it was, Niki Lauda seized back his crown.

Hunt began 1978 with real hopes of becoming champion again. But it was not to be. Nineteen seventy-eight was the year of ground effects, and the M26 was rendered obsolete. He never won again, getting on the podium just once, in France. He scored only eight world championship points.

His last season with McLaren was greatly affected by Ronnie Peterson's fatal crash in the Italian Grand Prix, for which he was partly responsible. Afterwards he blamed a young Italian driver, Ricardo Patrese, for causing the crash. He began a lifelong feud with Patrese, although later video evidence showed Hunt was as much to blame for the crash as was he.

Disillusioned with McLaren, he left for Walter Wolf's team in 1979, in effect his old Hesketh team, after being offered a $1 million salary by Wolf. But the Wolf car, designed by Harvey Postlethwaite, the old Hesketh designer, was terrible, and after he received the first half of his $1 million salary, he abruptly retired midseason at the Monaco Grand Prix.

Retirement proved a mistake, and he considered a comeback more than a few times but couldn't bring himself to make the decision to return. Instead he became a commentator for the BBC, a role that continued for 13 years right up to his death. Viewers loved him, and the combination with Murray Walker, although fractious initially, developed into something that was cherished by the audience. Eventually Hunt became better known for his commentary role on television than for his driving.

Two years after he retired, he decided to forgo tax exile and move back to Britain, buying a house in the leafy suburbs of Wimbledon, near London. But his retirement was dominated by three things: money, women, and his dog, Oscar. Hunt formed a very close relationship with his German shepherd dog, and the two became a familiar presence around London.

His private life was increasingly turbulent. Despite being with Jane Birbeck for six years, he was associated with a succession of beautiful women, whom he squired to various social functions. He always preferred to turn up to formal functions in bare feet and jeans. The Birbeck liaison lasted for six years, but she was well aware that he was incapable of being faithful to her. Many times she would open a newspaper or magazine and see a photo of her boyfriend with a glamorous woman on his arm.

During that time, Hunt had many high-profile relationships, including Valentine Monnier, a supermodel. Monnier was a serious rival to Jane, who took a long time to adjust to her boyfriend's chronic unfaithfulness. Hunt tried to hide it from her, but there were too many affairs. Jane Birbeck never spoke publicly about it, but it was often impossible to hide her disappointment, and she had to endure some pretty humiliating, and sometimes very public, putdowns.

Eventually they settled down to a form of domestic bliss, disturbed by her frequent miscarriages. The miscarriages initially brought them closer together, and many people say Hunt's time with Jane Birbeck was his happiest, including his close friend David Gray. Gray recalls: "They were both very funny together—very. It was all extraordinarily funny, and he was very loyal to her."

After he split with Jane, he gave her the London mews they had shared and left her very secure.

He then met a vivacious girl named Sarah Lomax, fell in love and married her, and they had two children, Freddie and Tom. But it was a high-maintenance, turbulent relationship that involved far too much alcohol and was destined to end in divorce. He continued to be an extensive user of alcohol, tobacco, and also cocaine and marijuana.

During that period of his second divorce, Hunt fought depression and alcoholism. He also ran into severe money problems, as Sarah took him for everything he had in the divorce. He had previously lost a lot of money on the Lloyds insurance market.

But he took his new frugal circumstances well, changing from a Mercedes car to an Austin A35 van and virtually ending his hectic social life, which included giving up drinking. Where he could, he chose to cycle around London. By then he was a very highly regarded and highly paid broadcaster at the BBC, and he and Murray Walker had become a national institution.

In the final years of his life, he met Helen Dyson, a struggling artist. She eventually moved in with him, and on his last night alive, he reputedly proposed marriage.

He died of a heart attack at the age of 45 on June 15, 1993, in the early morning, at his home in Wimbledon. His death led the news bulletins that day and was largely blamed on his past overexuberant lifestyle. Ironically, at the time of his death, he had given up drugs, drink, and cigarettes. He was cremated at Putney Vale Crematorium, and later in the year, there was a memorial service in London, notable for the number of women of a certain age sitting in the pews.

APPENDIX I

Brazilian Grand Prix

Interlagos, January 25, 1976

Race Result

Result	Driver	Car	Laps	Grid Position
1	Niki Lauda	Ferrari 312T/76	40	2nd - 2m 32.52s
2	Patrick Depailler	Elf Tyrrell-Ford 007	40	9th - 2m 34.49s
3	Tom Pryce	Shadow-Ford DN5	40	12th - 2m 34.84s
4	Hans-Joachim Stuck	March-Ford 761	40	14th - 2m 35.38s
5	Jody Scheckter	Elf Tyrrell-Ford 007	40	13th - 2m 35.02s
6	Jochen Mass	Marlboro McLaren-Ford M23	40	6th - 2m 33.59s
7	Clay Regazzoni	Ferrari 312T/76	40	4th - 2m 33.17s
8	Jacky Ickx	Wolf-Williams-Ford FW05	39	20th - 2m 37.62s
9	Renzo Zorzi	Wolf-Williams-Ford FW04	39	17th - 2m 37.07s
10	Carlos Pace	Martini Brabham-Alfa Romeo BT45	39	10th - 2m 34.54s
11	Ingo Hoffman	Copersucar Fittipaldi-Ford FD	39	19th - 2m 30.25s
12	Carlos Reutemann	Martini Brabham-Alfa Romeo BT45	37	15th - 2m 35.97s
13	Emerson Fittipaldi	Copersucar Fittipaldi-Ford FD04	37	5th - 2m 33.33s
14	Lella Lombardi	Lavazza March-Ford 761	36	22nd - 2m 40.95s
Ret	Jean-Pierre Jarier	Shadow-Ford DN5	33	3rd - 2m 32.66s
Ret	James Hunt	Marlboro McLaren-Ford M23	32	Pole - 2m 32.50s
Ret	Vittorio Brambilla	Beta March-Ford 761	15	7th - 2m 33.63s
Ret	Jacques Laffite	Gitanes Ligier-Matra JS5	14	11th - 2m 34.67s
Ret	Ronnie Peterson	John Player Special Lotus-Ford 77	10	18th - 2m 37.19s
Ret	Mario Andretti	John Player Special Lotus-Ford 77	6	16th - 2m 36.01s
Ret	John Watson	First National City Penske-Ford PC3	2	8th - 2m 33.87s
Ret	Ian Ashley	Stanley BRM P201B	2	21st - 2m 40.94s

Fastest Lap: Jean-Pierre Jarier on lap 31: 2m 35.07s

Points Standings after Round 1

1	Niki Lauda	9
2	Patrick Depailler	6
3	Tom Pryce	4
4	Hans Joachim-Stuck	3
5	Jody Scheckter	2
6	Jochen Mass	1

APPENDIX II

South African Grand Prix
Kyalami, March 6, 1976

Race Result

Result	Driver	Car	Laps	Grid Position
1	Niki Lauda	Ferrari 312T/76	78	2nd - 1m 16.20s
2	James Hunt	Marlboro McLaren-Ford M23	78	Pole - 1m 16.10s
3	Jochen Mass	Marlboro McLaren-Ford M23	78	4th - 1m 16.45s
4	Jody Scheckter	Elf Tyrrell-Ford P007	78	12th - 1m 17.18s
5	John Watson	First National City Penske-Ford PC3	77	3rd - 1m 16.43s
6	Mario Andretti	Vel's Parnelli-Ford VPJ4B	77	13th - 1m 17.25s
7	Tom Pryce	Shadow-Ford DN5	77	7th - 1m 16.84s
8	Vittorio Brambilla	Beta March-Ford 761	77	5th - 1m 16.64s
9	Patrick Depailler	Elf Tyrrell-Ford 007	77	6th - 1m 16.77s
10	Bob Evans	John Player Special Lotus-Ford 77	77	23rd - 1m 19.35s
11	Brett Lunger	Chesterfield Surtees-Ford TS19	77	20th - 1m 18.36s
12	Hans-Joachim Stuck	March-Ford 761	76	17th - 1m 17.44s
13	Michel Leclere	Wolf-Williams-Ford FW05	76	22nd - 1m 18.82s
14	Chris Amon	John Day Model Cars Ensign-Ford N174	76	18th - 1m 17.73s
15	Harald Ertl	Hesketh-Ford 308D	74	24th - 1m 22.11s
16	Jacky Ickx	Wolf-Williams-Ford FW05	73	19th - 1m 18.13s
17	Emerson Fittipaldi	Copersucar Fittipaldi-Ford FD04	70	21st - 1m 18.40s
Ret	Clay Regazzoni	Ferrari 312T/76	52	9th - 1m 16.94s
Ret	Jacques Laffite	Gitanes Ligier-Matra JS5	49	8th - 1m 16.88s
Ret	Jean-Pierre Jarier	Shadow-Ford DN5	28	15th - 1m 17.35s
Ret	Carlos Pace	Martini Brabham-Alfa Romeo BT45	22	14th - 1m 17.26s
Ret	Gunnar Nilsson	John Player Special Lotus-Ford 77	18	25th - 1m 22.70s
Ret	Carlos Reutemann	Martini Brabham-Alfa Romeo BT45	16	11th - 1m 17.09s
Ret	Ronnie Peterson	March-Ford 761	15	10th - 1m 17.03s
Ret	Ian Scheckter	Lexington Tyrrell-Ford 007	0	16th - 1m 17.40s

Fastest Lap: Niki Lauda on lap 6:1m 17.97s

Points Standings after Round 2

1	Niki Lauda	18
2	Patrick Depailler	6
=	James Hunt	6
4	Jochen Mass	5
=	Jody Scheckter	5
6	Tom Pryce	4
7	Hans-Joachim Stuck	3
8	John Watson	2
9	Mario Andretti	1

US Grand Prix West

Long Beach, March 28, 1976

Race Result

Result	Driver	Car	Laps	Grid Position
1	Clay Regazzoni	Ferrari 312T/76	80	Pole - 1m 23.099s
2	Niki Lauda	Ferrari 312T/76 80	80	4th - 1m 23.647s
3	Patrick Depailler	Elf Tyrrell-Ford 007	80	2nd - 1m 23.292s
4	Jacques Laffite	Gitanes Ligier-Matra JS5	80	12th - 1m 24.442s
5	Jochen Mass	Marlboro McLaren-Ford M23	80	14th - 1m 24.541s
6	Emerson Fittipaldi	Copersucar Fittipaldi-Ford FD04	79	16th - 1m 24.779s
7	Jean-Pierre Jarier	Shadow-Ford DN5	79	7th - 1m 24.163s
8	Chris Amon	Norris IndustriesEnsign-Ford N174	78	17th - 1m 24.803s
9	Carlos Pace	Martini Brabham-Alfa Romeo BT45	77	13th - 1m 24.472s
10	Ronnie Peterson	March-Ford 761	77	6th - 1m 24.157s
Ret	Alan Jones	Durex Surtees-Ford TS19	70	19th - 1m 25.214s
Ret	John Watson	First National City Penske-Ford PC3	69	9th - 1m 24.170s
Ret	Jody Scheckter	Elf Tyrrell-Ford 077	34	11th - 1m 24.344s
Ret	Tom Pryce	Shadow-Ford DN5	32	5th - 1m 24.677s
Ret	Mario Andretti	American Racing Wheels Vel's Parnelli-Ford	15	15th - 1m 24.566s
Ret	James Hunt	Marlboro McLaren-Ford M23	3	3rd - 1m 23.420s
Ret	Hans-Joachim Stuck	Theodore March-Ford 761 2	2	18th - 1m 25.122s
Ret	Gunnar Nilsson	John Player Special Lotus-Ford 77	0	20th - 1m 25.277s
Ret	Carlos Reutemann	Martini Brabham-Alfa Romeo BT45	0	10th - 1m 24.265s
Ret	Vittorio Brambilla	Beta March-Ford 761	0	8th - 1m 24.168s

Fastest Lap: Clay Regazzoni on lap 61: 1m 23.076s
Did not qualify: Michel Leclere, Ingo Hoffman, Arturo Merzario, Bob Evans, Jacky Ickx, Harald Ertl, Brett Lunger

Points Standings after Round 3

1	Niki Lauda	24
2	Patrick Depailler	10
3	Clay Ragazzoni	9
4	Jochen Mass	7
5	James Hunt	6
6	Jody Scheckter	5
7	Tom Pryce	4
8	Hans-Joachim Stuck	3
=	Jacques Lafitte	3
10	John Watson	2
11	Mario Andretti	1
=	Emerson Fittipaldi	1

Spanish Grand Prix
Jarama, May 2, 1976

Race Result

Result	Driver	Car	Laps	Grid Position
1	James Hunt	Marlboro McLaren-Ford M23	75	Pole - 1m 18.52s
2	Niki Lauda	Ferrari 312T-2/76	75	2nd - 1m 18.84s
3	Gunnar Nilsson	John Player Special Lotus-Ford 77	74	7th - 1m 19.35s
4	Carlos Reutemann	Martini Brabham-Alfa Romeo BT45	74	12th - 1m 20.12s
5	Chris Amon	Ensign-Ford N176	74	10th - 1m 19.83s
6	Carlos Pace	Martini Brabham-Alfa Romeo BT45	74	11th - 1m 19.93s
7	Jacky Ickx	Wolf-Williams-Ford FW05	74	21st - 1m 21.13s
8	Tom Pryce	Shadow-Ford DN5	74	22nd - 1m 21.19s
9	Alan Jones	Durex Surtees-Ford TS19	74	20th - 1m 20.87s
10	Michel Leclere	Wolf-Williams-Ford FW05	73	23rd - 1m 21.29s
11	Clay Regazzoni	Ferrari 312T-2/76	72	5th - 1m 19.15s
12	Jacques Laffite	Gitanes Ligier-Matra JS5	72	8th - 1m 19.39s
13	Larry Perkins	HB Bewaking Boro-Ensign-Ford N175	72	24th - 1m 21.52s
Ret	Jochen Mass	Marlboro McLaren-Ford M23	65	4th - 1m 19.14s
Ret	Jean-Pierre Jarier	Shadow-Ford DN5	61	15th - 1m 20.21s
Ret	Jody Scheckter	Elf Tyrrell-Ford 007	53	14th - 1m 20.19s
Ret	John Watson	First National City Penske-Ford PC3	51	13th - 1m 20.17s
Ret	Arturo Merzario	Ovoro March-Ford 761	36	18th - 1m 20.63s
Ret	Mario Andretti	John Player Special Lotus-Ford 77	34	9th - 1m 19.59s
Ret	Patrick Depailler	Elf Tyrrell-Ford P34	25	3rd - 1m 19.11s
Ret	Vittorio Brambilla	Beta March-Ford 761	21	6th - 1m 19.27s
Ret	Hans-Joachim Stuck	March-Ford 761	16	17th - 1m 20.40s
Ret	Ronnie Peterson	March-Ford 761	11	16th - 1m 20.34s
Ret	Emerson Fittipaldi	Copersucar Fittipaldi-Ford FD04	3	19th - 1m 20.71s

Fastest Lap: Jochen Mass on lap 52: 1m 20.93s

Did not qualify: Brett Lunger, Loris Kessel, Emilio Zapico, Emilio Villota, Harald Ertl, Ingo Hoffman

Points Standings after Round 4

1	Niki Lauda	33
2	Patrick Depailler	10
3	Clay Regazzoni	9
4	Jochen Mass	7
5	James Hunt	6 (9 points deducted)
6	Jody Scheckter	5
7	Tom Pryce	4
=	Gunnar Nilsson	4
9	Carlos Reutemann	3
=	Hans-Joachim Stuck	3
=	Jacques Lafitte	3
12	John Watson	2
=	Chris Amon	2
14	Mario Andretti	1
=	Emerson Fittipaldi	1
=	Carlos Pace	1

Belgian Grand Prix
Zolder, May 16, 1976

Race Result

Result	Driver	Car	Laps	Grid Position
1	Niki Lauda	Ferrari 312T-2/76	70	Pole - 1m 26.55s
2	Clay Regazzoni	Ferrari 312T-2/76	70	2nd - 1m 26.60s
3	Jacques Laffite	Gitanes Ligier-Matra JS5	70	6th - 1m 27.14s
4	Jody Scheckter	Elf Tyrrell-Ford P34	70	7th - 1m 27.19s
5	Alan Jones	Durex Surtees-Ford TS19	69	16th - 1m 28.44s
6	Jochen Mass	Marlboro McLaren-Ford M23	69	18th - 1m 28.50s
7	John Watson	First National City Penske-Ford PC4	69	17th - 1m 28.44s
8	Larry Perkins	HB Bewaking Boro-Ensign-Ford N175	69	20th - 1m 28.81s
9	Jean-Pierre Jarier	Shadow-Ford DN5	69	14th - 1m 28.38s
10	Tom Pryce	Shadow-Ford DN5	68	13th - 1m 28.37s
11	Michel Leclere	Wolf-Williams-Ford FW05	68	25th - 1m 29.46s
12	Loris Kessel	Tissot/ Thursdays Brabham BT44B 63	63	23rd - 1m 29.09s
Ret	Brett Lunger	Chesterfield Surtees-Ford TS19	62	26th - 1m 29.76s
Ret	Carlos Pace	Martini Brabham-Alfa Romeo BT45	58	9th - 1m 27.66s
Ret	Chris Amon	Ensign-Ford N176	51	8th - 1m 27.54s
Ret	James Hunt	Marlboro McLaren-Ford M23	35	3rd - 1m 26.74s
Ret	Hans-Joachim Stuck	John Day Model Cars March-Ford 761	33	15th - 1m 28.41s
Ret	Harald Ertl	Hesketh-Ford 308D	31	24th - 1m 29.40s
Ret	Patrick Depailler	Elf Tyrrell-Ford P34	29	4th - 1m 26.91s
Ret	Mario Andretti	John Player Special Lotus-Ford 77	28	11th - 1m 27.75s
Ret	Patrick Neve	Tissot/ Thursdays Brabham BT44B	24	19th - 1m 28.80s
Ret	Arturo Merzario	Ovoro March-Ford 761	21	21st - 1m 28.84s
Ret	Carlos Reutemann	Martini Brabham-Alfa Romeo BT45	17	12th - 1m 28.30s
Ret	Ronnie Peterson	March-Ford 761	16	10th - 1m 27.72s
Ret	Gunnar Nilsson	John Player Special Lotus-Ford 77	7	22nd - 1m 28.99s
Ret	Vittorio Brambilla	Beta March-Ford 761	6	5th - 1m 26.93s

Fastest Lap: Niki Lauda on lap – : 1m 25.98s

Did not qualify: Emerson Fittipaldi, Jacky Ickx, Guy Edwards

Points Standings after Round 5

1	Niki Lauda	42
2	Clay Regazzoni	15
3	Patrick Depailler	10
4	Jochen Mass	8
=	Jody Scheckter	8
6	Jacques Lafitte	7
7	James Hunt	6 (9 points deducted)
8	Gunnar Nilsson	4
=	Tom Pryce	4
10	Carlos Reutemann	3
=	Hans-Joachim Stuck	3
12	Chris Amon	2
=	John Watson	2
=	Alan Jones	2
15	Carlos Pace	1
=	Mario Andretti	1
=	Emerson Fittipaldi	1

APPENDIX VI

Monaco Grand Prix
Monaco, May 30, 1976

Race Result

Result	Driver	Car	Laps	Grid Position
1	Niki Lauda	Ferrari 312T-2/76	78	Pole - 1m 29.65s
2	Jody Scheckter	Elf Tyrrell-Ford P34	78	5th - 1m 30.55s
3	Patrick Depailler	Elf Tyrrell-Ford P34	78	4th - 1m 30.33s
4	Hans-Joachim Stuck	John Day Model Cars March-Ford 761	77	6th - 1m 30.60s
5	Jochen Mass	Marlboro McLaren-Ford M23	77	11th - 1m 31.67s
6	Emerson Fittipaldi	Copersucar Fittipaldi-Ford FD04	77	7th - 1m 31.39s
7	Tom Pryce	Shadow-Ford DN5	77	15th - 1m 31.98s
8	Jean-Pierre Jarier	Shadow-Ford DN5	76	9th - 1m 31.65s
9	Carlos Pace	Martini Brabham-Alfa Romeo BT45	76	13th - 1m 31.81s
10	John Watson	First National City Penske-Ford PC3	76	17th - 1m 31.14s
11	Michel Leclere	Wolf-Williams-Ford FW05	76	18th - 1m 32.17s
12	Jacques Laffite	Gitanes Ligier-Matra JS5	75	8th - 1m 31.46s
13	Chris Amon	F&S Properties Ensign-Ford N176	74	12th - 1m 31.75s
14	Clay Regazzoni	Ferrari 312T-2/76	73	2nd - 1m 29.91s
Ret	Gunnar Nilsson	John Player Special Lotus-Ford 77	39	16th - 1m 32.10s
Ret	Ronnie Peterson	March-Ford 761	26	3rd - 1m 30.08s
Ret	James Hunt	Marlboro McLaren-Ford M23	24	14th - 1m 31.88s
Ret	Vittorio Brambilla	Beta March-Ford 761	9	10th - 1m 31.47s
Ret	Alan Jones	Durex Surtees-Ford TS19	1	19th - 1m 32.33s
Ret	Carlos Reutemann	Martini Brabham-Alfa Romeo BT45	0	20th - 1m 32.43s

Fastest Lap: Clay Regazzoni on lap 60: 1m 30.28

Did not qualify: Jacky Ickx, Henri Pescarolo, Larry Perkins, Harald Ertl, Arturo Merzario

Points Standings after Round 6

1	Niki Lauda	51
2	Clay Regazzoni	15
3	Patrick Depailler	14
=	Jody Scheckter	14
5	Jochen Mass	10
6	Jacques Lafitte	7
7	James Hunt	6 (9 points deducted)
=	Hans-Joachim Stuck	6
9	Tom Pryce	4
=	Gunnar Nilsson	4
11	Carlos Reutemann	3
12	Chris Amon	2
=	John Watson	2
–	Alan Jones	2
=	Emerson Fittipaldi	2
16	Carlos Pace	1
=	Mario Andretti	1

Swedish Grand Prix
Anderstorp, June 13, 1976

Race Result

Result	Driver	Car	Laps	Grid Position
1	Jody Scheckter	Elf Tyrrell-Ford P34	72	Pole - 1m 25.659s
2	Patrick Depailler	Elf Tyrrell-Ford P34	72	4th - 1m 26.362s
3	Niki Lauda	Ferrari 312T-2/76	72	5th - 1m 26.441s
4	Jacques Laffite	Gitanes Ligier-Matra JS5	72	7th - 1m 26.773s
5	James Hunt	Marlboro McLaren-Ford M23	72	8th - 1m 26.958s
6	Clay Regazzoni	Ferrari 312T/-276	72	11th - 1m 27.157s
7	Ronnie Peterson	March-Ford 761	72	9th - 1m 27.040s
8	Carlos Pace	Martini Brabham-Alfa Romeo BT45	72	10th - 1m 27.133s
9	Tom Pryce	Shadow-Ford DN5	71	12th - 1m 27.527s
10	Vittorio Brambilla	Beta March-Ford 761	71	15th - 1m 27.640s
11	Jochen Mass	Marlboro McLaren-Ford M23	71	13th - 1m 27.568s
12	Jean-Pierre Jarier	Shadow-Ford DN5	71	14th - 1m 27.618s
13	Alan Jones	Durex Surtees-Ford TS19	71	18th - 1m 28.207s
14	Arturo Merzario	Ovoro March-Ford 761	70	19th - 1m 28.221s
15	Brett Lunger	Chesterfield Surtees-Ford TS19	70	24th - 1m 29.343s
Ret	Harald Ertl	Hesketh-Ford 308D	54	23rd - 1m 29.885s
Ret	Hans-Joachim Stuck	John Day Model Cars March-Ford 761	52	20th - 1m 28.230s
Ret	Mario Andretti	John Player Special Lotus-Ford 77	45	2nd - 1m 26.008s
Ret	Chris Amon	Ensign-Ford N176	38	3rd - 1m 26.163s
Ret	Michel Leclere	Wolf-Williams-Ford FW05	20	25th - 1m 29.597s
Ret	Larry Perkins	HB Bewaking Boro-Ensign-Ford N175	18	22nd - 1m 28.815s
Ret	Emerson Fittipaldi	Copersucar Fittipaldi-Ford FD04	10	21st - 1m 28.670s
Ret	Loris Kessel	Tissot/Thursdays Brabham BT44B	5	26th - 1m 30.020s
Ret	Gunnar Nilsson	John Player Special Lotus-Ford 77	2	6th - 1m 26.570s
Ret	Carlos Reutemann	Martini Brabham-Alfa Romeo BT45	2	16th - 1m 27.762s
Ret	John Watson	First National City Penske-Ford PC4	0	17th - 1m 28.065s

Fastest Lap: Mario Andretti on lap 11: 1m 28.002s

Did not qualify: Jac Nelleman

Points Standings after Round 7

1	Niki Lauda	55
2	Jody Scheckter	23
3	Patrick Depailler	20
4	Clay Regazzoni	16
5	Jochen Mass	10
=	Jacques Laffite	10
7	James Hunt	8 (9 points deducted)
8	Hans-Joachim Stuck	6
9	Gunnar Nilsson	4
=	Tom Pryce	4
11	Carlos Reutemann	3
12	Chris Amon	2
=	John Watson	2
=	Alan Jones	2
=	Emerson Fittipaldi	2
16	Carlos Pace	1
=	Mario Andretti	1

French Grand Prix
Paul Ricard, July 4, 1976

Race Result

Result	Driver	Car	Laps	Grid Position
1	James Hunt	Marlboro McLaren-Ford M23	54	Pole - 1m 47.89s
2	Patrick Depailler	Elf Tyrrell-Ford P34	54	3rd - 1m 48.59s
3	John Watson	First National City Penske-Ford PC4	54	8th - 1m 49.22s
4	Carlos Pace	Martini Brabham-Alfa Romeo BT45	54	5th - 1m 48.75s
5	Mario Andretti	John Player Special Lotus-Ford 77	54	7th - 1m 49.19s
6	Jody Scheckter	Elf Tyrrell-Ford P34	54	9th - 1m 49.63s
7	Hans-Joachim Stuck	John Day Model Cars March-Ford 761	54	17th - 1m 50.31s
8	Tom Pryce	Shadow-Ford DN5	54	16th - 1m 50.27s
9	Arturo Merzario	Ovoro March-Ford 761	54	20th - 1m 51.79s
10	Jacky Ickx	Wolf-Williams-Ford FW05	53	19th - 1m 51.41s
11	Carlos Reutemann	Martini Brabham-Alfa Romeo BT45	53	10th - 1m 49.79s
12	Jean-Pierre Jarier	Shadow-Ford DN5	53	15th - 1m 50.12s
13	Michel Leclere	Wolf-Williams-Ford FW05	53	22nd - 1m 52.29s
14	Jacques Laffite	Gitanes Ligier-Matra JS5	53	13th - 1m 50.06s
15	Jochen Mass	Marlboro McLaren-Ford M23	53	14th - 1m 50.10s
16	Brett Lunger	Chesterfield Surtees-Ford TS19	53	23rd - 1m 52.41s
17	Guy Edwards	Penthouse/Rizla Hesketh-Ford 308D	53	25th - 1m 52.63s
18	Patrick Neve	Ensign-Ford N176	53	26th - 1m 52,82s
19	Ronnie Peterson	March-Ford 761	51	6th - 1m 49.07s
Ret	Alan Jones	Durex Surtees-Ford TS19	44	18th - 1m 51.11s
Ret	Vittorio Brambilla	Beta March-Ford 761	28	11th - 1m 49.83s
Ret	Emerson Fittipaldi	Copersucar Fittipaldi-Ford FD04	21	21st - 1m 52.11s
Ret	Henri Pescarolo	Norev Surtees-Ford TS19	19	24th - 1m 52.60s
Ret	Clay Regazzoni	Ferrari 312T-2/76	17	4th - 1m 48.69s
Ret	Niki Lauda	Ferrari 312T-2/76	8	2nd - 1m 48.17s
Ret	Gunnar Nilsson	John Player Special Lotus-Ford 77	8	Pole - 1m 49.83s
Ret	Harald Ertl	Hesketh-Ford 308D	4	-

Fastest Lap: Niki Lauda on lap 4: 1m 51.0s
Did not qualify: Damien Magee, Ingo Hoffman, Loris Kessel, Harald Ertl

Points Standings after Round 8

1	Niki Lauda	55
2	Patrick Depailler	26
3	Jody Scheckter	24
4	James Hunt	17 (9 points deducted)
5	Clay Regazzoni	16
6	Jochen Mass	10
=	Jacques Laffite	10
8	Hans-Joachim Stuck	6
=	John Watson	6
10	Gunnar Nilsson	4
=	Carlos Pace	4
=	Tom Pryce	4
13	Carlos Reutemann	3
=	Mario Andretti	3
15	Chris Amon	2
=	Alan Jones	2
=	Emerson Fittipaldi	2

British Grand Prix
Brands Hatch, July 18, 1976

Race Result

Result	Driver	Car	Laps	Grid Position
1	Niki Lauda	Ferrari 312T-2/76	76	Pole - 1m 19.35s
2	Jody Scheckter	Elf Tyrrell-Ford P34	76	8th - 1m 20.31s
3	John Watson	First National City Penske-Ford PC4	75	11th - 1m 20.41s
4	Tom Pryce	Shadow-Ford DN5	75	20th - 1m 21.84s
5	Alan Jones	Durex Surtees-Ford TS19	75	19th - 1m 21.42s
6	Emerson Fittipaldi	Copersucar Fittipaldi-Ford FD04	74	21st - 1m 22.06s
7	Harald Ertl	Hesketh-Ford 308D	73	23rd - 1m 22.75s
8	Carlos Pace	Martini Brabham-Alfa Romeo BT45	73	16th - 1m 21.03s
9	Jean-Pierre Jarier	Shadow-Ford DN5	70	24th - 1m 22.72s
Ret	Gunnar Nilsson	John Player Special Lotus-Ford 77	67	14th - 1m 20.67s
Ret	Ronnie Peterson	March-Ford 761	60	7th - 1m 20.29s
Ret	Brett Lunger	Chesterfield Surtees-Ford TS19	55	18th - 1m 21.30s
Ret	Patrick Depailler	Elf Tyrrell-Ford P34	47	5th - 1m 20.15s
Ret	Carlos Reutemann	Martini Brabham-Alfa Romeo BT45	46	15th - 1m 20.99s
Ret	Arturo Merzario	Ovoro March-Ford 761	39	9th - 1m 20.32s
Ret	Bob Evans	Tissot/ Thursdays Brabham BT44B	24	22nd - 1m 22.47s
Ret	Vittorio Brambilla	Beta March-Ford 761	22	10th - 1m 20.36s
Ret	Henri Pescarolo	Norev Surtees-Ford TS19	16	26th - 1m 22.76s
Ret	Chris Amon	First National Ensign-Ford N176	8	6th - 1m 20.27s
Ret	Mario Andretti	John Player Special Lotus-Ford 77	4	3rd - 1m 19.76s
Ret	Jochen Mass	Marlboro McLaren-Ford M23	1	12th - 1m 20.61s
Ret	Hans-Joachim Stuck	John Day Model Cars-Ford 761	0	17th - 1m 21.20s
Ret	Guy Edwards	Penthouse/Rizla Hesketh-Ford 308D	0	25th - 1m 22.76s
Disq	James Hunt	Marlboro McLaren-Ford M23	76	2nd - 1m 19.41s
Ret	Clay Regazzoni	Ferrari 312T-2/76	36	4th - 1m 20.05s
Ret	Jacques Laffite	Gitanes Ligier-Matra JS5	31	13th - 1m 20.67s

Fastest Lap: Niki Lauda on lap 41: 1m 19.91s

Did not qualify: Jacky Ickx, Divina Galica, Mike Wilds, Lella Lombardi

Points Standings after Round 9

1	Niki Lauda	58
2	James Hunt	35
3	Jody Scheckter	30
4	Patrick Depailler	26
5	Clay Regazzoni	16
6	Jochen Mass	10
=	Jacques Laffite	10
=	John Watson	10
9	Tom Pryce	7
10	Hans-Joachim Stuck	6
11	Carlos Pace	4
=	Gunnar Nilsson	4
=	Alan Jones	4
14	Mario Andretti	3
=	Carlos Reutemann	3
=	Emerson Fittipaldi	3
17	Chris Amon	2

APPENDIX X

German Grand Prix
Nürburgring, August 1, 1976

Race Result

Result	Driver	Car	Laps	Grid Position
1	James Hunt	Marlboro McLaren-Ford M23	14	Pole - 7m 6.5s
2	Jody Scheckter	Elf Tyrrell-Ford P34	14	8th - 7m 12.0s
3	Jochen Mass	Marlboro McLaren-Ford M23	14	9th - 7m 13.0s
4	Carlos Pace	Martini Brabham-Alfa Romeo BT45	14	7th - 7m 12.0s
5	Gunnar Nilsson	John Player Special Lotus-Ford 77	14	16th - 7m 23.0s
6	Rolf Stommelen	Martini Brabham-Alfa Romeo BT45	14	15th - 7m 21.6s
7	John Watson	First National City Penske-Ford PC4	14	19th - 7m 23.5s
8	Tom Pryce	Shadow-Ford DN5	14	18th - 7m 23.3s
9	Clay Regazzoni	Ferrari 312T-2/76	14	5th - 7m 9.3s
10	Alan Jones	Durex Surtees-Ford TS19	14	14th - 7m 19.9s
11	Jean-Pierre Jarier	Shadow-Ford DN5	14	23rd - 7m 30.9s
12	Mario Andretti	John Player Special Lotus-Ford 77	14	12th - 7m 16.1s
13	Emerson Fittipaldi	Copersucar Fittipaldi-Ford FD04	14	20th - 7m 28.0s
14	Alessandro Pesenti-Rossi	Gulf Tyrrell-Ford 007	13	26th - 7m 48.5s
15	Guy Edwards	Rizla/ Penthouse Hesketh-Ford 308D	13	25th - 7m 38.6s
Ret	Arturo Merzario	Wolf-Williams-Ford FW05	3	21st - 7m 28.8s
Ret	Vittorio Brambilla	Beta March-Ford 761	1	13th - 7m 17.7s
Ret	Patrick Depailler	Elf Tyrrell-Ford P34	0	3rd - 7m 8.8s
Ret	Carlos Reutemann	Martini Brabham-Alfa Romeo BT45	0	10th - 7m 14.9s
Ret	Ronnie Peterson	March-Ford 761	0	11th - 7m 14.9s
Ret	Niki Lauda	Ferrari 312T-2/76	1	2nd - 7m 7.4s
Ret	Brett Lunger	Campari Surtees-Ford TS19	1	24th - 7m 32.7s
Ret	Harald Ertl	Hesketh-Ford 308D	1	22nd - 7m 30.0s
Ret	Hans-Joachim Stuck	Jagermeister March-Ford 761	1	4th - 7m 9.1s
Ret	Jacques Lafitte	Gitanes Ligier-Matra JS5	1	6th - 7m 11.3s
Ret	Chris Amon	Ensign-Ford N176	1	17th - 7m 23.1s

Fastest Lap: Jody Scheckter on lap 13: 7m 10.8s
Did not qualify: Henri Pescarolo, Lella Lombardi (car impounded by the police)

Points Standings after Round 10

1	Niki Lauda	58
2	James Hunt	44
3	Jody Scheckter	36
4	Patrick Depailler	26
5	Clay Regazzoni	19
6	Jochen Mass	14
7	Jacques Laffite	10
=	John Watson	10
9	Carlos Pace	7
=	Tom Pryce	7
11	Hans-Joachim Stuck	6
=	Gunnar Nilsson	6
13	Alan Jones	4
14	Carlos Reutemann	3
=	Mario Andretti	3
=	Emerson Fittipaldi	3
17	Chris Amon	2
18	Rolf Stommelen	1

APPENDIX XI

Austrian Grand Prix
Österreichring, August 15, 1976

Race Result

Result	Driver	Car	Laps	Grid Position
1	John Watson	First National City Penske-Ford PC4	54	2nd - 1m 35.84s
2	Jacques Laffite	Gitanes Ligier-Matra JS5	54	5th - 1m 36.52s
3	Gunnar Nilsson	John Player Special Lotus-Ford 77	54	4th - 1m 36.46s
4	James Hunt	Marlboro McLaren-Ford M23	54	Pole - 1m 35.02s
5	Mario Andretti	John Player Special Lotus-Ford 77	54	9th - 1m 36.68s
6	Ronnie Peterson	March-Ford 761	54	3rd - 1m 36.34s
7	Jochen Mass	Marlboro McLaren-Ford M23	54	12th - 1m 37.22s
8	Harald Ertl	Hesketh-Ford 308D	53	20th - 1m 39.09s
9	Henri Pescarolo	Norev Surtees-Ford TS19	52	22nd - 1m 39.84s
10	Brett Lunger	Chesterfield Surtees-Ford TS19	51	16th - 1m 37.62s
11	Alessandro Pesenti-Rossi	Gulf Tyrrell-Ford 007	51	23rd - 1m 40.67s
12	Lella Lombardi	Lavazza Brabham-Ford BT44B	50	24th - 1m 42.25s
Ret	Hans Binder	Raiffeisen Ensign-Ford N176	47	19th - 1m 38.36s
Ret	Loris Kessel	Tissot Brabham-Ford BT44B	44	25th - 1m 56.01s
Ret	Vittorio Brambilla	Beta March-Ford 761	43	7th - 1m 36.59s
Ret	Emerson Fittipaldi	Copersucar Fittipaldi-Ford FD04	43	17th - 1m 37.76s
Ret	Jean-Pierre Jarier	Tabatip Shadow-Ford DN5	40	18th - 1m 37.88s
Ret	Carlos Pace	Martini Brabham-Alfa Romeo BT45	40	8th - 1m 36.66s
Ret	Alan Jones	Durex Surtees-Ford TS19	40	15th - 1m 37.60s
Ret	Hans-Joachim Stuck	Jagermeister March-Ford 761	26	11th - 1m 36.95s
Ret	Patrick Depailler	Elf Tyrrell-Ford P34	24	13th - 1m 37.24s
Ret	Arturo Merzario	Wolf-Williams-Ford FW05	17	21st - 1m 39.33s
Ret	Tom Pryce	Tabatip Shadow-Ford DN5	14	6th - 1m 36.56s
Ret	Jody Scheckter	Elf Tyrrell-Ford P34	14	10th - 1m 36.91s
Ret	Carlos Reutemann	Martini Brabham-Alfa Romeo BT45	0	14th - 1m 37.24s

Fastest Lap: James Hunt:1m 35.91s

Points Standings after Round 11

1	Niki Lauda	58
2	James Hunt	47
3	Jody Scheckter	36
4	Patrick Depailler	26
5	John Watson	19
6	Clay Regazzoni	16
=	Jacques Laffite	16
8	Jochen Mass	14
9	Gunnar Nilsson	10
10	Carlos Pace	7
=	Tom Pryce	7
12	Hans-Joachim Stuck	6
13	Mario Andretti	5
14	Alan Jones	4
15	Carlos Reutemann	3
=	Emerson Fittipaldi	3
17	Chris Amon	2
18	Rolf Stommelen	1
=	Ronnie Peterson	1

Dutch Grand Prix

Zandvoort, August 29, 1976

Race Result

Result	Driver	Car	Laps	Grid Position
1	James Hunt	Marlboro McLaren-Ford M23	75	2nd - 1m 21.39s
2	Clay Regazzoni	Ferrari 312T-2/76	75	5th - 1m 21.55s
3	Mario Andretti	John Player Special Lotus-Ford 77	75	6th - 1m 21.88s
4	Tom Pryce	Shadow-Ford DN5	75	3rd - 1m 21.55s
5	Jody Scheckter	Elf Tyrrell-Ford P34	75	8th - 1m 21.91s
6	Vittorio Brambilla	Beta March-Ford 761	75	7th - 1m 21.88s
7	Patrick Depailler	Elf Tyrrell-Ford P34	75	14th - 1m 22.27s
8	Alan Jones	Durex Surtees-Ford TS19	74	16th - 1m 22.51s
9	Jochen Mass	Marlboro McLaren-Ford M23	74	15th - 1m 22.48s
10	Jean-Pierre Jarier	Shadow-Ford DN5	74	20th - 1m 23.18s
11	Henri Pescarolo	Norev Surtees-Ford TS19	74	22nd - 1m 23.55s
12	Rolf Stommelen	Rizla/Penthouse Hesketh-Ford 308D	72	25th - 1m 24.71s
Ret	Jacky Ickx	Ensign-Ford N176	66	11th - 1m 22.13s
Ret	Bob Hayje	F&S Properties Penske-Ford PC3	63	21st - 1m 23.26s
Ret	Carlos Pace	Martini Braham-Alfa Romeo BT45	53	9th - 1m 22.03s
Ret	Jacques Laffite	Gitanes Ligier-Matra JS5	53	10th - 1m 22.06s
Ret	Ronnie Peterson	March-Ford 761	52	Pole - 1m 21.31s
Ret	Harald Ertl	Hesketh-Ford 308D	49	24th - 1m 24.37s
Ret	John Watson	First National City Penske-Ford PC4	47	4th - 1m 21.62s
Ret	Larry Perkins	HB Bewaking Boro-Ensign-Ford N175	44	19th - 1m 24.37s
Ret	Emerson Fittipaldi	Copersucar Fittipaldi-Ford FD04	40	17th - 1m 22.55s
Ret	Carlos Reutemann	Martini Brabham-Alfa Romeo BT45	11	12th - 1m 22.16s
Ret	Gunnar Nilsson	John Player Special Lotus-Ford 77	10	13th - 1m 22.16s
Ret	Conny Andersson	Chesterfield Surtees-Ford TS19	9	26th - 1m 24.74s
Ret	Hans-Joachim Stuck	March-Ford 761	9	18th - 1m 22.59s
Ret	Arturo Merzario	Wolf-Williams-Ford FW05	5	23rd - 1m 24.71s

Fastest Lap: Clay Regazzoni on lap 49: 1m 22.59s

Did not qualify: Alessandro Pesenti-Rossi

Points Standings after Round 12

1	Niki Lauda	58
2	James Hunt	56
3	Jody Scheckter	38
4	Patrick Depailler	26
5	Clay Regazzoni	22
6	John Watson	19
7	Jacques Laffite	16
8	Jochen Mass	14
9	Gunner Nilsson	10
=	Tom Pryce	10
11	Mario Andretti	9
12	Carlos Pace	7
13	Hans-Joachim Stuck	6
14	Alan Jones	4
15	Carlos Reutemann	3
=	Emerson Fittipaldi	3
17	Chris Amon	2
18	Rolf Stommelen	1
=	Ronnie Peterson	1
=	Vittorio Brambilla	1

APPENDIX XIII

Italian Grand Prix
Monza, September 12, 1976

Race Result

Result	Driver	Car	Laps	Grid Position
1	Ronnie Peterson	First National City March-Ford 761	52	8th - 1m 42.64s
2	Clay Reggazoni	Ferrari 312T-2/76	52	9th - 1m 42.96s
3	Jacques Laffite	Gitanes Ligier-Matra JS5	52	Pole - 1m 41.35s
4	Niki Lauda	Ferrari 312T-2/76	52	5th - 1m 42.09s
5	Jody Scheckter	Elf Tyrrell-Ford P34	52	2nd - 1m 41.38s
6	Patrick Depailler	Elf Tyrrell-Ford P34	52	4th - 1m 42.06s
7	Vittorio Brambilla	Beta March-Ford 761	52	16th - 1m 43.94s
8	Tom Pryce	Shadow-Ford DN8	52	15th - 1m 43.63s
9	Carlos Reutemann	Ferrari 312T-2/76	52	7th - 1m 42.38s
10	Jacky Ickx	Tissot Ensign-Ford N176	52	10th - 1m 43.29s
11	John Watson	First National City Penske-Ford PC4	52	26th - 1m 13.95s
12	Alan Jones	Durex Surtees-Ford TS19	51	18th - 1m 44.41s
13	Gunnar Nilsson	John Player Special Lotus-Ford 77	51	12th - 1m 43.30s
14	Brett Lunger	Chesterfield Surtees-Ford TS19	50	23rd - 1m 46.48s
15	Emerson Fittipaldi	Copersucar Fittipaldi-Ford FD04	50	20th - 1m 44.57s
16	Harald Ertl	Hesketh-Ford 308D	49	19th - 1m 44.56s
17	Henri Pescarolo	Norev Surtees-Ford TS19	49	22nd - 1m 45.12s
18	Alessandro Pesenti-Rossi	Gulf Tyrrell-Ford 007	49	21st - 1m 44.62s
19	Jean-Pierre Jarier	Shadow-Ford DN5	47	17th - 1m 44.05s
Ret	Rolf Stommelen	Martini Brabham-Alfa Romeo BT45	41	11th - 1m 43.29s
Ret	Hans-Joachim Stuck	John Day Model Cars March-Ford 761	23	6th - 1m 42.18s
Ret	Mario Andretti	John Player Special Lotus-Ford 77	23	14th - 1m 43.34s
Ret	James Hunt	Marlboro McLaren-Ford M23	11	24th - 2m 8.76s
Ret	Larry Perkins	HB Bewaking Boro-Ensign-Ford N175	8	13th - 1m 43.32s
Ret	Carlos Pace	Martini Brabham-Alfa Romeo BT45	4	3rd - 1m 41.53s
Ret	Jochen Mass	Marlboro McLaren-Ford M23	2	25th - 2m 11.06s

Fastest Lap: Ronnie Peterson on lap 50: 1m 41.3s

Did not qualify: Otto Stuppacher, Guy Edwards, Arturo Merzario

Points Standings after Round 13

1	Niki Lauda	61
2	James Hunt	56
3	Jody Scheckter	40
4	Clay Regazzoni	28
5	Patrick Depailler	27
6	Jacques Laffite	20
7	John Watson	19
8	Jochen Mass	14
9	Ronnie Peterson	10
=	Gunnar Nilsson	10
=	Tom Pryce	10
12	Mario Andretti	9
13	Carlos Pace	7
14	Hans-Joachim Stuck	6
15	Alan Jones	4
16	Carlos Reutemann	3
=	Emerson Fittipaldi	3
18	Chris Amon	2
19	Rolf Stommelen	1
=	Vittorio Brambilla	1

Canadian Grand Prix

Mosport Park, October 3, 1976

Race Result

Result	Driver	Car	Laps	Grid Position
1	James Hunt	Marlboro McLaren-Ford M23	80	Pole - 1m 12.389s
2	Patrick Depailler	Elf Tyrrell-Ford P34	80	4th - 1m 12.837s
3	Mario Andretti	John Player Special Lotus-Ford 77	80	5th - 1m 13.028s
4	Jody Scheckter	Elf Tyrrell-Ford P34	80	7th - 1m 13.191s
5	Jochen Mass	Marlboro McLaren-Ford M23	80	11th - 1m 13.439s
6	Clay Regazzoni	Ferrari 312T-2/76	80	12th - 1m 13.500s
7	Carlos Pace	Martini Brabham-Alfa Romeo BT45	80	10th - 1m 13.438s
8	Niki Lauda	Ferrari 312T-2/76	80	6th - 1m 13.060s
9	Ronnie Peterson	March-Ford 761	79	2nd - 1m 12.783s
10	John Watson	First National City Penske-Ford PC4	79	14th - 1m 13.973s
11	Tom Pryce	Shadow-Ford DN5	79	13th - 1m 13.665s
12	Gunnar Nilsson	John Player Lotus-Ford 77	79	15th - 1m 14.397s
13	Jacky Ickx	Tissot Ensign-Ford N176	79	16th - 1m 14.461s
14	Vittorio Brambilla	Beta March-Ford 761	79	3rd - 1m 12.799s
15	Brett Lunger	Chesterfield Surtees-Ford TS19	78	22nd - 1m 16.201s
16	Alan Jones	Durex Surtees-Ford TS19	78	20th - 1m 15.652s
17	Larry Perkins	Martini Brabham-Alfa Romeo BT45	78	19th - 1m 15.598s
18	Jean-Pierre Jarier	Shadow-Ford DN5	77	18th - 1m 15.113s
19	Henri Pescarolo	Norev Surtees-Ford TS19	77	21st - 1m 15.846s
20	Guy Edwards	Rizla Penthouse Hesketh-Ford 308D	75	23rd - 1m 17.217s
Ret	Jacques Laffite	Gitanes Ligier-Matra JS5	43	9th - 1m 13.425s
Ret	Emerson Fittipaldi	Copersucar Fittipaldi-Ford FD04	41	17th - 1m 14.47s
Ret	Hans-Joachim Stuck	John Day Model Cars March 761	36	8th - 1m 13.322s
Ret	Arturo Merzario	Wolf-Williams-Ford FW05	11	24th - 1m 17.288s

Fastest Lap: Patrick Depailler on lap 60: 1m 13.817s

Did not qualify: Otto Stuppacher

Points Standings after Round 14

1	Niki Lauda	64
2	James Hunt	56
3	Jody Scheckter	43
4	Patrick Depailler	33
5	Clay Regazzoni	29
6	Jacques Laffite	20
7	John Watson	19
8	Jochen Mass	16
9	Mario Andretti	13
10	Ronnie Peterson	10
=	Gunnar Nilsson	10
=	Tom Pryce	10
13	Carlos Pace	7
14	Hans-Joachim Stuck	6
15	Alan Jones	4
16	Carlos Reutemann	3
=	Emerson Fittipaldi	3
18	Chris Amon	2
19	Rolf Stommelen	1
=	Vittori Brambilla	1

US Grand Prix
Watkins Glen, October 10, 1976

Race Result

Result	Driver	Car	Laps	Grid Position
1	James Hunt	Marlboro McLaren-Ford M23	59	Pole - 1m 43.622s
2	Jody Scheckter	Elf Tyrrell-Ford P34	59	2nd - 1m 43.870s
3	Niki Lauda	Ferrari 312T/76	59	5th - 1m 44.257s
4	Jochen Mass	Marlboro McLaren-Ford M23	59	17th -1m 46.067s
5	Hans-Joachim Stuck	John Day Model Cars March-Ford 761	59	6th - 1m 44.265s
6	John Watson	First National Penske-Ford PC4	59	8th - 1m 44.791s
7	Clay Regazzoni	Ferrari 312T/76	58	14th - 1m 45.534s
8	Alan Jones	Durex Surtees-Ford TS19	58	18th - 1m 46.402s
9	Emerson Fittipaldi	Copersucar Fittipaldi-Ford FD04	57	15th -1m 45.646s
10	Jean-Pierre Jarier	Shadow-Ford BN5	57	16th -1m 45.979s
11	Brett Lunger	Chesterfield Surtees-Ford TS19	57	24th - 1m 51.373s
12	Alex Ribeiro	Rizla Penthouse Hesketh-Ford 308D	57	22nd - 1m 49.669s
13	Harald Ertl	Hesketh-Ford 308D	54	21st - 1m 49.418s
14	Warwick Brown	Wolf-Williams-Ford FW05	54	23rd - 1m 51.124s
Ret	Henri Pescarolo	Norev Surtees-Ford TS19	48	26th - 2m 5.211s
Ret	Tom Pryce	Shadow-Ford DN8	45	9th - 1m 45.102s
Ret	Jacques Lafitte	Gitanes Ligier-Matra JS5	34	12th - 1m 45.324s
Ret	Vittorio Brambilla	Beta March-Ford 761	34	4th - 1m 44.250s
Ret	Carlos Pace	Martini Brabham-Alfa Romeo BT45	31	10th - 1m 45.724s
Ret	Larry Perkins	Martini Brabham-Alfa Romeo BT45	30	13th - 1m 45.353s
Ret	Mario Andretti	John Player Special Lotus-Ford 77	23	11th - 1m 45.311s
Ret	Jacky Ickx	Norris Ensign-Ford N176	14	19th - 1m 46.605s
Ret	Gunnar Nilsson	John Player Special Lotus-Ford 77	13	20th - 1m 46.776s
Ret	Ronnie Peterson	March-Ford 761	12	3rd - 1m 43.941s
Ret	Arturo Merzario	Wolf-Williams-Ford FW05	9	25th - 1m 44.0932s
Ret	Patrick Depailler	Elf Tyrrell-Ford P34	7	7th - 1m 44.516s

Fastest Lap: James Hunt on lap 11: 1m 42.851s

Did not qualify: Chris Amon, Otto Stuppacher

Points Standings after Round 15

1	Niki Lauda	68
2	James Hunt	65
3	Jody Scheckter	49
4	Patrick Depailler	33
5	Clay Regazzoni	29
6	Jacques Lafitte	20
=	John Watson	20
8	Jochen Mass	19
9	Mario Andretti	13
10	Ronnie Peterson	10
=	Gunnar Nilsson	10
=	Tom Pryce	10
13	Hans-Joachim Stuck	8
14	Carlos Pace	7
15	Alan Jones	4
16	Carlos Reutemann	3
=	Emerson Fittipaldi	3
18	Chris Amon	2
19	Rolf Stommelen	1
=	Vittorio Brambilla	1

Japanese Grand Prix
Fuji International Speedway, October 24, 1976

Race Result

Result	Driver	Car	Laps	Grid Position
1	Mario Andretti	John Player Special Lotus-Ford 77	73	Pole - 1m 12.77s
2	Patrick Depailler	Elf Tyrrell-Ford P34	72	13th - 1m 14.15s
3	James Hunt	Marlboro McLaren Ford M23	72	2nd - 1m 12.80s
4	Alan Jones	McLaren/Durex Surtees-Ford TS19	72	20th - 1m 14.60s
5	Clay Regazzoni	Ferrari 312T-2/76	72	7th - 1m 13.64s
6	Gunnar Nilsson	John Player Special Lotus-Ford 77	72	16th - 1m 14.35s
7	Jacques Laffite	Gitanes Ligier-Matra JS5	72	11th - 1m 13.88s
8	Harald Ertl	Hesketh-Ford-Ford 308D	72	22nd - 1m 15.26s
9	Noritake Takahara	Surtees-Ford TS19	70	24th - 1m 15.77s
10	Jean-Pierre	Jarier Shadow-Ford DN5	69	15th - 1m 14.32s
11	Masahiro Hasemi	Kojima-Ford KE007	66	10th - 1m 13.88s
Ret	Jody Scheckter	Elf Tyrrell-Ford P34	58	5th - 1m 13.31s
Ret	Hans Binder	Wolf-Williams-Ford FW05	49	25th - 1m 17.36s
Ret	Tom Pryce	Shadow-Ford DN5	46	14th - 1m 14.23s
Ret	Vittorio Brambilla	Beta March-Ford 761	38	8th - 1m 13.72s
Ret	Hans-Joachim Stuck	John Day Model Cars March-Ford 761	37	18th - 1m 14.38s
Ret	Jochen Mass	Marlboro McLaren Ford M23	35	12th - 1m 14.05s
Ret	John Watson	First National City Penske-Ford PC4	33	4th - 1m 13.29s
Ret	Kazuyoshi Hoshino	Uni-Pex Tyrrell-Ford 007	27	21st - 1m 14.65s
Ret	Arturo Merzario	Wolf-Williams-Ford FW05	23	19th - 1m 14.41s
Ret	Emerson Fittipaldi	Copersucar Fittipaldi-Ford FD04	9	23rd - 1m 15.20s
Ret	Carlos Pace	Martini Brabham-Alfa Romeo BT45	7	6th - 1m 13.43s
Ret	Niki Lauda	Ferrari 312T-2/76	2	3rd - 1m 13.08s
Ret	Larry Perkins	Martini Brabham-Alfa Romeo BT45	1	17th - 1m 14.38s
Ret	Ronnie Peterson	March-Ford 761	0	9th - 1m 13.85s

Fastest Lap: James Hunt on lap 25:1m 18.23s

Did not qualify: Masami Kuwashima, Tony Trimmer

Points Standings after Round 16

1	James Hunt	69
2	Niki Lauda	68
3	Jody Scheckter	49
4	Patrick Depailler	39
5	Clay Regazzoni	31
6	Mario Andretti	22
7	John Watson	20
=	Jacques Laffite	20
9	Jochen Mass	19
10	Gunnar Nilsson	11
11	Ronnie Peterson	10
=	Tom Pryce	10
13	Hans-Joachim Stuck	8
14	Carlos Pace	7
=	Alan Jones	7
16	Carlos Reutemann	3
=	Emerson Fittipaldi	3
18	Chris Amon	2
19	Rolf Stommelen	1
=	Vittorio Brambilla	1

Index